LEARNING DISABILITIES

The Struggle from Adolescence toward Adulthood

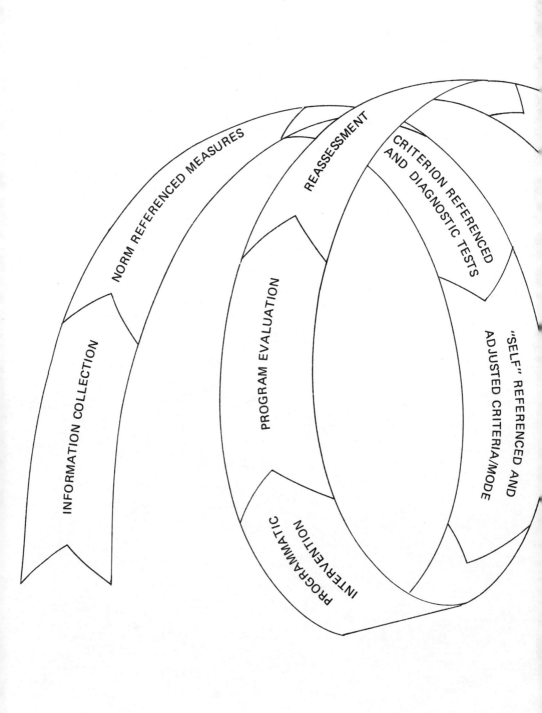

LEARNING DISABILITIES

The Struggle from Adolescence toward Adulthood

WILLIAM M. CRUICKSHANK
WILLIAM C. MORSE
JEANNIE S. JOHNS

SYRACUSE UNIVERSITY PRESS • 1980

Library of Congress Cataloging in Publication Data

Cruickshank, William M
    Learning disabilities.

    Includes bibliographies and index.
    1. Learning disabilities. I. Morse, William
Charles, joint author. II. Johns, Jeannie S., joint
author. III. Title.
LC4704.C77   371.9′2   79-23529
ISBN 0-8156-2220-1
ISBN 0-8156-2221-X pbk.

Manufactured in the United States of America

Contents

Figures

Tables

In order to maintain the anonymity of the young persons referred to in this book, their names, and those of all their family members, friends, and associates, have been changed. We have also changed the names of schools, streets, institutions, and places of work. In several instances, we have substituted an actual job title with one of comparable level and vocational area. Several persons should be acknowledged by name because they have been helpful in providing us with background and institutional information, but to do so would have made it possible to identify one or more of the youths. Those who have assisted us know of our appreciation and our reason for not including them by name.

Preface

THE FOCUS ON LEARNING DISABILITIES over the years has been toward early identification and elementary education programs. These children become adolescents, and adolescents do reach adulthood. Parents have not forgotten this, but they have had to force professional people to the realization. Now the New York State Association for Children with Learning Disabilities has changed its name to include children and adults. This tells something to professional people who listen. Delinquency, probably erroneously, is "linked" to learning disabilities. But are learning disabled children prone to delinquency, or do the studies begin with delinquent youth who after the fact are determined by some ill-defined definition to be learning disabled? Some data appears to refute the implied causal relationship between these two issues, at least for children who have had a reasonable experience with clinical teaching programs in their early school years. Is there hope or defeat within this confusing issue for parents and learning disabled youth alike in the years of adolescence and early adulthood? We believe that forces can be placed in motion which will result in positive adult adjustment for the great majority of learning disabled young people.

In this book (Part I) we choose to examine the problem creatively, not, we hope, emotionally, but with logic and calm. We intend to permit young adults, most of whom have achieved reasonable lives, to speak for themselves about their struggles. Against the backdrop of normal adolescent growth and development, some youths (Part II) will share observations with us regarding their growth and development, often skirting the tragic. One will tell us that he didn't make it, and probably never will. Others have found solutions. These anonymous young men share their lives in often brutally frank ways.

Finally, we will turn (Part III) to the junior and senior high school educators, and ask, "How can you help? Can you turn from content-oriented teaching to a concern for youth with problems? Can individualization of instruction become a reality in your time, in your school, and with youth you legally and professionally must serve? Can you devise an educational regimen which will truly prepare all children for life, and which will insure the integrity of the individual personality in so doing? Can you defend yourselves against the law suits which are inevitable if you don't?" At the date of this writing secondary educators have not accomplished these things. There are isolated exceptions, but the rule is opposite to the spirit of the questions we ask.

There is a growing literature on the nature and needs of the adolescent with learning disabilities. We hope that this volume will add another dimension to this effort, and that it may assist in the creation of a climate which will see the needs of all those with learning disabilities met in an honest, mature, and realistic manner.

Books such as this are completed not just by the authors, but with the help of many people. We wish here to recognize those who have been of particular assistance to us. Mary McElhone and Sylvia McIntosh have carried a great responsibility for the development of the initial typescripts from which a final manuscript was prepared. Personnel of the Word Processing Center, Institute for the Study of Mental Retardation and Related Disabilities, University of Michigan, through the use of their remarkable machines and personal efforts have delivered a long series of "final" drafts. These and they are much appreciated. Mary Frances Ingram managed the production of typescripts all along the way.

Mary Pedley, teacher of Social Studies, Latin and English, and Patricia DeYoung, Special Education teacher-consultant, are members of the faculty of the Tappan Intermediate School, Ann Arbor Public Schools, Michigan. It is general education and special education teachers such as these who will be the reason learning disabled adolescents will make it, if they do. Conversations with Ms. DeYoung provided insights gleaned from her years of experiences with secondary students.

Finally, to the young men and women, youth with learning disabilities, with whom the authors have worked closely over many years and from whom we have learned much of what we know, we extend a very sincere "thank you."

All figures, except those which depict children's writing, were conceptualized and prepared by Jeanne Bright, graphic artist.

Ann Arbor, Michigan   WMC
Summer 1979   WCM
                                                                       JSJ

LEARNING DISABILITIES

The Struggle from Adolescence toward Adulthood

Part I

ADOLESCENCE AS A TIME OF LIFE

1

The Enormity of It All

W<small>E WERE ONCE VISITING</small> with a teen-aged youth and his parents. Following a very lengthy discussion of the young man's learning problems, he stretched his legs, reached out as far as his arms would extend into the air around him, stifled a nervous yawn, and groaned, "Oh wow! The enormity of it all! Why me, and not some other guys?" The "Why me" aspect of his frustration can be discussed with careful counseling in which understanding and insight can replace frustration and discouragement. But the complexity and enormity of the problem is not so easy for young people to understand; it is confusing also to a vast number of adults and professional people.

Learning disabilities is not just a single thing. The failure to realize this accounts for more misunderstanding than almost any other of its aspects. It is little wonder that adolescents express confusion over a problem which is theirs, but for which no one gives them very adequate answers.

In Figure 1 will be found most, if not all, of the aspects of learning disabilities which in combination make this problem complex. It is important first to recognize that "learning disabilities" is a generic term encompassing a whole family of related problems. It is not a clean-cut term referring to a specific type of problem. Within the broad classification one can speak of dyslexia, aphasia, minimal cerebral dysfunction, specific learning disabilities, hyperactivity, and numerous other subsets. Figure 1 focuses on the enormity of the problem while at the same time isolating its many characteristics.

There are two major types of learning disabilities, broadly defined. First, and probably the largest group, are those problems in children and youth which are environmentally produced, not related specifically to central nervous system dysfunction. In a later chapter we shall

3

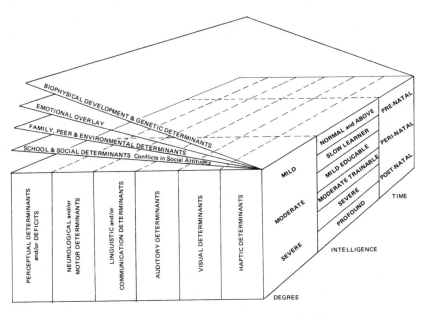

FIGURE 1 The complexity of learning disability

meet a young man by the name of Tom whose problems stem essentially from a disorganized family living arrangement, from a lack of good adult modeling behavior, from racial tension, from the lack of any schedule around which his young life could be organized, and from an educational system which was unable to respond to his problems over which the school personnel had little or no control.

Tom's problems are learning disabilities of a particular type and are represented in Figure 1 as conflicts in social attitudes reflected in problems of learning in school. Familial and peer determinants are particularly significant with Tom. These issues are also noted in Figure 1. Together these issues produced an emotional overlay in Tom which complicated his learning problems. While emotional problems may play a secondary role to school achievement and learning problems, they are dynamic factors inhibiting learning.

Environmentally produced problems of learning may result from many causes. On entering pre-school or kindergarten the child may have experienced great difficulty in mother-child separation. As a result the child may have been unable to respond adequately to the breadth of academic readiness activities which had been prepared for him. The elements necessary for future academic progress were not assimilated properly. In another instance the child may have been struggling through the first grade at a time when his or her parents were undergoing separation or divorce. The emotional tensions of the home may have made it impossible for the child to respond to the basic teaching of reading, number concepts, spelling, and writing.

Environmentally produced problems of learning may be seen in hungry children, and there are many of these youngsters in the United States as well as other countries. Lack of family structure due to poverty reaches into the child, and makes it difficult, if not sometimes impossible, for the child to learn properly. The recent exposures regarding child abuse —both psychological and physical—make us realize that here, too, is a cause of problems of learning which many had not realized was as significant as it is. Hard drug use on the part of the mother during pregnancy may also have significant impact on the developing fetus. This is one of the biophysical causes of learning disabilities noted in Figure 1. The issues of environmental determinants are addressed in the next three chapters of this book.

As adolescence and its unique characteristics take over, new dimensions of the learning disabilities become apparent, if the school and the home have been unable to provide the important clinical teaching program, the individual counseling, and parental support which are so necessary. Then the peer pressures of adolescence, the need for independence coupled with the lack of a long history of success experiences in childhood, and the need to experiment with little-understood adult behaviors combine to produce hazards for the youth with learning disabilities. Adolescence is a difficult time for most young people; for the young man or woman with learning disabilities it can often truly be at least a purgatory on earth. The situation is of particular concern for the youth whose learning problems are environmentally produced because these pressures—home and neighborhood disorganization, distraught parents, poor adult models, economic desperation, and other comparable situations —continue with the child into adolescence, already a difficult time. Each youth maintains his or her own characteristics, own way of integrating a hostile world into their developing personalities, their own way of responding to the social pressures around them as they seek to develop day-to-day and year-to-year survival techniques. Problems arise when these survival techniques do not harmonize with the concepts of right or wrong as pronounced by the youth's parents or school personnel. The end result is the reflection of environmental disturbances and pressures in the youth's ability to read, write, spell, or deal with numerical concepts. The learning disability is measured by the discrepancy between what the youth can do with academic concepts and a performance expectancy which is established for him by a society which is not the same one as originally produced his problems! Social conflicts of conflicting social groups produce learning problems too.

In contrast to environmentally produced problems of learning, learning disabilities may be related to perceptual, perceptual motor, and cognitive deviance (see Figure 1). These may be of an auditory order, visual, tactile, or related to another sensory modality. Since perception is a manifestation of the neurological system of the human organism, disturbances or dysfunctions of the neurophysiological system produce perceptual processing deficits. These in turn result in very specific and often very complicated learning disabilities. This group of problems historically antedated and produced the concept of learning disabilities, a term felt by parents to be acceptable to them in understanding and speaking about their children. In reality the term has produced confusions which have added to an already complex problem, and indeed which constitute the reason for a discussion of this nature. It is almost impossible to consider learning disabilities without first presenting an elaborate statement of definition.

The concept of learning disabilities started with neurologically oriented conditions in children and youth. Beginning in 1963 the term was created and expanded almost immediately to encompass environmentally determined problems of learning. In more recent years as attempts have been made to make logic out of the chaos which ensued, more clearly defined subsets to the term "learning disabilities" have appeared: perceptual processing deficits, environmentally produced problems of learning; and in more specific limitations aphasia, accurately defined dyslexia, perceptual problems in cerebral palsy, and related clinical problems. Unless learning disabilities is viewed in terms of these appropriate subsets, confusion will continue, and the result will be an ever-declining service program for children, youths, and their families. The problem is indeed complex, but it need not be confusing.

Figure 1 contains further information essential to an understanding of learning disabilities, namely characteristics pertaining to the degree of severity of the problem, to intelligence, and to the time of occurrence. The characterizations of mild, moderate and severe are purely arbitrary. The impact of learning disabilities on development may occur in varying degrees of severity from the most mild to the most severe and complicated. They may involve one sensory modality in a minor way, or they may be observed to involve multiple sensory systems in an extreme manner.

Intersensory relationships may be disturbed in other individuals. For example, the teacher of driver education says to youth with learning disabilities who is attempting to drive an automobile, "Listen to me. See that white line. You are to bring the car to a complete stop at the white line. Do it." "Listen" means the auditory system must be employed; "see" involves the visual system; "do it" involves motor activities localized in still another portion of the brain. Intersensory organization or reorganization is difficult and sometimes seemingly impossible for some individuals with severe learning disabilities. The concept of degree includes the concept of variance in severity and also the number of sensory modalities which may be involved. Diagnostic services must delineate each of these issues fully in order that educators and other professional persons who work with the youth will know where and how best to provide a good therapeutic attack.

There is considerable controversy regarding the relationship of intelligence and learning disabilities. In 1963, when the parents determined to call these children "learning disabled," they also arbitrarily set an intelligence quotient score as the lower limit to this problem and stated that learning disabilities was characteristic of children and youth with normal intelligence. This is a flagrant denial of fact. The cut-off point of an IQ of 80 (in many states), of 85 (in the Province of Saskatchewan), or of 90 (in California) has constituted not only misunderstanding of the problem per se, but an actual denial of services to thousands of children who present the multiple problem of learning disabilities and mental retardation. The reality of this situation cannot further be denied or tolerated, since it not only results in a lack of services to many children and young people, but also results in a form of discrimination which is blatantly illegal. Furthermore, it denies credit to the very children who loaned themselves to research and from whose efforts the early beginnings of an understanding of this problem of learning disabilities was formed.

Figure 2 may assist the reader further to visualize the complexity of learning disabilities. Children with environmentally produced problems of learning appear as a subset of the total school population, but the size unknown. While this group is frequently included within the popular term learning disabilities, the still smaller subset of children labeled Learning Disabilities is also noted. These are those who are defined as such from both the points of view of historical accuracy and from the neurophysiological base which is inherent in perceptual processing deficits. However, Figure 2 also illustrates the relationships of several clinical

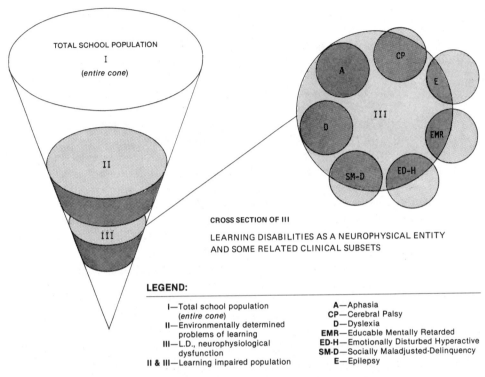

CROSS SECTION OF III

LEARNING DISABILITIES AS A NEUROPHYSICAL ENTITY
AND SOME RELATED CLINICAL SUBSETS

LEGEND:

I—Total school population (*entire cone*)	A—Aphasia
	CP—Cerebral Palsy
II—Environmentally determined problems of learning	D—Dyslexia
	EMR—Educable Mentally Retarded
III—L.D., neurophysiological dysfunction	ED-H—Emotionally Disturbed Hyperactive
	SM·D—Socially Maladjusted-Delinquency
II & III—Learning impaired population	E—Epilepsy

FIGURE 2 Relationship of learning impaired children
to the general school population

Schema illustrating theoretical relationships among total school population,
learning impaired populations, and selected subsets of the specific learning disability group.

categories to learning disabilities. Dyslexia, aphasia, a high percentage of
children with cerebral palsy, and other clinical categories noted in Figure
2 each are characterized by perceptual processing deficits similar to those
in children with learning disabilities. The relationship proportionally (estimated) of mental retardation to learning disabilities is likewise indicated.

Figure 1 indicates that these problems may stem from causes at
any level of human development, namely, prenatal (before birth), perinatal (during the birth process), and during later postnatal life. Environmentally produced problems of learning are essentially related to postnatal
life, whereas perceptual processing deficits may be related to prenatal and
perinatal life periods. Accidents, illnesses, or injuries can, of course, produce neurological damage and dysfunction during postnatal years as well.

This is not a book of the usual textbook type. It is prepared for teachers and for parents who in some manner are responsible for adolescent young men and women who are also learning disabled. This book will not deal with diagnostic techniques, causation, or treatment procedures. It is built around the lives of five young men, each of whom presented severe learning disabilities at one time in his life. Other adolescent youth, both boys and girls, will appear in the book from time to time, but the major focus will be on five with whom we have worked closely for many years. You will meet Andy, Scott, Ronald, John and Tom. We hope from them you will become acquainted with some of the educational, social, growth, and home problems of children with learning disabilities, and view these problems with us and with the young men as they look back into their childhood and see themselves in a more reasonable perspective.

We believe that the stories these young men tell have meaning for secondary school educators, particularly in consideration of the emphasis on mainstreaming and normalization of the educational experience so often being advocated. Some youth in our high schools face double jeopardy daily. These young people are first faced with the complications of physical and emotional growth about which they know and understand little. Secondly, they are at the same time faced with the perceptual processing deficits, if their learning disability is neurophysiologically based, or with achievement failures of great magnitude, if their problems are environmentally determined. The impact of the one set of problems on the other is little understood by the adults who live or work closely with them, and this inability to obtain clarity from those who should know adds to the insecurity and frustration in which the adolescent with learning disabilities lives daily. Perhaps from John, Andy, Scott, and their friends we can learn something of the nature of adolescent life for some youth with learning disabilities. From them we may be able to draw conclusions and form some understandings which will make life easier for the young man or woman for whom we are particularly responsible.

2

The Adolescent Years

Aʟʟ ʏᴏᴜᴛʜ ᴀɴᴅ ᴍᴏsᴛ ᴘᴀʀᴇɴᴛs realize only too well that adolescence in America is a trying developmental period. Many adults still harbor vivid memories of this time many of which they would like to forget. The interesting examination of the imprinting which takes place at adolescence is found in *Is There Life After High School?* (Keyes, 1976). The author suggests that our high school experience shapes our destiny for the rest of our lives. What happens during this impressionable age is so intense that we go through life with a view of ourselves as one who "made it" or as an "outsider" coming from how it was with us. Our social role and personal expectations are conditioned by what happened to us during these years.

Perhaps a more comprehensive way to look at the matter is to recognize why the adolescent time is so critical. The answer is clear: this is a critical time because adolescents are making decisions and evolving patterns which set the course of their lives. What is to be my vocation? What about careers and marriage? What about sexual behavior? High school behavior may condition future opportunities—poor grades and no college career for example. A teenage pregnancy leaves scars. Inability to cope results in drifting and alienation. Drugs may be a temporary escape. As we shall see, the import of adolescent decisions is the real source of parental and youth anxiety and fears at this time. Every parent with a learning disabled adolescent knows that the normal hazards of the age are considerably increased by the disability. By understanding the adolescent process as it affects the growth of learning disabled youngsters, parents and teachers can help provide support.

Adults always compare and the comparison takes many forms. The mistakes we may have made ourselves come back to haunt us in the lives of the young. Thus being a parent at this time is living two lives at once: reworking our own memories and trying to live the new life by proxy

11

though is really not ours to live. Parents and any upbringing adult, such as a teacher, thus walk the tightrope doing a delicate balancing act. There are many ifs. *If* we have absorbed our own growing up experience and forego the "when I was your age" advice with a thousand inappropriate moralisms, we will be seen as useful adults. *If* we ourselves represent a reasonable moral stance, the model will be far more important than the preaching as a source of influence. *If* we have lived productive and satisfying lives, we will have demonstrated the possibility for the next generation. Since their need for a given amount of support alternates by the day, if indeed not by the hour or minute, being an effective parent or teacher for this age demands a great deal of insight. We cannot be amateurs. To help us become professional caring adults is what this chapter is about.

Three issues are important here: The first has just been alluded to and that is know thyself, or at least thy adolescent self. When this is clear, we can monitor what we put in from our own past, whether fears, frustrations, or hopes so that we can help the youngster with his life rather than re-enact our past life. The second issue is that we know (sometimes with great fear) how much life has changed since we grew up. Jobs and employment patterns are new and foreboding. Sexual behavior ranges from strict adherence to conservative codes to a degree of freedom for the many which in the past was managed only by the iconoclastic few. The whole contemporary youth life style may be foreign to the young person's parents and yet the mass media (and perhaps neighborhood examples) make it clear that adults are very often doing their own thing too. And it would be a mistake to stereotype all young people as giving up old values: many do maintain parental values. As we list how different their life forces are, we must not recoil at the challenge "How do you know? You aren't growing up in my high school. All the kids do what I do." They rightfully reply, these young raised by TV and the other mass media in a violent time, that we do not understand their lives. But we can understand the process of growing up with its blows and assists even if the substance is different. It is sharing the information about a time of life where we have gone before which helps to keep the communication channel open. It is easy to panic or become depressed as a parent. There is often a feeling of hopelessness and helplessness. We may easily ignore the reality. If we are emphatic, we will have observations to contribute to adolescents who are groping for solutions to their problems. They do listen to adults as well as their peers. We will need to study how to keep communication open and what to do when communication atrophies. But any sober adult who can keep a rein on his or her own unfinished adolescent business, as described here, can certainly learn to help the new generation through the process of growing up.

Then there is the question of our particular children, the learning disabled adolescents. They are first of all adolescents with more typical than special, but the range of even typical adolescence adjustment is great. The focus on disability must not dominate our appreciation of their lives. It is the goal of this book to blend the two conditions of adolescence and adolescence with learning disabilities as the latter struggle into adulthood.

ADOLESCENCE AS A POSITIVE FORCE

When parents are asked about their most significant burdens in life, they say "raising children." When they are asked about their greatest joys in life they reply "raising children." Such a potent experience has both the bitter and the sweet and being able to cope with the bitter can be a source of tremendous gratification to any parent. We recognize there are many intrinsically positive aspects to the culture at large and to us as parents in our association with this time of life.

Adolescence, because it is such a crucial and fluid time of life also has the potential for correcting past problems and starting a new psychological as well as a new physical life. The awakening of affectional urges, the increased intellectural capacity, especially the ability to reason and solve problems, the direction which comes from goals—all of these and more offer opportunities.

One of the reasons for the ominous feeling adults have about adolescents is the separatist culture teenages create or have created for them. They cling together, have their own codes, and use peers as a basic verification source, sometimes along with, but often in contrast to, adults. It has been found that commercial taste makers and fad purveyors exploit the young person's need to belong to the adolescent cult society. Folk heroes are engineered by commercial enterprise. Taste in clothes is manipulated; since adolescents spend a lot of money they are a coveted market. In fact it is clear that the mores of their society are wished on them as well as created by them. There comes to be a sort of cold war between youth and adult cultures, though in truth the youth culture is an exaggerated mirror image of elements of the large society, represented by families, schools and churches, trying to control and manage the young with minimal success. It has also been said by some that society does not need adolescents. Their schools are expensive, jobs are hard to come by, and they are bent upon enjoying life. They have no functional role in this in between time.

But on the positive side adolescents make a tremendous contribution to society. They provide spontaneity and hope for the future. Without their idealism, the process of change would be slowed to a virtual standstill. Many are creative and contribute a great deal to others. What parent has not had his or her education extended and world view expanded by interaction with young people? They are the greatest adult education force in the society. We adults may be more influenced than influencing. It is easy to overlook the buoyant influence they provide families, institutions, and society as a whole. Sometimes they drag adults into the real world in which we live. Rather than seeing them as the enemy, we can benefit by accepting them as colleagues and growing even as they grow. It should not be all pain. The adventure can be exciting and exhilarating for us all. We take courage from the realization that, in one way or another, most adolescents do cross over into reasonable adulthood.

CONTINUITY OF DEVELOPMENT

Adolescence is sometimes seen as a completely dissociated period, split off from the youngster's past. ["Old moorings are broken loose."] One hardly knows what to expect from the "stranger" who has replaced the child we knew. Familiar patterns seem lost.

Such an interpretation is but half a truth. It is a period of experimentation. Many new behaviors are tried out. Roles are played. The adolescent may hardly even recognize himself at times. But we are seeing a metamorphosis and not a new creature. We are witnessing the drastic reworking of the self in search of a new identity. If we see only the surface behavior, we miss the connection with the past.

The truth is, the best preparation for adolescence is a successful pre-adolescence. If communication has been good with parents before, it will more likely be good at adolescence. The child who has learned to cope and has a reasonable self-concept is in the best shape to meet the challenges of youth. If the child has security and self-esteem, peer group socialization, trust in authority figures, and energy devoted to school tasks, the forecast is good. There will be disruptions to be sure, but the recovery rate is high. If a child goes into adolescence with age level patterns not mastered, the on rush of adolescent development brings a double hazard. The underlying core attributes of personality are established in the earlier stages which precede adolescence.

Our first consideration, then, is with the pre-adolescence of the learning disabled pupil, but even this should not be considered fatalistically. There is a second chance, and it is adolescence.

THE LEARNING DISABLED YOUTH AND THE HERITAGE OF PRE-ADOLESCENCE

Both parents and youth who come to the time of turmoil unready and filled with defeatist expectation can well find the new challenge disastrous. Each developmental period rests on what has been achieved before though always the new is added and changes are possible. The reason there is so strong a continuity of behavior, good or poor, probably rests upon the fact that we change so little of the external condition as children grow. Some authors hold that those learning disabled children who evidence inadequacy in motor alternatives and emotional control end up with difficulties in integrating inner life and developing stable personality even with good family support.

This matter is shown on Figure 1 as the biophysical dimension. The classic work on this has been done by Thomas and Chess (1977). Basically their position is as follows. There are certain high-risk, hard-to-raise children who have temperaments which make living with them difficult. When parents do not recognize these inclinations as basic biogenetic patterns and try to change or moderate the behavior too rapidly, there is tension. This is especially likely if the parent temperament and child temperament are incompatible. In such instances the child fails to meet expectations, friction results, and adjustment deteriorates. Thomas and Chess feel that abrasion is not necessary and parents can adjust, making only reasonable, gradual demands. While the child maintains his or her biological temperamental nature, growth and careful learning experiences can allow for reasonable moderation. They found adolescents functioning normally when a reasonable balance was achieved by parents.

A study of hyperactive youngsters (Ackerman et al. 1977) indicates that half of the hyperactive children at adolescence had major conflicts with authority. It takes concerted effort to prevent this from happening. We must admit they will not become normal. We cannot "cure" all children of being themselves," and individual differences will not be eliminated.

Usually the earlier stages of childhood are less strenuous than adolescence for youngsters. Such is not the typical situation for the learning disabled child, especially since the disabilities affect school achievement as well as overall conceptualization. If there are motor manifestations, this adds further burden. Any atypicality in our culture creates an added hazard for normal adjustment. In this connection it is very important to separate out the behavior which is specifically generated by adolescence from that which is exacerbated by the period but has deep roots in earlier times.

Comparison with others starts very early both by parents and the children themselves. Parents who reflect negatively on the child's achievement encourage a feeling of being rejected and a sense of inability to meet expected standards. On the other hand, those who overprotect create a sense of inadequacy as well: here the child senses that he cannot be trusted on his own as other children are. The fortunate parent who has balanced expectations and ability has not yet won the campaign: the child's own self-appraisal goes on its independent way. Peers and siblings introduce judgments and the teacher-authority figure and other parent surrogates put on an imprint as well.

It is not even enough to go on a policy of "do as well as you can: It's okay." The learning disabled pre-adolescent needs to recognize the reality of his disability and be accepted as the worthwhile person he is. There are so many sad cases where the conclusion the youngster comes to is that he is dumb. He may label himself "retarded." Since the feedback the child gets from those about him comes in both overt messages (things said) and covert messages (innuendos and gesture language) there is only one safe course. That is in discussing the situation with the youngster. Parents, teachers, guidance personnel, social workers, and psychologists can discuss these matters. The best person is the one with adequate knowledge and who is trusted. In some instances group discussion with others having the same problem can relieve the anxiety which builds up around "Am I normal?" It is no wonder there is so much depression, hyperactivity, and defensiveness in these children. They live a secret, or if the secret is out, they live with negative social response.

With the best of intentions, demands may be put on a child to motivate him and get the maximum performance. "You can do it if you only will try." When the child tries and cannot do it, he is still criticized.

One youngster was to be retested by the teacher, a part of the new accountability requirement in special education. He said he knew and she knew and everybody knew he could not read much at all so why did they have to test him over all the time. The subtle balance necessary to provide good feelings and a realistic perception of one's disability is seldom easily obtained, but it can be done. Even those youths well managed by the family are likely to suffer lower feelings of self-worth than normal children, probably because parents and teachers themselves are subject to anger, denial, and self-blame. Many adults who are "self made" successes find it hard to believe that the child could not change if he tried hard enough.

If the family has managed reasonably well, it is an excellent start but not enough. School is one long, extended-stress nightmare when you can't compete. Frequently teachers are not well informed, and diagnostic services may be lacking. If he is not mentally handicapped, why doesn't he learn as the other children do? Is it deliberate negativism? An emotional block? Since other children in his class are doing reasonably well, the child cannot attribute his failure to the teaching. None of the explanations are pleasant when you are different, but the explanation the child uses is most important. One of the first explanations is often "developmental lag," which covers a multitude of sins and implies wait until the pupil matures. Since this is not the situation with the learning disabled youngster, the waiting only puts him further behind.

If the trauma of first-grade failure is not enough to do the child in, it often gets worse by the mid grades where rote learning is reduced and conceptual thinking becomes more important. If the learning disabled youngster lacks the facility with symbols, this will affect, not only the cognitive accomplishment, but the ability to solve problems and generalize in social interaction skills as well. The long and short of it is, if the adolescent is having severe coping difficulty, start the search for the origins. Talk to the youngster about the first time he remembers failing, being upset and hiding his difficulty, being laughed at and so on.

How negative ideas got started, and what the causes were can be openly discussed. Fortunately, most of the harm was done through ignorance and not maliciousness. It still hurts, but the youngster learns it was not his fault or that maligning was unwitting. A junior high student who finally discussed with his doctor what his problem really was, asked his mother (also a teacher) why she had whipped him when he did not learn. The mother, in tears, told him of her ignorance and frustration which led to such counter-productive behavior. The sorting out would help the child re-establish self-esteem.

But it is only half enough to clarify and correct erroneous ideas a child may accumulate about his condition. To believe in one's self, there must be some actual progress. This necessitates specific assistance. Tutorial sessions, special classes, and teaching aids minimizing the limitations must be employed if self-esteem is to be solid. These are discussed in the educational section of this book. But it is discouraging to know you must work twice as hard on some tasks as your peers and still gain much less than they do for your efforts.

Parents and teachers can check off the normal tasks of pre-adolescence. One is the mastery of school learning as we have been describing. Another is the development of peer relationships, especially with the same sex. If failure in school tasks results in acting-out behavior, the peer relationship may suffer doubly—first from the relative inability to pick up nonverbal nuances and make generalizations about social relationships; second from the behavior which no one likes. The pre-adolescent lives in a world where game skills are very important. It is a "bike culture" with increases in mobility and independence. This age loves to hang around in groups, talking over real and imagined adventures or last night's TV shows. In addition to these tasks, there is usually some special attribute the youngster develops as a unique extension of the self. It may be a motor skill, a particular talent, or the biggest collection of beer cans, to add to one's status and individuality. Watching a frightening series on TV tests your ability to stand fear: addiction to the tube is common.

Few pre-adolescents (or adolescents for that matter) are strongly inner directed. They require concrete personal achievement along with love and recognition from both adults and peers to maintain their self-esteem. When they can cope reasonably well in meeting the developmental tasks of their own age, they can feel good about themselves. They have achieved positive self-esteem. A core of postive self-worth will tide over the normal temporary discouragements which are bound to be part of growing up.

If one arrives unready and inadequate to adolescence as with learning disabilities, then the situation is one of double indemnity. But adolescence will come, ready or not, and to the learning disabled youngster at the same pace as for the others.

The studies of adjustment of pre-adolescence learning disabled youngsters are not all consistent, and the findings deserve review. There is no single pattern of personality style or formulation common to all learning disabled pre-adolescents. While the shape of the problem behavior may differ, one is likely to see variation in mood (sometimes happy, sometimes sad), reduced frustration tolerance, difficulty with body image, poorer than average appraisal of reality, more dependence and diffi-

ganizing abstract attitudes. Comparison with siblings is often u.. ble, thus adding to the low self-concept. Going to school is usually traumatic even for those with good family relationships.

It is easy to see how fear of failure can lead to many defensive reactions resulting in a negative attitude. Refusal to do what is asked can be interpreted as hostility. Parents, as well as teachers, can give assignments which the child cannot carry out. Rather than admitting this, some youngsters refuse to comply. A great deal of the disruptive behavior stems from such condition.

One common solution to pressure by learning disabled pupils is withdrawal, especially in the face of overbearing cultural expectations. But just as common is aggressive behavior. One learning disabled group of youths with very low self-images felt much denial, leading to confrontation with those in power. Another group was depressed, worried, quiet, and withdrawn. One learning disabled student said he could not stand it any longer, sitting there and not able to do the work. He would get frustrated then angry, and start a fuss with the teacher or his classmates with the aim of being excluded. A great deal of shame is common which accounts for denial and attempts to hide disabilities. The result is anxiety. There is often a loss of hope by adolescents. The feeling of being dumb, worthless, and bad is hardly the desired start for adolescence.

It has been found that youngsters with learning disabilities are lower in sociometric status, give and get more aggressive responses with peers, and give and get fewer supportive statements. It is not surprising that they are, on the average, both more dependent and more hostile at the same time. They come to believe that what happens to them is a consequence of external events rather than what effort they put in themselves. They are at the mercy of things beyond their control.

One of the aspects of the learning disabled youngster which can become lost in the concentration on academic difficulties is social adjustment. There are two ways to think about this. If a youngster is low in achievement he will usually think less of himself. This low self-concept results in behavior which is socially self-defeating. The other position is that there are inherent limitations of the learning disabled child in conceptualizing social situations and reading cues appropriately. Whatever the cause, the result is difficulty in the social environment.

In summary, what is likely to be the preparation for adolescence for the seriously learning disabled child? The results will range from disaster to reasonable prognosis, but there will be high risk. It is dependent upon the complex of support factors. Frauenheim (1975), considering 40 youths, found that more than 25 percent of the referrals were made for learning disabilities and behavior problems combined. Seventy percent were negative or ambivalent about elementary school and 60 percent about junior high. Three quarters had repeated one or more grades before high school. They saw this as having a negative impact on them. It is no wonder school was difficult, for the average reading age of Frauenheim's adult group was the fourth grade, and spelling was worse. Many of these young people blamed themselves for their failure and continued in this disposition later as adults. Rosenthal's (1973) interesting study compared the self-esteem of children for whom dyslexia was no mystery and no mystery to their families with those who were uninformed. Self-esteem is higher for those who understood. However, being "told" does not mean "informed." The explanation must be understood and accepted.

When we examine the pre-adolescent preparation of the learning disabled youth who are discussed in later chapters of this book, many facets of the problem are revealed. Several had adequate counseling, which made the difference. In the case of Scott, being told that he had the "brains" to succeed is still remembered in adulthood. However, he feels the special education program put him behind. He failed again, and "a kid can only take so much failure." Raymond failed two grades in elementary school. He was thought to be cheating because, while he could not write, he could do certain math percentages. He had tutors all the way through grade school—seven of them who all concentrated on phonics. He understood the content, but could not write it down in acceptable form. He felt people in elementary school were easier to get along with than in high school. With all of this, one can predict self-feelings of a person growing up with learning disabilities, but not for all. Not Raymond described in Chapter 13. He developed a very strong ego and maintained a good self-concept. It is to be noted he did have compensating abilities. He has kept pushing through high school, college, and graduate school! But he is an exception.

When a learning disabled child is deprived of adequate care because of a poor family as were Ron and Scott, the impact is even more devastating than for the average youngster with the same background. If there is no identification model or expectation pattern which is realistic, stress is added. The example of Ron, who could never be the baseball player of his father's dream, spells problems. Again he remembers and appreciates those who helped him. It was hard in school. He remembers not being able to sit still, feeling he just had to move about. The school tried everything. "Boy I had problems," starting with the first grade. School was too hard. This was excellent preparation for a poor adolescent self-concept!

John's father realized the pain of failure for his boy. But John was a hard-to-raise child, one on whom everything was tried. Teachers were then negative to him. His aggression, hyperactivity and destructiveness were hardly endearing. As he said, "Reading was always a problem for me."

Andy remembers being a "ruffian" as a child. He was scapegoated, and he came to feel the other kids were crazy and should be avoided. He failed a couple of years in the elementary school and one later. His interest in the Civil War—a preservation obsession—he explains as reflecting concern about freedom and rights and protecting himself. The dependency of these children started early, and we will see that it continues late. Some of this is related to over-protective families, but there is also the fact of being less able to cope than most children. Andy learned to ask teachers for help, a necessary dependency.

Tom is an example of everything being wrong—not one thing but everything. Brutalized and living by his wits, his psychopathology dominates his learning inadequacies, as he put it "problems from day one," from the cradle to the grave. Tough, hardened, and delinquent, Tom's life goes on. It is interesting that his pre-adolescence might have been a time to help, for he was responding to the help which was given.

Scott is the wonder child who had adversity on every side and managed to end up a wonderful adult. He remembers the talk with an adult which he used to give himself a rudder in life. As he remembers his pre-adolescence it was nothing but trouble, always being called wrong. There were periods of destructive acting out. Things happened to him, but he never understood why: "I was a clumsy little bastard." Yet his life is the most profoundly disturbed of the youth considered here, as will be noted.

What have we learned except that the "learning disability life" is a very hard one for a pre-adolescent? The need for supportive school programs for the student and counseling for both pupil and family are clear. Failure besets them. Low self-esteem is a natural consequence.

The point of this chapter is this: whenever possible we should resolve problems in or before adolescence. The youngsters at this age may not express their appreciation, but it is clear from their memories of those who helped them, that they do, at this time, care and feel under a great deal of stress. Counseling and guidance from loving parents are crucial. When this takes place, adolescence may still be a bitter time, but the youngster has the best preparation we can provide.

3

The Adolescent
with Learning Disabilities

Many a learning disabled youngster enters the turbulence of this adolescent cycle with less than an even start because of what has happened in pre-adolescence and childhood. Stress continues to be the lot of the learning disabled adolescent. One of the dangers of adolescence for youngsters with learning disabilities is being free to develop. So much is usually put into the emotional struggle of covering up and dealing with the learning disability issue that forthright dealing with adolescent problems is never accomplished. The normal youngster has to work through adolescent dilemmas, and so does the special youngster as well. One of the best things we could do for them is to make available *conflict-free energy to apply to the normal developmental tasks.* This is where counseling and acceptance become so critical.

So far we have been discussing adolescence as a psycho-social event. But adolescence is also a biological phenomenon as represented in Figure 1. In fact real adolescence has its generator in biological change, fostered by two hormones from the pituitary gland. One regulates growth; the other is the hormone which stimulates sexual growth. The reproductive organs reach their maturity; girls mature, on the average, two years before boys.

The range of "normal" puberty in girls is about 3 years, but may take place over a span of about 10 years: breast development begins close to 11 years, pubic hair at 11.5, and as of 1970 the menarche average age is just over 13 years. Boys' natural range is two to four years, based upon voice change, pubic hair, and ejaculation. Just prior to puberty, a growth spurt takes place. The rate of skeletal development increases dramatically at this point. The important thing to remember is the range of time involved.

PHYSICAL GROWTH AND IMPLICATIONS FOR ADOLESCENCE

Adolescence has been so associated with acne that the essential physical change which are the motivational wellsprings for the period are often neglected. What is important is the objective condition of change in size, shape, and sexual maturity, the subjective meaning of these changes to the person, and finally the change in response from the social environment. The average time when growth takes place which was reported earlier means nothing really to the individual adolescent. Rather, we should look at how the individual pattern is assimilated by each youngster. Early growth may be a source of satisfaction or chagrin. If growth is late, it can carry the stigma of immaturity for a long period. Secondary sexual changes force more specific decisions with regard to one's own sexual role and brings up the question of moral stance. What do I believe? In this sexually aware society, we may think there is nothing new, but for each youngster it is new. It is personal. Knowledge alone is not enough. Contraception information gives a new degree of freedom. Yet there is ever growing illegitimacy at all socioeconomic levels in many communities approaching epidemic proportions. Sexual involvement can be an effort to solve other problems of personal worth and capacity for personal caring. Twenty percent of the babies born are unwanted. Adults who are not concerned are either uncaring or uninformed. But adult fears and anxiety must be expressed carefully lest this be translated into mistrust by the teenager.

While adolescence is a period of life with maximum health, it is also a time of special health problems. Auto accidents, homicide and suicide take their toll. Obesity is a plague on many youth whether it be unfortunate body chemistry or eating as a compensation for feelings of failure. Efforts to be beautiful and manly are preoccupations well attended by commercial enterprises. Venereal disease has increased markedly. While one can be alarmed, the fact is, this period is one of high energy and overall good health compared to others.

One of the specific problems for adolescents is the way society equates height and sexual attributes with maturity. Youngsters are expected to act their physical age. There are many "ages"—chronological, mental, physical, and social, to name a few. It is no help to be told, "A big boy like you should be able to read much better than that" when you may be in a struggle to decode even simple symbols. This increases the shame. Adolescence is a very bad time to feel even dumber than before. One program for virtually non-reader learning disabled adolescents started with great hopes on the part of everyone. But progress was so slow as the boys inched toward the third grade level of reading skill. While the teachers were pleased with what they knew was a great deal of effort, the youth themselves became depressed and lost hope. "So what is it to read at 2.5 grade level at my age?" We can expect that failure will be more difficult to accept in the teen years. Denial, hiding, devaluation ("who needs to read anyway?"), and shame occur.

We must realize that youth as well as children can often accept more pain than we acknowledge. Why is it that conveying the facts to a child is often so garbled? There seem to be three reasons. First, we adults explain poorly because we are ignorant or are afraid to be honest. Second, to be told you have a handicap, but are not accepted as an equal and worthwhile person by parents, teachers, and peers erodes the value of the explanation. Third, the youngster has to understand and plan ahead so that the handicap is not condemnation for life. Examples of how others with like potentials have succeeded becomes the essence of counseling with them. A symbol is worth more than many admonitions.

The major resolution of physical change for adolescents is the incorporation of a sex role image which is satisfactory to the peer culture and the self as well as important adults. This usually means being valued by the opposite sex as well. Since most adolescent societies splinter off into cliques, there are usually several resolutions which are acceptable, depending on the sub-group. For the typical adolescent there are choices of athletic skills, academics, special talents, and sexual exploration. One asks adolescents to describe the various high school sub-groups, and they can usually define them quite well. There are the leaders and the followers. The range of experience and behavior is startling. Some date constantly, while others sit at home. There is no substitute for knowing "your" adolescent as the variation of behavior in the youths presented in subsequent chapters so clearly shows.

Looking back briefly to the preschool age, where identity begins, we see a spiraling sequence of body identification which requires physical explanation. The concept of self derives from the body image, the physical separation from the supporting caregiver. The learning disabled child finds this more difficult because of greater dependency needs. One's name, family name, place of abode, gender identity all begin to merge into a sense of self. Favorite toys and possessions become woven into an extension of self.

Because the source of food, shelter, love, concern and discipline is the parents, usually the mother, the degree of one's self-esteem is largely a function of the parent-child relationship. Children who are different may be less gratifying to parents. If the learning disabled youth's temperament is over-excitable, fearful, or less independent than the typical child the parent may consciously or unconsciously find it difficult to respond positively. Also, there may be a disaffinity between the child's temperament and the particular parent's temperament which results in abrasive interaction. Parents may resent and reject the youngster. The result is low self-esteem and even a feeling of being bad. When the talk content is reasonable, the nonverbal communication through gesture, attention, and physical contact cues may give away an attitude of deep rejection. All of this adds up to feelings of failure on the child's part. Some parents, when they recognize the child has a problem, will protect too much. The result is a lack of independence and a feeling of inadequacy. But worse than this, the child comes to feel he has failed, compared to other children. Over protection, even from the highest of motives, cause a child to question his ability to cope, encourages fear of exploration, and nets a condition of low self-esteem.

Some children who have had very well-modulated care in their homes enter a new world when they go to school. The problems are accentuated, and peer comparisons regarding the ability to cope cannot be ignored by the youngster, the teacher, and the parent. Now it is not only how the parents regard the child, but peers and the teacher as well. Children begin to judge themselves as well, based upon standards of expectation. Low self-esteem is sometimes reflected in hostile, defensive behavior in some youngsters who come to terrorize their classrooms and families with unmanageable behavior. Other children deal with their low self-esteem through depression and withdrawal. It is hard to be different and slower and still feel good about oneself. There is so much to sort out that the child can become overwhelmed. It has been estimated that a child has 2,500 transactions with things and people a day!

The adolescent comes to think of himself or herself as a social person, increasingly with the opposite sex. The physical attributes become critical—will others see the adolescent as attractive? Can the teenager cope with school and environment? What are his or her future goals? Is the person's family role satisfactory? Must adolescents have a public self (what the individual wants to be seen as), a private self (what he thinks he really is), and an ideal self (what he or she aspires to be)? These concerns arise from introspection, mulling over these matters, which is so characteristic of the adolescent.

The recognition of being different often erodes self-esteem. Since the adolescent now determines for himself how well he is doing, even though there is pathological need for reinforcement from peers, what others say is routed through his own appraisal system. If parents or teachers say the student's achievement is satisfactory, but he knows it is less than others of his age, their praise does little to alleviate his tension.

Special education increases the youth's feelings of being different in the wrong way. Lacking compensations, depression results. Most learning disabled youngsters later indicate that they had to compromise their personal goals for professions or employment because of their disability. There is much hiding of the inability to read. Finding one's way around town, reading menus, filling out job applications, and getting a driver's license—everywhere there are words and more words. No wonder words become the enemy. Even locating the TV program time for a favorite program becomes a task.

This chapter is designed to help the reader appreciate the dilemma: How does an adolescent develop sufficient ego strength so that there will be no need to hide? Often even peers are tolerant and concerned. But hiding prevents this. Many pupils report the effort to protect one's self-image by rejecting the "stupid" assignment, at the same time feeling everyone else was in better shape. Usually the self-hate is projected, and others are seen as hating the student. Teachers and parents "accuse" the youngster of not trying when he is, so he puts down "any old thing." Others come to ignore the learning disabled child who in turn gives out more negative messages.

Because of the physical changes and the social demands, the adolescent undergoes a change of what he is and whether or not this is a good image to have. While some youngsters can compensate for a failure in one area by success in others, others find this difficult or impossible. The important elements of a positive self-concept at this age usually include a reasonable level of social success, school success, owning some more or less unique talent or skill (in athletics or music, for example), a level of independence of action (which involves control over resources like money), and the ego strength to make decisions and follow them. An adolescent may deny caring what teachers or parents think and then become anxious and sad when they criticize. One may go along with the crowd for security and yet feel depressed when one's behavior violates one's own conscience.

Most of us have a low tolerance for low self-esteem and the depression which accompanies it. We look for ways to build up our esteem by finding others who will support our behavior. We create illusions. One learning disabled adolescent "played it cool" at adolescence by being aloof and sophisticated. He thought his peers saw him as a very "cool cat" until he overheard some girls talking about him as a "creep," not to be seen with, an "odd ball" type, a "psycho." He was devastated to find his mask was not successful, and reacted by becoming a real loner. The energy taken to defend one's self-esteem is lost to productive work, and the learning disabled youth will need to spend more rather than less energy on keeping up.

Many psychologists and educators have discussed methods of reversing negative self-images, but one should remember several conditions when making applications. The first is that self-concept and self-esteem represent the unique individuality of each one of us. Therefore the mode of intervention must be a relevant match of what we do and what the individual is like. If tutoring and skill learning meet the pupil's needs, then they can be the significant channel to self-esteem. When a boy needs the respect of his father to feel good about himself, pretense of this by artificially paired activities will not be enough.

Sol Gordon (1970) deals intensively with this issue. He gives an example of a multiply handicapped youngster who was helped by a multiple approach through group counseling, parent counseling, and socialization. Probably the key was having his first real friends. Around this came a rejuvenation of the self. What is interesting is that many of the stigmata of learning disabled adolescents such as "hyperactivity," "short attention span," and "emotional lability" disappeared too as psychological adjustment improved. Gordon lists the elements to reverse a negative self-image with learning disabilities in youngsters: good parental relationships, peer relationship, activated interest, at least minimum function in academic skills, and knowledge of what to do in social situations. Gordon is frank about the difficulties in achieving these essential relationships, yet they are clear goals for all who work with learning disabled adolescents. He emphasizes that the attitude toward the handicap is more crucial than the fact of the handicap itself. It is unfortunate that, as is shown in problems illustrated by youths in a later section, many of our children do not find themselves until after being free of the school regime. Often partial success comes only when they can join the wide variance found and accepted in adult life patterns. The talents they do have can then be used to best advantage, away from the failures imposed by formal schooling.

SPECIAL PROBLEMS OF SOCIALIZATION AND
THE LEARNING DISABLED ADOLESCENT

There may have been difficulty in finding friends at pre-adolescence, but we can be assured it will be a more significant problem at adolescence.

The reason is the general insecurity of the learning disabled youth at this age. The sensitivity of boys and girls about themselves and risking friendship knows no limits. The increasingly subtle cues one has to read for properly testing out and learning how to relate often are missed by the learning disabled adolescent.

While there are many reasons for social problems, one is improper reading of social cues of a nonverbal type, from both adults or from peers. Learning disabled youngsters are poorer than normals in registering the positive or negative affect cues displayed in a film. In an adolescent peer group, rapid accurate cue pick up is the essence of "being with it." Bryan (1977) believes that we have an obligation to teach such cues to the learning disabled child and not expect this skill to develop normally.

McGlannan (1977) carries this a step farther and indicates that learning disabled children are more deficient than normals in ability to empathize with peers because they were "less able to perceive social situations appropriately." They cannot recognize or label emotions well.

AFFECTIVE EDUCATION AS A PROPHYLACTIC

One recent development which schools can utilize is affective education. These programs have to do with the non-cognitive aspects of growth— attitudes, feelings, values, and self esteem. We should build strength in pupils so that they can deal with situations in a more healthy fashion. We must teach pupils how to respond to those with disabilities, to deal with the peer culture values and behavior.

Parents can ask that these components be explored for school curricula where they do not now exist. A review of the most prevalent procedures can be found in Morse and Ravlin (in press). Cautions include avoidance of reliance on gimmicky programs or the involvement of teachers who are not trained to do this type of work.

It is especially important to avoid creating a climate of relationships which learning disabled students are less accepted socially than their classmates.

It is easy to lose sight of the essential issue in concentrating on programs. If we are to get pupils to accept those who are different without denigration, the most effective intervention will be through the way the teacher models acceptance without prejudice. It is essential that the teacher demonstrate proper attitudes and clarify the essence of acceptance.

SEXUALITY AT ADOLESCENCE

The degree to which sexual behavior has actually changed in American society over the past two decades may be open to question. It is well documented that some of the most conservative communities have always had considerable teenage sexual activity, pretend what they might. In Jessor's (1977) study 21 percent of the boys and 26 percent of the girls had sexual intercourse by the tenth grade; and by the 12th grade, 33 percent and 55 percent. Several cautions are necessary here. One is the need to protect those—the majority—who are not sexually active. Another is to remember the experience in many instances is accompanied by pressure and guilt. The trauma can be a life scar. Also, a sexual experience does not mean constant or continual sexual activity in all instances: the figures represent the loss of virginity. By the end of college the percentages are 82 percent and 85 percent. It appears that the biggest change in sexual ideology and freedom come during the college years (Dreyer 1975).

But two things are different without question. One is the broad social sanction of sexual freedom in the culture at large and contraceptive information which is available, sometimes in school courses. But the condition of sex and the teenager is anything but satisfactory. The high increase in teenage pregnancies is a national scandal. While the girl, for biological reasons, has the severe experience, both the girl and the boy have had a traumatic experiment in human relationships, responsibility, social acceptability, and personal morality as well. The willingness to take a chance is one factor, the need for close relationships of which sexual involvement is the quintessence is another. But it appears that ignorance combined with street misinformation is the most significant cause. Since they are high risk adolescents, we have a particular obligation to provide sex education to these learning disabled youth. The five youths who report in the following chapters are not exceptions. They are less likely to be able to get accurate information on their own by reading. Yet their need for love and intimate relationship may be even stronger than that of the regular adolescent. Because of social relationship difficulties they may be more prone to masturbatory fantasy with potential anxiety. Since it is known that some confrontation with homosexual sex is likely for young people, this too needs to be discussed. Further, in a society where sadism, rape, and exhibitionism are rampant, the educational domain is large and must include morality, love, social relationships, one's body feelings, and one's self-regard. So few young people are given even the basic information. Sol Gordon (1975) has an excellent paperback manual for adolescents which is particularly useful with learning disabled youngsters because of the low reading level and pictorial presentation. It is called *You*.

THE IMPORTANCE OF THE PSYCHO-SOCIAL SUPPORT SYSTEM FOR ADOLESCENTS

That is adolescence in general. What of the learning disabled? We know that school achievement is a severe risk area. When parents are not understanding and supportive, the danger of delinquent patterns increases. Many youth, judging themselves outside the achieving group, look for friends where they can find understanding and support; one solution is to gravitate to other alienated peers.

One of the important recent developments in understanding adolescence is in the analysis of the social system which surrounds each youngster. Jessor and Jessor (1977) have not only catalogued the incidence of problem behavior in typical adolescent populations, through college, but they have also given us a picture of what conditions lead to problematic behavior.

As to the incidence, they found that marijuana use rose from about 30 percent at the 10th grade to about 70 percent by the end of college. Sexual intercourse increases from over 20 percent in the 10th grade to about 45 percent in the 12th grade (girls being higher than boys), and 84 percent by the end of college. Alcohol use starts at about 68 percent in the 10th grade to 95 percent in the college group. The figures for problem drinking are somewhat under half for the high school age and about one-third of the college drinkers. Their analysis of general deviant behavior indicates that males are considerably more involved than females, and start at 38 percent the 10th year with increases throughout until college, but the actual percents are not reported.

Jessor's study involved a follow-up of the same clientele over the years, and, in addition to yearly intensive reports from the teenagers, parents also provided information. Their general conclusion is that teenagers and young adults differ on an essential dimension which they call conventionality—unconventionality. The unconventional are more likely to engage in deviant behaviors; the conventional, less likely. Conventionality is reflected by a value for academic achievement and expectation to be successful in this area; less concern for personal independence; seeing society as acceptable; the maintenance of a positive family and religious affiliation; and less tolerance of deviancy in others. They also tend to have peer group friends who are similar and, together with parents, support their beliefs. In short, they have both internalized and socially supported substantiations for their views. The alienated youth also have peer support for their oppositional views, and tend to be rather rejecting of parents or have parents who condone or tolerate their values. Environmental and personality factors tend to be reinforcing, positively or negatively.

Now this sounds fatalistic, but that is *not* the correct interpretation. There are the big ifs—*if* parents do not accept and support, *if* school achievement is impossible, *if* they are left to migrate to antisocial subgroups in the peer culture. *The message is clear.* If we are to prevent the frustration which would lead to such affiliation, the school has work to do, and that is to allow for success experiences in the school. Social agencies will need to provide a group life experience with positive peers. Friends (whoever they are) constitute models, which can be delinquent or normal in what they represent. And above all, parents will have to be certain they are seen as helpful. Can it be done? One of the best examples is Raymond, introduced later in this book, where being learning impaired did not convert risk into failure. One encouraging aspect of this example was the fact that independence did not have to be sacrificed. Parents who care and have faced their anxieties do not need to encourage dependency. If they help the youth learn how best he can solve his problems, they will be assured he can go much more on his own. Raymond's parents did this. The result was a strong, independent ego, an insurance policy against alienation. Finally, we should not allow independence to be at the expense of academic achievement. It would help if academic achievement came to be represented by school success with a properly adjusted curriculum. As with all adolescents, desirable behavior for learning disabled youth is one aspect of the personal attitudes and forces in the whole life space and not the product of a single condition. Learning impairment increases the hazards. Counseling will help those children appraise their condition, but will not be enough in itself to produce good mental health without an adequate social support system.

4

Resolving the Identity Crisis

THE CRISIS IN IDENTITY is to be resolved by the evolution of a new self. This implies independence, being the executor of one's destiny, making decisions, and being more self-sufficient. In our society all of this most frequently has to take place while the teenager is still living at home. Few move out into the world of work to support themselves. Some marry young (frequently to escape stress). Some go to college (and may manage to delay decisions for a time). But most struggle through to a new identity in the family setting. Parents and siblings are all too eager to provide painful commentary.

Youth need a psychosocial moratorium in order to accomplish the new identity. A pause is required to reorganize the self. The period of freedom is useful to test our new ideas and explore possibilities without making an irrevocable commitment. Many youth are driven by competitive anxiety to push on without a period of reflection. When one considers the significance of this process, is it any wonder that learning disabled youth find it especially difficult? We turn now to some of the specifics in young adult identity formulation.

INDEPENDENCE AND THE RELATIONSHIP TO AUTHORITY

Perhaps the most essential need which evolves in the normal adolescent is for a sense of power to manage and control his or her own affairs. Until this takes place, the adolescent remains a child. While independence does not always mean going one's own way in opposition to parents and teachers, it does mean being able to make one's own judgments based upon one's own goals.

33

Parents and teachers must realize that teenagers defy, go their own way, and resist stubbornly to feel they are arriving at some state of independence. If we realize this is a growth process we will handle it with consideration rather than defensive counter demands. Adults listen, discuss, raise issues related to the teenager's goals, and quietly counsel, saving the nonnegotiable items for those few crucial times when a possible mistake would very likely be disastrous. For the most part it is less a matter of *what* is decided, though at times that is the only recognized battle, than *who* decides which of the options to follow.

One limitation to the development of self-directedness and independence is being "outer directed," that is, depending upon external direction rather than inner direction for decision making. There is some evidence to suggest that school failures make the learning disabled adolescent reduce inner directedness right at the time when dependence is abhorred (MacMillan and Cauffield 1977).

It is clear that adolescents are often ambivalent about decisions. Following close on the heels of "I don't care. I'm going to the party anyway," may come a request for parental verification or assistance. Too assertive adult behavior often generates only more opposition. When the contest gets to the "as long as you live in this house you will do as I say," adult gamesmanship takes over. Absurd arguments and threats become the focus. When the youngster has to have "that jacket like all the kids have," best find a way to help them earn all or part of it rather than argue cost of clothes. Save the argument for the really tough decision.

For an adult to be accused of being unfair, not understanding, "you don't know what it's like today," "you are just mean," and the like is enough to throw most parents and teachers into a defense panic. To the young person's delight, we move from the real issue to the secondary one of our own defense. Adolescents still need adult authority but in new ways—co-equal discussion rather than autocratic dicta. The balancing act is not easy.

Independence, executive decision-making power, is the very core of normal adolescent development. Making reasonable decisions does not spring full fledged with the growth spurt of adolescence. One could hope for reasonable decision-making stemming from pre-adolescence, increasing along with the years. Most parents say they want the youth's independence, but it turns out they want independence only in certain things: taking care of the teenager's room and possessions, earning money, doing helpful things for the family. Independent decisions about values, where one goes and when one comes back, choice of friends, assigning a value to school attendance or sexual behavior calls for the exercise of veto power. The adolescent's underlying task runs deep: the development of a serviceable moral code. They must do this in a society where general morality is not usually clearly defined, with fractionated adult values exhibited all around them.

One of the tribal rites for both boys and girls is getting a driver's license. Even more than graduating from high school, this has come to be the sign of adulthood. For the severe learning disabled youngster this poses a special threat, since in addition to the driving, one has to pass a verbal test. Here it may take all year just to learn how to respond adequately. And then perhaps the intercession of a teacher is needed so that the authorities will "talk it" to the youth who cannot read. Some cannot read the signs to find their way about, and going downtown is a hazard.

Curriculum and Two Central Life Decisions

While today marriages are often delayed, living together and sexual behavior has increased. Life work decisions often require long preparation, and the time for commitment is being pushed up to earlier ages. The big decisions are what kind of a person do I want for a living partner and what is to be my career?

Is it to be marriage alone, or some new combination? Will the person I want, want me? Am I worthy? Am I secure enough to even explore the possibilities? With the many cultural values to which youngsters are exposed, all of these matters constitute moral decisions as well. While adequate knowledge of contraceptive methods is spotty, combined with what they do know and the willingness to take a chance, there are many new sexual issues faced by present-day adolescents. In spite of the drive for and publicity on sexual equality, many communities still adhere to traditional sex roles.

Too many adolescents find their family security dissolving around them. Parents who have only stayed together until the children have grown up may take this time to separate with less guilt, thinking the adolescent will be better able to handle it. But the teenager usually feels deserted when the need for support is highest. One youth put it in terms of wondering why after seventeen years of marriage his parents suddenly discovered they could not live together anymore. This can come at just the time the adolescent is seeking to know how one tells about love and long-term commitment or a temporary infatuation. Adolescents have been left more to their own resources and fewer stable models.

The decision about life work is complex too. What do I want to be? What can I possibly be? Who says yes and who says no? Do I have the money and ability needed? Once again, if the teenager is poor, he feels the double jeopardy of poverty and adolescence. Can I develop the skills to get a job? All work is noble, but some is more noble than other in this society. With high unemployment, any job may look good until one learns how to get along on welfare. Youth asks that the work opportunity be useful, in a social setting, bring in money, require active involvement, and offer security. Not many such opportunities come along.

Entering any field of work is difficult today. Fortunately vocational rehabilitation has begun to give attention to the learning disabled adolescent. There are all kinds of limitations in even using the resources available in the high school, resources which are supposed to be for everyone. Regardless of mechanical ability, material must first be read in order to get to auto shop. Apprenticeship is hard to come by. Serious reading retardation makes it difficult even to be a stock boy. Parental ambitions for the youth may have to be scrapped. Sheltered workshops and on-the-job training may become the major channel for many.

Recreational Needs

Since adolescence is a motor-active time, recreational pursuits should involve more than passive (or even active) watching. There should be the catharsis of play and group life for adolescents. While some of the activities will not be life long, they have a definite transitional role to play during this period.

One thing often overlooked, especially for youngsters with learning disabilities, is that the stratified society of a large high school is very difficult to penetrate. There are other activities—religious, athletic, and social groups—which may not be as rigid as the school environment.

DATA FROM THE LEARNING DISABILITIES LIFE EXAMPLES

We turn now to see how some of these adolescent tasks hit the learning disabled youngsters in the series of semi-autobiographical interviews and other related material. Much depends upon the severity of the learning disability when the pupils go to junior or senior high. Adolescence is not known as a period of high frustration tolerance for the normal child.

Frauenheim's subjects never learned to read even as adults. After ten years —some with over five years of help—gains averaged 1.3 years. Only one of the 40 ever read above the sixth grade level. And over half were negative to school—reading being their biggest problem. Still, 62 percent graduated from high school or were passed along from grade to grade regardless of skill achievement. Ten percent tried junior college. The percentage who quit high school is high, more than 37 percent. Reading scores correlate with grades completed. It is interesting that high school graduation is delayed at least a year for this group. As adults, 95 percent blamed themselves for their inability to do academic work; only a few said it was consequence of neurological factors.

In the youths reported in this book, Ron says English and History were the worst, but writing and reading were close behind. John found junior high the worst. He says he can learn best from what others say, not reading. Though he failed a course or two, things went better when they finally learned he had a reading problem. He appreciates the fact his problem was explained; it meant survival.

Raymond had real difficulty in high school in spite of his spurt and drive. He got "D" grades and could not write, but got a waiver graduation. Surprisingly, he did satisfactorily on the college boards which did not require writing. He usually managed until an exam was given, and then if it were oral he could perform. While he reads, and understands the content, he cannot write. High school people were especially difficult to get along with for him.

Raymond illustrates many of the hazards to reasonable emotional development which face the learning disabled youngster. Failing grades and having tutors in elementary school would be enough to produce discouragement in most children. But here we see the combination of supportive conditions which can keep the hope up. First of all, parents were supportive advocates and kept the school from underestimating his potential. Second, he was very bright overall and had more mature judgment. He believes in himself to the point he is ready to go to court for his rights. The difficult—some would say insurmountable—task of going on to law school does not seem too much, and he has looked at various aspects of the situation with considerable care. As a young adult, he has achieved a great deal of self-insight and, what is equally important, insight about the society in which he must function. Perhaps the best indicator of his ego strength is found in his desire to have "no more back doors." From now on, he wishes to confront the condition directly with an open honesty plus a recognition of his rights, since he knows his talents and limitations, he can plan realistic strategies. Along the way, he has found the rare person who understands, such as the college professor. These he cultivates. It is interesting how discriminating he is about help— no more tutors who do the wrong thing.

Are there cues to how adolescents develop such strength? In this case his high personal ability and his accepting and supporting parents seem to have been crucial in contributing to unusual strength. Then his problem-solving ability sustained him and brought him the successes which breed confidence. Through it all one sees the strong personal motivation. Nothing can stop him from trying. One sees in the news the rare blind person who becomes a doctor. Here is a similar situation, for Raymond says that his learning disability cannot prevent him from becoming a lawyer. One suspects that the specificity of his deficit contrasts with many who have more impairment. For example, if you can do percents but not algebra, you are in a better position to develop confidence than the youngster who can do no math.

For Andy, the 10th grade graduation was to the navy. But this "messed his life up with drugs and trouble," so he was discharged as unable to adapt. Scott felt bad about being older than the others and was anti-school in junior high. The counselors, an understanding principal, and helpful teachers were a godsend because his family was in a traumatic state at the time. Scott ran away. He quit school, became involved with drugs and went into the service. He got an exciting tour in Europe which was very maturing. The army, he says, made him, and he became a diesel mechanic.

It is interesting how important a high school diploma is, and even if it is "general," John wants no "waivers" for reading.

Finding the World of Work

A most critical issue for the learning disabled youngster is finding a job. Most of the current examples have moved around in jobs, trying one thing and then another. Like most of us, Ron has his dreams—to be a jockey. Time and time again John says he would like to do something constructive, and his parents want him to find a job. The army would only frustrate him. Andy shows confusion about the work world. He would like to be a CPA or run a truck stop. He has been a short order cook and taxi driver, among other things. Tom's real occupation is being a con man. Scott has the most independent and persistent goals, developed from the service. He is a transmission repair man working for a master technician's rating which will take him another two years.

Extracurricular Activities

Several of the men became involved in sports. John played football, but he got hurt often. Apparently, he was willing to quit and his folks were adamant that he do so. He says sports are one place you can make friends.

It is worth noting that all of these young men compensated in the manual arts areas. They had hobbies and jobs; this could be emphasized more with the learning disabled adolescents.

Drugs are available and for many almost the downfall. They know where to find them. Whether they are more frustrated than the typical teenager is hard to know. But they try what the others try. The struggle for independence from drugs is clear in several instances. They get drunk and smoke marijuana like many others.

Like many adults, they find their social life in bars, rock music concerts, bowling, and playing cards with friends. As one said, "I don't read much except the paper." Most of them say that they enjoy dancing.

Sex

Without normative information, one cannot tell the differences between learning disabled men and other men with regard to sexual behavior. The examples here range from sexual athletes to being restrictive in their behavior. There is evidence that they learn most from peers and the locker rooms. Parents are not a main source, but one of the youths did say that when you are 18, you can talk to your mother frankly about such matters. Tom began sex play as a pre-adolescent. Some exploit women; others are thoughtful about what love means, and the excitement over one's child is important to share. One can say that being learning disabled does not predicate different sexual behavior than for the normal. The number with homosexual experiences, often connected with fear in our group, may be higher than average. As one reads the summaries, it is again clear that for each individual, the introduction to sexual experience is unique and usually accompanied by anxiety.

For many learning disabled youngsters, dating is difficult. The usual anxiety about girls is accentuated by poor self-concepts. While they all reported successes, one wonders a bit. The difficulty of reading a menu, a movie announcement or a map, are not encouraging for social activity. Even the TV guide is a mystery. When it comes to the responsibility of marriage, there is often a sober, "I'm-not-ready-yet" approach before making a final decision. But we do see that marriage and children suggest the same role for these young adults as for any other.

But as things move along, there is maturing here as well. A caring wife is part of a support system critical to the welfare of these youth, and dependency here sometimes replaces the dependency on parents. Wives work. They manage the checking accounts. Scott knows and reflects on the importance of the support he gets from his wife.

Independence

The struggle for independence takes a different form for many of these young people with learning disabilities. Even when married, they may live at home. Fathers teach drivers education and how to cook. Mothers are a definite point of reference. Scott's concern for his siblings is clear evidence that we need not fear the empathetic potential of the learning disabled youngster. It is an individual matter relating to moral development. This potential is independent of the learning disability condition.

Learning disability does not stand alone. It must be seen as one aspect of life. As Scott says, "I wonder why I am, who I am; why all those problems; why not someone else?" But Scott has reached a mature level of young adulthood. Would that they all had come this far.

COUNSELING WITH TEENAGERS

When Things Go Sour

Adolescents are playing for keeps. Even non-handicapped adolescents get mixed up at times, and the high risk youth are even more likely to be confused.

Unfortunately, adolescents behave like adults when they lose hope and cannot cope. For this reason they look for what they expect will be an easy way out—even suicide. And whatever they would do, they see adults leading the way.

1. *A feeling of alienation:* Every human being is essentially a world to himself. We only dimly really know another or share. The feeling of "no one understands me" is common. This encourages alienation, not being a part of this society.

Since learning disabled youngsters tend to focus on the concrete, help is best given in relationship to specific problem situations. This is why talks with children about real conditions must supplement any formal counseling or group work. It also means that teachers, parents, and those in charge of various activities have to work through problems of life when and where they happen. We cannot depend on transfer from general discussions or that the youngster will always see similarities of conditions. They have to be pointed out without anger, again and yet again.

2. *Embracing delinquent behavior:* With the old values changing in many countries of the world and in the behavior of leaders, it is easy to rationalize and follow the models in the news into delinquency. Aggressive behavior is depicted every day. Gang behavior allows operation of one's own values. Since more than 5 percent of youth are legal delinquents every year, this is one clear pathway.

The three subdivisions are destruction of one's self through drug abuse, through attacks on people, and through the destruction and appropriation of property. These are usually signs of frustration and failure. The supposed linkage of learning disability and delinquency is a case in point. *It should be put the other way around.* Youngsters who cannot achieve using symbols in this culture are at high risk. More of them become delinquent than one expects on the basis of averages although, of course, only a few of all learning disabled youth are delinquent.

Considerable delinquency results from the schools' curriculum, teachers and administrators. Compulsory education makes the place look like a prison. One learning disabled youngster complained that the superintendent of schools ought to come around and see what school is really like. If he cannot do the work he has to sit there anyway. If you give any lip, you get kicked out. And it's all your fault! As mainstreaming increases with little commitment to or adjustment for variant ability in that mainstream, we can expect more problems. One administrator has heart-to-heart talks with the learning disabled youngsters encouraging them to drop out as soon as they are of age! Who needs them? Not the school and not the job market.

Like other children with low life satisfaction, high in anger and frustration for whatever cause, the learning disabled adolescent may turn to delinquent behavior. Social associations, impulsivity, and poor judging of cues can end up that way. But parents and teachers should know that the cause of delinquency is one's value system and *there should be no fatalistic and no generalized assumptions made about the learning disabled youngster being prone to delinquency.*

3. *Persistent procrastination:* One way to avoid responsibility is to remain undecided. Without commitment, one cannot be held account-

able. These youth take a moratorium on work. They are in hot water most of the time, but this is better than decision. Sometimes they become dedicated to fun and play. It is as if growing up is too frightening or too impossible to achieve.

COUNSELING ADOLESCENTS

The adult role starts by not being or acting like an adolescent. Adolescents need benign symbols of understanding—adults who exemplify sound behavior. More than that, they need adults who act on the basis of principles, models who both enjoy life and have mastered its trials reasonably well. There are cross age relationships which youth need and value.

It is important to keep communication as open and frank as possible. While it is true that adolescents become independent partly by their opposition to parents, the situation is more complex. Adults expect to be pressured, but they do not give up listening. We need to do less talking and more listening. We need to discover how each adolescent perceives his situation.

There are many times when the parents, the teachers or natural events are not enough help. Professional counseling is required. Counselors, psychologists, social workers, psychiatrists can be used. If the knots do not unravel, expert help must be sought.

One good means of helping learning disabled youngsters who have major conflicts is through family intervention. The most progressive approach is not family therapy where the family is the "patient" and all which that implies, but through family problem solving. The vast majority of parents both consciously and unconsciously wish the best for their learning disabled youngster, but are held back by lack of knowledge, anxiety, and immature patterns of response. Rather than making out the family is "ill" and in need of deep analysis, helping people are recognizing that the family is under stress and needs help in how to proceed. Thus more "learning" and problem solving, rather than the typical therapy role, is indicated. By meeting together (or in visits to the home), mental health workers can help the family find itself. Sometimes this requires conscious recognition of attitudes or feelings of various types which bind people together in unuseful ways. The strain on the family of hyperkinetic offspring is very real. A youngster who cannot do the things the family expects is liable to fight back. Because of the critical impact of the family, poor relationships are devastating to all members. The goal is find better ways to live together.

One caution: check to see that any public or private therapy available is of a reputable and useful nature. It is not getting therapy, but getting *proper* therapy which makes the difference.

Often the total adolescent is overlooked as the "helpers" concentrate on problem aspects. The same youngster who may be giving parents a hard time may be very helpful to a younger sibling. A youth who is giving the school trouble may be fine at home. To be seen in total perspective is a right of an adolescent.

Part II

FIVE DIFFERENT PATHS

Introduction

BETWEEN 1962 AND 1967 one of the authors had an opportunity to work closely with some thirty children with specific learning disabilities, and to do so intensively over an extended period of time. These children, all boys from a medium-sized metropolitan area, were referred for psycho-educational treatment by personnel in a typical American urban public school system. Each of the children was characterized by very severe learning disabilities and adjustment problems which were proving beyond the capacity of the neighborhood schools to handle. The families of these boys likewise were extremely agitated because of their inability to cope and their perception of the inability of the teachers of the children to meet the extreme and apparent needs of the children. These families were both professional and non-professional in terms of training and job activities, and represented a cross-section economically of what might be termed the middle income group in the United States.

The boys were placed in a highly structured program and remained in it on the average for two and one-half years. This elementary education program has been fully described in the literature (Cruickshank et al. 1961; Cruickshank 1977), so it will not be elaborated upon here again. Suffice to say that structure as it has been defined included a total concept of environment and space program, thoughtful relationships between the child and adults, and the utilization of structured teaching materials. Discussion groups with fathers and mothers were regularly held throughout the period of clinical teaching experienced by the children. Social services, psychiatry, pediatrics, neurology, audiology, speech pathology, and a spectrum of educational services were available to the children and to their families.

When it was judged that the child could return to the regular classroom to compete at age in grade, a carefully supervised transfer back to the neighborhood school was undertaken.

Although some liaison was maintained with the neighborhood schools for a relatively short period of time following transfer from the clinical teaching program, this was not felt to be necessary for any extensive period of time. It was determined by the staff of the clinical program —an interdisciplinary staff comprised of all the necessary basic disciplines —that the children were ready for transfer and were capable of competing in the regular grades to which they were assigned. Thus, continued supervision of them by the clinical teaching staff was judged to be neither necessary nor appropriate. A psychological as well as an administrative transfer was appropriate at that time, and it was effected. The children and their families were believed able to function within the usual facilities of the community school system. No further contact was planned with respect to the children concerned, and none was made.

Between ten and twelve years elapsed, and a follow-up on the children, now youths or young adults, was undertaken. In this book five of the thirty youths have been selected for somewhat detailed consideration. Of the thirty who were originally in the project, only one is reported to have had any serious contact with the police or with legal authorities of his community. His story is included in this section of the book, not to scare the reader, but to acknowledge that the best in educational effort may not always be sufficient. All the others in varying degrees have been able to maintain an adjustment in the community which has not brought them into direct conflict with the law-enforcement agencies. Not all have achieved completely independent lives.

A sixth youth consulted for some time with another of the authors. His story and that of Jim's are referred to in the final section of the book, not only because they add another dimension to the adjustment spectrum in learning disability, but because they highlight the need for advocacy which may be an important ancillary service required for these children and youths throughout much of their lives. Success and good adjustment may well be within the grasp of many who have learning disabilities. Hurdles to these accomplishments, however, often reside outside the child or youth—in the attitudes of teachers, school officials, parents, employers, and others who cannot be moved by the youth alone.

The youths selected for discussion here illustrate a spectrum of adult adjustment, from being in conflict with society through varying degrees of moderate and successful personal and community adjustment. Each of these young men volunteered to provide us with two hours of recorded interviews which probed at times rather mercilessly into many aspects of their social and educational growth since they returned to the regular school programs of their communities.

At the time of the interviews, the youths were between the ages of 19 and 23 years of age. The youngest was a senior in high school; one was employed part-time; one was self-employed; one was employed in a competitive type job in industry; one was unemployed and in prison.

In the following chapters the young men will tell their stories. Their comments will be interlaced with some data taken from their clinical records of a dozen years earlier, and with professional comments aimed at providing as full a picture of the youths as possible. They tell much of significance to professional educators, to psychologists, parents, and others who have responsibilities for implementing programs in junior and senior high schools for young people with perceptual processing deficits and concomitant learning disabilities. Each of the youths at one time in his life was seen as a child with all of the classical symptomatology of perceptual processing deficits based on firm or highly suspected neurological dysfunction. Each met the critieria of definition of specific learning disability.

5

Ronald: Success through Structure

As a child Ronald was almost beyond the control of adults; as a young man he is nervous and tense. As a boy he had an inadequate father model; as an adult he is still tied to his mother and to family controls. As a boy Ron needed extreme structure to survive; as an adult he has profited from a structured home, a dominant mother, and a structured religion. Ron is making it in a modest way. His parents still provide him strength, but he has demonstrated his ability for limited achievement. He has unresolved problems, the chief of which is what will he do when his parents die? His sexual repressions, which appear very controlling, have never been verbalized.

When the first telephone contact was made after a twelve-year lapse, Ron's mother answered. Following identification of the caller and a few comments, the conversation ceased. It was quiet on the phone for a few seconds, and then the mother rushed to speak: "Ron's made it. It was awful when he was a boy, but he's made it. He's made it. Come for Friday night dinner and you'll see".

Ronald was first seen in a special training program at the age of nine, and thirteen years later at twenty-two years of age. In his and the succeeding studies all of the early boyhood material is indented and is in smaller type.

Author	Ron, I believe it's a good ten or eleven years since we have seen each other. You didn't have a mustache when I knew you then!
R	No, I couldn't grow one then.
Au	No, you sure couldn't, but now you are twenty-three, and it's growing in great shape. What are you doing these days?
R	Well, right now I run my mother's delicatessen.

49

The social worker's comments regarding Ron's parents are of interest not only to provide background information about Ron, but in the light of his continued living in his parents' house at the age of twenty-two.

"Mr. and Mrs. Creason have been quite preoccupied with their difficulties, both marital and business, since Ron's birth. They have had financial difficulties, hence the necessity of Mrs. Creason going to work. As a result, Ron was cared for by three older sisters who were not capable of giving him the type of care that he needed. His power struggle with the mother is probably the result of, first of all, a desire to have her home to care for him, and secondly, her own guilt about not supplying him with the kind of care he really needed. Mr. Creason is, at best, quite ineffectual in the role of a father. He maintains a peer relationship with Ron, which takes away from Ron any opportunity for identification. In this way Ron also has no outside controls for his impulsivity, and this necessitates further acting out. This lack of an identification model is also evident in Ron's feminine behavior.

"The hyperactivity, distractibility, decreased attention span, and facial myclonic movements are suggestive of an organic brain impairment, according to the neurologist. These symptoms, however, become exaggerated in the home situation, since the care is quite inconsistent and very little structure is provided for him. In addition to this, Ron and Mr. Creason seem to be one family, and Mrs. Creason and the girls are another family. She has, for example, consented to having the girls attend therapy sessions at the Jewish Family Center, but for some reason this has never been supplied for Ronald. Mr. Creason has not been interested in involving himself in any kind of therapeutic situation. Mr. Creason has difficulty in handling his own aggression and, as indicated by several comments, he doesn't know his own strength, which would also suggest his inability to really help Ron handle his own impulses and aggression. Mr. Creason hopes to make a baseball player out of Ron. He has been molding him in this direction by taking him to ball games three times a week and providing him with considerable baseball equipment. This seems to be quite unrealistic in view of Ron's poor coordination. Ron may also be reacting to his father's providing this molding type of activity while supplying him with very little else in any other area of life."

Au   What do you mean, you run the delicatessen? You manage or operate it?

R   Well, my Mother's retired, and she had a back injury two years ago where she can't really work anymore. So, my Father comes in and helps out once in a while, but like I'm there. I run it—make it go.

Au   The whole operation is within your own store. You don't have the food preparation done outside?

R   Right, most everything is done right there.

Au   I see. Do you have any other employees working for you?

R   Just one.

Au   You supervise that person?

R   Right.

Au   Is this a man or a woman?

R   A woman.

Au   Is she older or younger than you?

R   Older.

Au   She's worked there for some time?

R   Ah, about a year and a half to two years.

Au   I see. Who hired her? Did you hire her?

R   Well, no; my mother did that. The cook that we used to have was a friend of hers. He brought her into the store for us.

Au   Do you do some of the cooking?

R   Yeah, but now we have people outside who send things in for sale.

Au   I see. Do you do the planning?

R   Yeah.

Au   Do you ask people to send food in for sale?

R   Yeah. I make the contacts.

Au   Ever get any complaints on the food?

R   Every now and then, not too many.

Au   When's the last complaint you got?

R   Mmmm, last week. Not often, we watch things.

Au   Do you mind my asking you if you pay your own income tax?

R   Right.

Au   Ah, how much did you pay in taxes last year, do you remember how many dollars?

R   You mean from the business or?

Au   No.

R   From myself?

Au   You, yourself. How much salary did you earn?

R   Ah, 6 something, 6 . . .

Au $6,000?

R $6,000 something, but I can't really place it exactly.

Au   That's all right. How much was the income from the business as a whole? Do you have any idea?

R   Gee, that I don't, 'cause I have my own, ya know, accountant that keeps the books.

Au   You have an accountant?

R Right.

Au You have never tried keeping the books yourself?

R Well I have, but as far as . . . like, um . . . like, I would keep the checks, and y'know, what bills to pay, but as far as taxes, withholding taxes, I just let my accountant do that.

Au You say, "*I*" have an account," "*my* accountant." Did you employ him?

R No, this one has been with my Mother, y'know, for years.

Au I understand. So, you didn't select the accountant?

R Right. He's been with us ever since we've been . . .

Au You have a pretty good business?

R Not bad; it's got its seasons.

Au Yes, of course. I would imagine so. Do your father and mother as well as yourself live off the income of the shop?

R Ah, no. They don't take anything out.

Au They have their own retirement income?

R Right. The Social Security and 'cause my mother's on disability from the work.

Au So that the whole business is entirely yours?

R Right, in a sense. Like I run it, but my mother is still the president of the corporation.

Au Do you contribute to your father and mother at all? Do you give them money from the business?

R No, I give them room and board for myself.

Au Sure, I can understand that. You've always lived with your dad and mother, have you?

R Except for one time when I moved out in the summer with about two friends, and that was right before I was gonna go to the community college. Then I had to move back. My mother said the summer was over, time to go back to school.

Au I see. So, this was more of a holiday kind of moving out . . .

R Right.

Au . . . than living on your own. Did you go to the community college?

R Just for about two months.

Au Why did you stop?

R Well, I had a lot of bills, and I was working two jobs, and I couldn't keep up with my studying. So, I dropped out, but I would like to go back someday, maybe night school.

Au Now let's back up. You'd been with us about two and a half years at the clinical program when you left us to go back to the public schools.

R Right.

Au　When I say "us" I mean the program. You left us to go back into the sixth grade, I believe.

R　Right.

Au　And went where after that?

R　Smith Junior High.

Au　After that you must have gone to Johnson High School?

R　Right.

Au　Johnson High School is essentially an academically oriented high school, isn't it?

R　Yeah, even when my sisters went there, it was very high.

Au　When you went there, it must have been equally as academically oriented.

R　Right.

Au　Ah, did you ever fail after you went into the fifth grade?

R　No.

Au　Did you ever fail a course?

R　No.

Au　Can you remember before you came to us at the program what kind of school experience you'd had there?

R　Before?

Au　Before you came to the clinical teaching program. Do you remember your early school days?

R　Well, let me think.

Au　We can talk about other things if you'd prefer.

R　No, I'll tell you. I had problems sitting in classes, like I was, I couldn't sit still, and I was always up and bothering the teachers and everything. Overactive, like.

Au　Overactive?

R　Right. It was like I couldn't ever be still—always moving or feeling I had to move.

The psychologist's comments here reinforce Ron's memory of his early behavior and his problems of adjustment. When Ron was nine years old, the psychologist reported that he, "was easily distracted by extraneous stimuli and had difficulty maintaining both his self-control and motivation for the testing procedures. A basic visual-motor disturbance is suggested by his performance on the Bender. Inconsistency of hand preference was also noted. His performance on the WISC indicates that Ron is of average intellectual ability. His thinking lacked conciseness and was usually concrete and peripheral to the problem. Difficulty was encountered on both the Object Assembly and Block Design test, which lends credence to the hypothesis that a visual-motor disturbance does exist. Hyperactive and distractible behavior in conjunction with the absence of critical evaluation of his own work suggests poorly established ego controls. Problems centering around the fear of rejection, feelings of inferiority, and overconcern with self-esteem permeate his protocols. Ronald appears to be driven to react to the immediate stimulus situation. Intrinsic motivation in terms of satisfaction to be derived from a sustained striving for a better performance was conspicuously missing. In view of a basic visual-motor disturbance and the incomplete establishment of hand dominance, a thorough neurological examination should be considered.

"Ron impressed me as being extremely immature and high-strung. His immaturity was manifested in the quality of his performance on the WISC, on those tasks requiring him to draw figures or copy designs, and his periodic use of 'baby talk' when failure on a task was iminent. He was behaviorally hyperactive and his body was in constant motion. A forced responsiveness to both visual and auditory extraneous stimuli resulted in poor test motivation when persistence was a necessary element in the successful solution of problems. Inconsistent hand preference was noted during his performance on the various drawing tasks. Poorly developed eye-hand control was also in evidence. Ron had a rather unusual gait which can best be described as a pronounced shuffle. Although he presents a rather happy and friendly appearance, he is lacking in both social skills and self-confidence."

Au   It is quite true that you were constantly on the move. You were all over the place at once. There was a window ledge. It held the air conditioning units and the heating units. It was just next to the study cubicle where you were, and for many, many weeks you used that window ledge as a "launching pad." Every time you got up from your chair, you would climb upon that and soar off into space. You were very hyperactive, I can assure you of that point. You had practically no attention span, but when you left us, you certainly were able to hold on.

R   No, but I still had some problems. You know, one of the problems I had was that I have always been confused about which hand to use. Sometimes the right and other times the left. I write with my left hand most of the time, but not always. Everybody was always talking to me about my writing and drawing. Those things come hard for me even now. I got by, but it wasn't easy.

The psychologist noted: "Ron's protocol suggests a basic visual-motor disturbance. Poor planning ability was evident in terms of his placement of the Bender designs. The dots on configuration 1 gradually increased in size, loops replaced dots on configurations 3 and 4 and poor angulation and gross distortion of the configurations were to be noted on designs 7 and 8. His configurations were crowded together on the top half of the page so closely as to form an actual merger. Inability to sustain motivation for the task and a rapid loss of impulse control characterized his behavior. These configurations were reproduced with Ron's left hand. He held the pencil in a rather awkward manner and had difficulty coordinating his eye-hand movements. Despite the number of errors and obvious distortions which appeared in his protocol, Ron failed to criticize his own performance or attempt to erase or correct these mistakes."

The pediatrician who examined Ron at the same time adds some additional comments reflecting the image he gave others when he was nine years old:

"The patient is left-handed, throws the ball with his left hand, and kicks with his left foot. Hyperactivity and restlessness are evident, but he cooperated well during the examination. His attention span is short with distractibility being present. The hyperactivity, distractibility, decreased attention span and facial myclonic movements are suggestive of an organic brain impairment. One additional feature is the occasional episodes of lack of contact lasting from 1 to 15 minutes. These symptoms have been noted regularly during the story-time sessions and would suggest a paroxysmal disorder."

The electroencephalographer commented: *"Mild to moderate abnormality due to isolated spike fossi from right frontal and right central areas. Record strongly suggestive of focal cortical convulsive disorder."*

Au   Can you think back to what your best and worst grades were at Johnson High?

R   My best would be math.

Au   What kind of grades did you get in that?

R   Well, probably about, I'd say, a "B," "B minus" average.

Au   That's good. For that high school, very good. What were your worst subjects?

R   Probably English and history.

Au   Well, why were English and history so difficult?

R   Ah, English was probably my worst. Reading is a problem still.

Au   What kind of grades did you get in English?

R   Well, that was my average. I got a "D" once in awhile. Where I had trouble putting paragraphs in, writing, like compositions. That's where my trouble was. As far as reading a book and that, I didn't have too many problems.

Au   Were you in athletics at all at Johnson?

R   No, I didn't have time. Just what, you know, was in gym. Outside, I always worked after I got out.

Au   At the delicatessen?

R   Yeah, or I worked once at a fast food place for almost two years.

Au   How did you get along there?

R   Good.

Au   We'll come back to that in a minute. You graduated from high school?

R   Right.

Au   With what kind of diploma? By that I mean the Regents' diploma or a general diploma, do you remember?

R   Well, I took the Regents, like I passed my Regents' English exam.

Au   You did, really?

R   Just barely.

Au   I don't care how you passed it. But you passed it. That's wonderful. And your history and math, did you take Regents' exams?

R   Ah, history, yes. I don't know about math 'cause in my twelfth year I took accounting, and I did real good in that.

Au   What grade did you get in accounting?

R   Well, I finished up, got a "B" on my final exam and an "A" as my final mark.

Au   Ron, that's great.

R   That's the only subject I'm really good at, math.

Au   Well, that's all right. Nobody is good in everything. That's wonderful.

R   That's what I'd like to go back into if I went back to school.

Au   Into accounting?

R   Yeah, bookkeeping, something like that.

Au   Really, my word! I would never had thought that you were going to excel in mathematics. That's just wonderful. You told me you owned a van?

R   Right.

Au   It's the company's van, isn't it?

R   Right.

Au   So, you obviously have a driver's license?

R   Yeah.

Au   Do you deliver food or is . . .?

R   Deliver, pick up.

Au   On top of that, you do the ordering and some cooking?

R   Right.

Au   You're a busy young man.

R   Keeps me busy.

Au   I'll bet. How many hours a day do you work?

R   Well, on the average of about seven. I go in at 7:00 in the morning, and I'm usually done at 2:00–2:30.

Au   Including the deliveries?

R   Well, no, the deliveries I do only twice a week after I close the store. I don't have that many. I used to have a big route where it'd take me an hour. But now I can do it in a half hour. I do that after I'm all done working at the store.

Au   Has business gone down?

R   Well, it's starting to pick up now. Last week, 'cause the kids were back in school, things are more regular.

Au   I see, this is part of the seasonal bit.

R   Right, the summer is the slowest part.

Au   How old were you when you got your driver's license?

R   Sixteen.

Au   Did you take the driver's education in high school?

R   Yeah, many years after. I took it last year.

Au   Why did you take it?

R   Just to bring down my insurance rates.

Au   Where did you learn how to drive?

R   My father taught me.

Au   Are your parents happy about your being able to learn to drive?

R   Oh, yeah.

Au   Were they worried about you?

R   No, I've been driving almost eight years now, eight years this February.

Au   Did you earn the license, pass the examination on the first attempt?

R   Yeah.

Au   The written part was not difficult for you?

R   No, I think I only missed three.

Au   That's great. You're how old now, Ron?

R   I'll be 24 next month.

Au   You must have been one of the older kids that we had in that program.

R   Yeah, I think I was.

Au   So, how old were you when you graduated from high school?

R   Oh, let's see, it would be four years now.

Au   So, you were 19 or 20 when you graduated from high school?

R   Right.

Au   The older age than what might be considered usual was a result of the failure experiences that you had when you were a little tyke?

R   Yeah, I had, in, um, first grade, too, a lot of trouble. Where they put me
        into second grade, second grade was too tough for me, so they put me
        back into first grade another year. I was set back, all together, two, no
        three years back then.

> The social worked reported: "Ron craves attention at school and
> in the home—will go to any length to get it—at home shows hostility by
> destroying toys and furniture; in school breaks up pencils and crayons,
> makes noises, sings, hums, laughs aloud at nothing when room is quiet.
> Extremely restless.
>
> "Parents have long history of financial and business problems—
> 1st chicken business; at present food market. This necessitated leaving
> children alone at times with Ronald supervised by his sisters. An older
> sister has suddenly shown symptoms of being extremely disturbed; an-
> other is very irritable and unhappy over small incidents that occur in the
> classroom. She has been referred to the Child Guidance Center. The
> family has followed through and is receiving counseling. Parents have
> sought help from that agency for Ron previously, but did not follow
> through because of pressures of business.
>
> "Now, however, both parents realize that all four children have
> been seriously damaged by family pressures and agree that both will be
> obliged to cooperate to the fullest extent.
>
> "The school has attempted in every way possible to help Ron in a
> regular classroom—has excluded him for half-day periods when neces-
> sary, transferred him to other teachers, and even accelerated him in
> order to stimulate his interests."

Au   Your mother is pretty excited about the fact that you were able to make
        it when you got into the fifth and sixth grades.

R   Yeah.

Au   She talked very warmly about the clinical teaching program.

R   Well, she loved the program; she thought it was great for me.

Au   Well, it was a good program. You did a good job there, too. The pro-
        gram was good because you guys settled down and really got going. You
        had an excellent teacher; you really had two teachers.

R   Two of them. Oh, what was her, Mrs. S., I remember. I can't think of
        the other.

Au   Miss G.?

R   Right, that's it. I couldn't think of it. They were both great. I owe a lot to
        them. My mother says so too. Mrs. S., she was a good teacher, and she
        was the one who really got me on the track. Yeah, she started me going.

Au   She sure did. You weren't the easiest guy to get on the track, either.

R   No. Boy, did I have problems—so many problems when I was little, before fifteen years old.

When Ron came to the clinical teaching program as a child with suspected convulsive disorders or epilepsy, serious specific learning disabilities, and behavioral problems, it was also reported that "he could barely read and had great difficulty with mathematical concepts." Actually under appropriate individual testing situations, his academic skills were found to be very good for his chronological age—indeed excellent in terms of the disruption of his early years. The behavioral manifestations and a serious emotional overlay clouded the teachers' perceptions of what he could really accomplish. Over the two-year period his achievements were measured as noted below:

CALIFORNIA ACHIEVEMENT TESTS

Date	Reading Grade	Arithmetic Grade	English Grade	Spelling Grade
5-30-63 (initial data on admission)	4.9	4.0	6.0	5.6
11-12-63	5.5	4.2	6.3	6.4
6-10-65	6.0	6.1	7.1	6.7
10-2-65	7.1	6.1	6.7	6.6

The achievement levels of this learning disabled boy cloud the problem. A child with classical symptoms of organicity and hyperactivity, Ron had somehow been able to put it together insofar as academic achievement was concerned. His original academic successes were completely lost to view, however, in his inability to control his irritating behavior and his emotional fluctuations.

Au   You've developed into a fine man. Let me ask you some other things. Do you live at home?

R   Right.

Au   But do you have outside friends?

R   Well, yeah.

Au   Of your own age?

R   Ah, it varies, you know, my age, a year younger, two years younger.

Au   Oh well, I recognize age at your age doesn't really make much difference, but your friends are not just your father's or mother's friends, I take it.

R   Oh no, I've got lots, I couldn't even start naming 'em all.

Au   Boys and girls, men and women?

R   Yeah.

Au   What do you do socially with your friends?

R   Go out to bars and go out to, y' know, like concerts, things like that.

Au   What kind of concerts do you attend?

R   Oh, the ones at the civic auditorium, like rock groups and stuff like that.

Au   Rock groups? Do you play a musical instrument?

R   No, never took that up.

Au   But you do like rock music?

R   Yeah.

Au   Any other kind of music?

R   I love disco music. Yeah. That's about it, I like oldies, too.

Au   Do you dance?

R   Mmm-hum.

Au   Do you go dancing?

R   Yeah.

Au   Ah, how frequently do you go dancing?

R   Probably once a month.

Au   How old were you when you learned how to dance?

R   Oh gee, it'd be awhile back, probably since I've been in high school, at least, junior high maybe.

Au   You weren't very well-coordinated when you were a little boy.

R   No, I really wasn't. I was all feet.

Ron's motor behavior and function was considerably less than smooth. Throughout his participation in the clinical teaching program he received approximately 30 minutes per day of individualized gross-motor training. The comments of those who worked with him in this area indicate a constant problem, however: "General awkwardness in gross movement. Non-rhythmic and jerky gait." "Rigidity in wrists and fingers." He involves gross body movements in speaking, reading, and writing." "He has obtained a degree of fluency with the Getman exercises. The leg movements have not improved as much as had the arm movements. Coordination is somewhat improving. Visual tracking has gained considerable fluency, although regressions have been noted. There is still a tendency to lose the object through distractibility and a tendency to jump ahead at the left and right extremes. He can be all feet at times."

Au   But you can dance now; you can keep time?

R   Yeah, it took me a little practice, but nowadays tunes are a little harder to keep up with.

Au   Well, that may be true. Where did you learn how to dance? Who taught you?

R   Just picked it up from friends, watching 'em, y' know.

Au   Did you have a girlfriend all through high school to go dancing with?

R   No, just on and off.

Au   On and off. Do you have a girlfriend now?

R   No, nothing steady.

Au   But you go with girls?

R   Yeah.

Au   Have you ever had sexual relations with girls?

R   Umm, once.

Au   How did that happen? Where was it at?

R   What do you mean by where? We were in a park near where our street is.

Au   Well, I mean how did it happen? Were you with a crowd of guys, were you drunk when it happened?

R   No, we were alone—no one else around.

Au   Were you not drunk?

R   No, this was when I was going out with this girl.

Au   In high school?

R   Yeah. I started it, and then I got scared. She dared me to keep on. I sort of had to keep going, she wanted it. I was really scared. I didn't know what to do. She showed me. It was good finally, but I was really scared. Sort of blew my mind.

Au   But you don't have sexual relationships regularly now?

R   No.

Au   Do you wish you would?

R   Well, it's funny, 'cause I'm a funny guy. Like I don't want to go to bed with any girl, ya know, I like to, I gotta feel something for them before.

Au   But you like to go with girls. It's not that you don't like to go with girls?

R   Right.

Au   If you don't mind my pursuing this just a little bit further, Ron, where did you get your information about girls and about your own sexual growth? It wasn't at the clinical teaching program.

R   We were pretty young then.

Au   Where was it?

R   Friends, books, y' know, different places.

Au   Did your dad and mom direct you at all? Did they give you any hints, help, or tell you where you could find out accurate information?

R   No, I just read on my own.

Au   How did you happen to get books which would give you information about your own sexual development?

R   Usually from friends. If they read them, they'd let me read them. I'd ask for them.

Au   These were scientific books, or were they pornography, or what?

R   They were scientific books, not dirty stuff.

Au   Did your own physical development as you were getting into adolescence bother you at all? Did you worry about it? Was there anybody you could ask questions?

R   I would just ask my friends, really. I did worry some. I'd watch the guys in the locker room and compare me with . . .

Au   Your friends?

R   Yeah.

Au   Any particular friends, or did you have some very close?

R   I had a couple close friends that I went to high school with, all through.

Au   Did you engage in any kind of sex play with them?

R   No.

Au   It was purely on a conversational basis?

R   Right.

Au   These were boys?

R   Right.

Au   Could you have talked with your parents about these things? Would they have advised you freely?

R   No, I wouldn't have felt easy talking with them. I guess this is about the first time right now that I've ever talked about this with someone like a parent—someone older than me, you know what I mean.

Au   Yes. I do. You're not going with a girl now?

R   No.

Au   When was the last time you were out dancing?

R   Ah, a week ago this past Wednesday. No, I was at a wedding Saturday. Saturday night I was at a wedding.

Au   But you went to the wedding by yourself, or did you go with somebody?

R   No, I went with myself and, y' know, it was one of my friend's wedding. So, a lot of my friends were there.

Au   When was the last time you went out with a girl?

R   That would be a week ago Wednesday.

Au   Did you ask her, or did you meet her someplace, or?

R   No, I picked her up at her house.

Au   So you are going with a girl from time to time, but not steady with a girl?

R   Right, not steady.

Au   Have you thought about marriage?

R   I have, but I'm not ready. I'm, I feel in another couple years, y' know, I don't want to get tied down right now.

Au   Is that why you're not going steady with a girl, or is the opportunity just not presenting itself?

R   Well, I don't really go out that much 'cause I work, so I usually, all I go out is once a week, twice a week on week-ends.

Au   So, once a week or twice a week on week-ends you go out, but what about the other five nights? What are you doing?

R   Well, I bowl in a league Monday nights.

Au   Good. What's your average?

R   Right now 168–169.

Au   Oh, that's good. By golly, you couldn't . . .

R   Yeah, I started bowling in junior high. I think I was about 16 or 15.

Au   Were you? You couldn't hit a barn door with a bowling ball when you were the little boy I knew.

R   Yeah, every year my bowling average keeps going up. All that stuff you made us do at the program ought to have helped us do something! Maybe that's why I can bowl good. Remember all those physical things we practiced?

Au   Certainly. That's great. What team do you bowl on?

R   Well, I belong to the Jewish organization, Beth Israel. We have a league on Monday nights.

Au   You go to a synagogue?

R   No, not really. Just on holidays.

Au   You observe the holidays?

R   Right.

Au   How many guys are on your bowling team?

R   Ah, four.

Au   And you're there every night, are you, every time?

R   Every Monday. Y' know, unless I come down sick, but I only miss maybe once or twice a year.

Au   That's great. So, Monday nights is bowling.

R   Right. Tuesday night is TV. Wednesday nights I go out sometimes, or I'll stay home. Thursday night I play cards.

Au   With whom?

R   With about six guys from my bowling league. That's our once a week fling, and then usually on Friday I go out—maybe with a girl or alone to a movie.

Au   What kind of cards do you play, poker?

R   Yeah, poker.

Au   Money involved?

R   Yeah.

Au   What do you play per point?

R   Ah, ten cents.

Au   Do you win ever?

R   Oh, yeah. Every now and then I usually . . . every other week, sometimes two weeks in a row.

Au   What's the most you ever won in a night?

R   Probably about $18.00.

Au   What's the most you ever lost?

R   Probably about $22.00.

Au   You think you're averaging out, so that your winnings are offsetting your losses?

R   It figures that way somehow. You never get ahead.

Au   Do you read much for pleasure?

R   Ah, not really books. I like to read the morning newspaper. As far as books, I don't really have time, 'cause when I come home at night, if I stay home I watch TV and by the time I get done watching it, I just go to sleep.

Au   Would you say you're good friends with your dad and mother?

R   Yeah, I'm very close to them.

Au   Do you have brothers or sisters? I don't recall.

R   Yeah, three sisters. I had a brother but he died very young.

Au   Do they, your sisters, live at home?

R   Well, two of them are married. One has her own house, and my other sister moved back about three months ago, 'cause she just had a baby about four months ago. They couldn't afford, she's not working right now. So they're living, she and her husband, with us.

Au   Her husband lives at your home, too?

R   Yeah.

Au   How do you feel about that?

R   It's not bad, 'cause you know, there's more people in the house. But sometimes it's sort of a hassle, you know, everybody gets in their way, but other than that . . .

Au Do you like your sister?

R Yeah. We're always fighting but, y' know, but basically as far as my family, we'd go out of our way for anybody.

Au That's great. Then your other sisters, they live nearby as well?

R Right.

Au And you see them often?

R About once a week, sometimes twice a week.

Au Will your family all be getting together for the holidays?

R Oh, they always do on holidays.

Au Have your father and mother and you always maintained or observed the religious holidays?

R Right.

Au Ron, have you ever thought of going into the armed services?

R Well, I really can't. I'm on, I have an illness where I can't go in.

Au What is your illness?

R Colitis and ileitis.

Au I can understand. Is that a chronic problem with you? By chronic I mean, is it something you experience constantly?

R Not if I stay on my diet. I'm on medication, too.

Au What kind of a diet are you on?

R Well, mostly a non-spice diet. Like Italian foods, fried foods and stuff like that—they're out.

Au Most of the foods out of your own kitchen, the holiday foods and the foods you would normally eat within a good Jewish family are . . .

R . . . all greasy and full of fat!

Au So, how do you handle that?

R Well, I eat that. 'Cause all I have it is like twice a year or three times a year. So, as long as I'm on a diet, you know, regularly, I can eat it one day; it won't upset me.

Au How long have you had this problem?

R Um, gotta be close to about seven or eight years now.

Au Does this have any relationship, do you think, to the hyperactivity that you experienced when you were a little boy?

R Well, I don't, I really can't say on that, but it has something to do with the Jewish cooking.

Au You think so?

R 'Cause my sister had it before I did. Now my aunt has it down in New York, and someone was reading a book where it says that it's from the Jewish cooking, like with all the fats, and plus nervousness. It's like when I get real nervous, my illness bothers me.

Au Do you consider yourself a nervous young man?

R Yeah.

Au How would you describe yourself, Ron, at this point? You sure look relaxed now.

R Well, y' know, I am relaxed. But when like things go wrong, y' know, don't go right in the store, and something is wrong where it's not busy and I got bills to meet, then I get nervous. That's about the only time. I've always been tense though—hyperactive when I was a little kid and nervous now. I'm not like I was, though. I've learned some ways to control the hyperactivity. Sometimes it gets to me. Sometimes I don't understand me. Like when I'm at the races.

Au The races, eh? Do you bet? What does that have to do with hyperactivity by the way?

R Oh yes, I love the races. I just get so nervous that my colitis steps up. I get tense and really jump around. Well, I used to go two, three times a week, unless I was sick.

Au You go with guys or go alone?

R Well, I go sometimes with friends. I've taken a couple girls out there. But they don't seem to like it.

Au Really? How are you doing financially at the race track?

R Well, I was winning for a year, but I gave up.

Au You mean you gave up while you were winning?

R Right.

Au Or because you . . .

R Well, the store was slow, so I wasn't on a full salary, so I stopped going. But when I left I was probably about $200 ahead for the year.

Au If the races make you nervous, why do you go?

R It gets in your blood. I love the races, and I guess I'd rather have my insides back up awhile than not go at all. They are a big release for me.

Au Oh, that's great! What were we talking about before we got off on car racing?

R Oh, about my . . . hyperactivity.

Au Oh yes, let's go back to that. How do you sleep at night? Do you sleep pretty well?

R Yeah, I would say so. I don't sleep that much though. I usually average about six hours a night. Then I get up and go to work.

Au Do you like what you're doing, Ron?

R Ah, as far as . . . I don't know if I really want to continue with it all my life, 'cause it is a hard-working job, standing around and doing all that, but ah . . .

Au   What would you like to do if you had your choice? What would you en-
      joy doing?

R   Do you want to know the truth?

Au   Yeah.

R   I would like to be a jockey, a race driver.

Au   A racer!

R   Yeah, believe it or not, a harness race driver and a jockey, too.

Au   Do you ride?

R   No, I have ridden when I was little, you know, on the trails, but that's
      my far-out dream, which I know I'll never get, but that's what I would
      really like.

Au   What's your second choice?

R   Ah, it's hard to say; I would like to go back to school though, I think. I
      would like some sort of desk job, y' know, where you sit down. 'Cause
      all the jobs I've worked at, I've been on my feet. And I don't know how
      long I'll last. 'Cause my mother's had problems with her feet, and she's
      been on her feet all her life. Y' know, it's too long a day on your feet. I go
      home at night sometimes and my feet are bothering me.

Au   Your father, though, also worked with the delicatessen, didn't he? Well,
      Ron, I'd like to go back to some of the work that you've done since
      you've gotten out of high school. You told me you worked for a couple
      of years in a fast food shop. What was your specific job? Busboy, or
      what?

R   Everything. Waited on the counter, made the hamburgs, stocked the
      shelves, and . . .

Au   Ran the cash register?

R   Yeah.

Au   Made change?

R   Made change, hand out the food, all of it.

Au   If you worked there for two years, you must have gotten along pretty
      well with people, is that right?

R   Yeah. Well, the last year I used to just make, ya know, work on the grill
      back there, just made 'em. But the first year I was doing everything,
      like . . .

Au   Was working on the grill a promotion or demotion?

R   Well, I told them that I really didn't care to wait on the counter. It got
      too hectic, y' know, during the lunch hour. Where the boss would al-
      ways yell at ya, "you're not going fast enough." So, at the time I was one
      of the best, y' know, grill people they had back there. So, I used to al-
      ways do that.

Au   You came to the decision yourself that . . .

R   Well, I asked 'em, y' know.

Au   But you must have made the decision that it would be more comfortable for you to work one place than another?

R   Right.

Au   Ah, that shows your good judgment, I think. I'm not criticizing at all. Did the change of job indicate a change of pay for you, or did you get the same amount?

R   No, I got the same amount.

Au   Same pay regardless of what you did. You worked there two years. Did you get any pay raises over the time you were there?

R   Yeah. I got, I think, when I started, I think it was minimum, then it jumped up, then it jumped up again. It was like I was getting raises like that, but I left there . . . I think I was earning like $2.10 or $2.20 an hour.

Au   Mmm-hum. Ron, why did you leave there and where did you go?

R   Let's see, that would be when I was getting out of high school. It would either be, well, finally I didn't really care for it, y'know. I knew I wasn't gonna go anywhere anyway. But I can't remember if it was in eleventh grade when I quit, or if it was after twelfth, or if it was in the summertime.

Au   I see. They didn't fire you, in other words.

R   No.

Au   You quit. Did you get another job right away?

R   Yeah, that's when I went to Carvel's.

Au   That's another fast-food kind of place?

R   No, just ice cream. It's an ice cream store.

Au   Ah, yeah. How long did you work there?

R   At the time I was working at my mother's delicatessen.

Au   I see. So, you had two jobs?

R   Right.

Au   An eight-hour shift at Carvel's.

R   No, not quite. I would go in about, I think 7:00 A.M., and I would get home, get done, about 11:30 A.M.

Au   Then you'd start working at the store?

R   Well, then I was going to school, so I would go in after. That's when I did my deliveries; it was like 3:00 P.M. until 7:00 P.M. that I worked.

Au   Then after you stopped working at Carvel's, what did you do?

R   Then I was working; then I went to community college for two months.

Au   Yeah.

R   Then I was working afterwards, at my mother's store.

Au   Somebody told me that you were working at a gas station once.

R   That was after college. That's when I needed money to pay off my bills and that. So I went to work for a forty-hour work week then.

Au   How long did you work at the gas station?

R   Through the winter.

Au   Did you like that kind of work?

R   Not really. It was cold. Cold and rainy, and it was standing on your feet. You couldn't sit down where I was. Couldn't sit down and it was eight hours on your feet every day. I was getting up at 5:00 in the morning then. I worked until 2:00. I worked an eight-hour shift.

Au   Did you get along all right with the boss?

R   Yeah, we're good friends.

Au   What kind of station was it?

R   Oh, it was just gas and oil.

Au   You said you were good friends with your boss?

R   Yeah.

Au   Do you still see him?

R   No, I think he moved away. Well, he wasn't too happy when I left. 'Cause I went back; then I went back with my mother, and since then I've been, that's gotta be three years now when I went back, and he wasn't too happy that I left.

Au   Why wasn't he so happy?

R   Well, he didn't sound, he said it was all right when I told him I'm gonna go back to work for my mother. But he says, "That's all right, go ahead." But the next day I pulled in to talk to him and he wouldn't talk to me. So, I figured he was a little upset with me.

Au   How much notice did you give him before you quit?

R   Ah, well I think I asked him, I said, "Did you want me to give you two weeks' notice?" and he said, "No." But I've always given notice to a job when I quit.

Au   Ron, permit me to change the topic again. I don't want to embarrass you, but I want to go back a little bit to a topic we were talking about before, your relationship with girls. I'd like to broaden that just a bit. Can you remember when you first became aware that you, as a boy, were different from girls?

R   When did I?

Au   Physically different? Of course you grew up with sisters, didn't you?

R   Right. I've known a long time. I've known, gee, it's gotta be even before I went to the program. Maybe when I was, even before eight years old.

Au   I'm sure that may be correct. Have you ever been concerned at all about such things as masturbation, playing with yourself?

R   What do you mean by "concerned"?

Au   Well, were you worried about it?

R   I've never thought about it much. I've tried not to think about it.

Au   Do you masturbate, or have you masturbated when you played with yourself?

R   No.

Au   You never have?

R   No.

Au   You don't now? [Ron's head shakes no.] Where do you get your sexual releases, Ron?

R   Well, like I said, all I, that one time. That's all.

Au   That's the only time?

R   Right.

Au   Do you have wet dreams at night?

R   No. I don't have any dreams of that sort that I can remember.

Au   In the morning you don't wake up with your pajamas wet?

R   No.

Au   Do you have fantasies about having relationships with girls?

R   Well, I've had a couple; I've had dreams like that.

Au   You do dream dreams.

R   Yeah.

Au   Do you think about girls during the daytime?

R   Yes.

Au   Have you ever had sexual relationships with boys?

R   No.

Au   With other men? Have you ever thought about that kind of sexual experience?

R   No.

Au   Not that I'm suggesting that you should, but I'm just asking if you do think in that direction.

R   I've thought of it, but you know it doesn't turn me on, like . . .

Au   So that the whole issue of sexuality isn't apparently a very important thing, as far as you're concerned?

R   Not like to other guys I know.

Au   Why do you think that is? Do you have any idea? Do you see yourself as different than other men?

R   Not really different. I just don't need sex, I guess. I've got friends who would go to bed with any girl, and it all depends on how you're raised. And I'm not like that.

Au   But you feel that you would be able to have sexual relations with a girl?

R   If I've got, if I was involved with a girl or was in love with her, then I would do it. But as far as that, I couldn't go to a bar and pick up any girl for the night.

Au   Do you feel that there is going to be an opportunity someday to find a girl? You're not adverse to being married? You would be able to engage in good, healthy relationships with the girl that will ultimately be your wife?

R   Right. I don't think I'll have any problems. I'm pretty sure of that.

Au   You're not running away from being married? Or from girls?

R   No. I just don't think I'm ready right now.

Au   Yeah. Mmm-hum.

R   Especially financially.

Au   Sure, I think I can understand that. Let's talk about something else now. Have you registered to vote?

R   Yeah, I did that when I was in high school.

Au   Did you? Have you ever voted?

R   Yeah, every year they allow, when there's been an election.

Au   Are you going to vote in the forthcoming presidential election?

R   I'm debating.

Au   Do you get involved politically, at all? Do you belong to a political group?

R   No. I just watch the papers and read the scandals! There's another important thing in my life since I saw you. I had a bar mitzvah when I was thirteen.

Au   You went through with the bar mitzvah, did you?

R   Yeah.

Au   Tell me about that, will you please? How did you prepare for it?

R   Well, I went to classes, I think, once a week where I would—they would teach this and that.

Au   Did you have to learn to read Hebrew?

R   I could never learn to, I never learned it; I could never pick it up.

Au   Do you speak it?

R   No.

Au   Just isolated words?

R   Right. But I could never pick up or read Hebrew. But I went through where I read mostly English in it.

Au   Great. During your bar mitzvah, is it not customary that the young man give a bit of a talk?

R   Right, a speech.

Au   Did you?

R   Yeah.

Au   Do you remember what you talked about?

R   Well, just like thanking my teachers, my parents, and ya know, for help-ing me along.

Au   Were you scared?

R   Always. I almost passed out. I had to go out for air.

Au   Tell me, how long did you speak?

R   Oh, probably about five or ten minutes.

Au   Where was the bar mitzvah held?

R   At my temple.

Au   How many people were there?

R   Oh, I would say probably 150 or 200.

Au   So, you had a rather large audience to speak before?

R   Yeah. Between my relatives and everybody and my friends. Then they had the regular people who go just on the Sabbath.

Au   This was on the Sabbath?

R   Right. On Saturday morning.

Au   Did you have a celebration after the bar mitzvah somewhere?

R   Right in the temple.

Au   That was a big day for you, wasn't it?

R   Yeah, one of the biggest days of my life.

Au   I'll bet it was. Well, I think we've talked long enough for now. I really appreciated talking with you, Ron. This is a very real pleasure for me. You have developed into a fine guy, a very wonderful young man.

R   Thank you. Will you be around here again sometime? I'd really like to talk to you some more.

Au   I am sure I will be back, and we could certainly talk some more. Is there something else you'd like to bring up now before you go?

R   No, not now. I want to think about it awhile. It's that sex bit though. That's really something we ought to talk about, I guess. I'm pretty up-tight about that. It's hard to talk about, but I should—if you would. I need to know who I am. Not tonight. Got to think some more. Will you call me next time you're here?

Ronald survived adolescence for several reasons, two of which were paramount. First, through a highly structured program, received when he was a young boy he was able to learn to control his behavior so that his academic skills, already quite well founded as a child, could be utilized to support his high school program. External controls became internal; the locus of control changed as Ron's perception of what people could provide him began to change. Second, Ron's mother has provided direction, support, and further structure. This has been to the point of control and dominance, but in Ron's case that may not have all been bad. He weathered adolescence, though in a very repressed manner. He is dependent, and he is sexually confused. His mother's dominance has stifled him emotionally, and he is not open. Yet, adolescence for Ronald, centered as it was in a heavy work schedule, in his home and synagogue, was nevertheless generally successful. He has brought himself to a point where an adulthood of limited scope is possible.

6

Andy: Perennial Adolescent in a Hostile World

A LEARNING DISABLED CHILD with evidence of neurological dysfunction, Andy early developed protective mechanisms and deep-seated emotional attitudes toward those around him. He was a child who could be led by others. As an adolescent he was always conscious of the presence of others. Paranoia and suspicion in the presence of others is evident in his adult life.

Andy at twenty-two is succeeding in a marginal way. The adult dominance he has experienced throughout his life has been important for him. As he will tell us, when he leaves the security of his home, his success experiences become fewer. He cannot deal well with authority figures outside the familiar surroundings of his home.

Once again, there is evidence that the structured educational program Andy experienced provided the things he needed to achieve academically so that he could move into secondary school, pass his examination for the navy and the written portion of his driving license, and read other things for his sporadic jobs and for pleasure. The neurotic and perseverative behaviors were not affected noticeably by his clinical teaching experience. As the reader will observe, Andy's adolescence was relatively uneventful. He will probably always remain the neurotic and somewhat paranoid Milktoast of his community.

Author   Andy, it's been at least ten years, maybe eleven years, since I've seen you. You tell me you are now twenty-three years of age, and that means that we saw you last either when you were eleven or twelve years old. I should know which but I don't remember. Can you remember the clinical teaching program you were in with us?

A   Quite a bit, I think. I enjoyed it, I remember. And it was nice. I was there

75

because I was a ruffian when I was younger. Didn't learn too good. I was slow on learning at the time, and I was sent to that program. I caught up from then.

Au   I don't think that we ever thought of you as a ruffian. You surely had some very severe learning problems, though, when you were with us.

Andy started to attend the clinical teaching program at 9.6 years, a somewhat older chronological age than the other boys. His intellectual ability was seen as good. Intelligence tests, administered approximately every six months for four years before and during his participation in the clinical teaching program, resulted in scores of between 87 and 106, usually in the upper range.

Referral characteristics included such statements as "short attention span," "cannot conform to rules," "doesn't seem to profit from punishment," "too much in need of help for his emotions and behavior to work up to his potential," "he flits from one thing to another. His span of attention is about that of a kindergarten child."

The referring psychiatrist stated that "there is a history of birth injury including a broken collar bone, mis-shapen head. It looked like a water-blister. Dr. P. reported then that he had a 50-50 chance." Subsequent pediatric neurological examinations and EEG records reported no gross neurological symptomatology, but suggested "minimal cerebral dysfunction undifferentiated." Other neurological assessments reported that Andy was "very hyperactive and talkative. He manifested clumsiness, poor diction, and a mild slurring of his speech."

Andy's reference to his being a ruffian is undoubtedly a reflection of the many references to his hyperactivity, which are to be found in referring statements from school teachers, school social workers, and child guidance personnel who worked with him prior to his entrance into the clinical teaching program.

Au   What happened after you left our program? Where did you go after that?

A   I went back to general schools in the city, and I found out that the kids are crazy.

Au   Kids were crazy, eh?

A   Kids are crazy. Now, in public schools the, I'm not down on anybody, but the colored people back when I went to high school and junior high and stuff, they were sort of like, crazy, and they tried to show themselves bigger and better than anyone else. I just learned to keep away from everybody who was going to do me any harm. Kids are crazy. They're always ready to fight.

Au   It wasn't all the black students, though, was it?

A   True, everybody was out there to get you. There's no peace.

> An early social work interview indicates that Andy's memory of
> his peer problems is probably an accurate one. The social worker com-
> ments: "Both Mr. and Mrs. Roberts said that Andy had friends, but that
> most of the kids pick on him because he is little for his age." Mr. Roberts
> stated that he is "the brunt of their plays" and added that "his feelings get
> hurt easily." Mrs. Roberts mentioned that they were Catholic and that
> they were living in a predominantly Protestant neighborhood. I inquired
> as to whether she felt that this was difficult for Andy and she said, "Yes, I
> do; the older boys resent this." Mr. Roberts stated that "Andy was very
> anxious to join the Boy Scouts, I feel that this will solve all of his difficul-
> ties in that he likes to camp, hunt, fish, hike with his father." But he was
> disappointed because a group of Cub Scouts appeared to be filled at
> present with delinquent kids.
> In the father's comments are to be seen shadings of criticism of
> anything which interferes with Andy's adjustment, displacement of re-
> sponsibility, and support of attitudes which in Andy as a growing adult
> borders at times on paranoia.

Au   Do you remember the name of the school that you were in? It was an ele-
      mentary school, was it?

A   At the time it was Power Elementary. Then I went to Smith Junior High,
      and I went out to the suburbs where I'm living now. I went to Roberts
      Junior High and then to the high school there.

Au   Did you graduate from high school?

A   No, I stuck it out to tenth grade; joined the navy.

Au   Did you? Well I want to come back to that in a few minutes. Let's go
      back to when you left the clinical teaching program. You would have
      been about eleven years old, and do you recall what grade you went into
      after you left us?

A   I think it was seventh or eighth grade.

Au   Seventh or eighth grade. That would have put you in junior high school.
      It was probably the fifth or sixth grades, somewhere there I would sus-
      pect. Now, let's assume it was the fifth grade, for a moment. Do you re-
      call, did you pass into the sixth grade? Did you fail at any place along in
      elementary school?

A   I've been passing ever since I've been out of that program.

> Andy was achieving well when he left the clinical teaching pro-
> gram for the regular school classroom. His records indicate the following:

CALIFORNIA ACHIEVEMENT TESTS

Pre-Admission Data 12-6-62	10-24-63	6-9-64	12-7-64	6-6-65	9-21-65
Reading Grade = 2.3	4.5	4.1	5.7	5.7	6.5
Arithmetic Grade = 2.2	4.1	4.2	5.2	5.4	5.8
English Grade = N.A.	3.8	4.0	3.9	4.8	6.7
Spelling Grade = 1.8	4.1	4.0	4.9	6.0	6.4

He was reassimilated into the fifth grade, primarily due to the continuation of chronic emotional problems and tensions in the home revolving around the deteriorating health of grandparents. Rather than to risk failure in the sixth grade, it was felt he should have a better opportunity to function with strength in the fifth grade.

Au   You passed ever since you've been out of the clinical program. So, between that time and the tenth grade when you went into the navy, you did not fail a school program. Is that right?

A   I didn't fail a school program that I know of. Once in a while I'd be back in a subject; naturally it happens. I passed most of the time.

Au   When you came to us you were about nine. That's a long while to remember, I know. But you had had some rather serious problems in elementary school, as I recall. Do you recall whether you failed grades before you came to us?

A   I failed a couple of years. Also, when I was younger I was mistaken for a what you might call a "fagottry," something like that.

Au   A what?

A   When I was in elementary school there was a situation that had happened.

Au   What was that?

A   Between a colored person and about four or five different white guys. They tried to make me commit what you would call, ah, bisexual, they had my pants off.

Au   Homosexual kinds of behavior? This was before when?

A   This was before I went to your school, I know. Yes, homosexual.

Au   So you were seven or eight years of age then. Is that right?

A   Somewhere around there, I guess.

Au   Have you been thinking about this ever since?

A   Not really, no, 'cause it doesn't bother me that much, because it's not me.

Au Did this experience happen . . .

A   Before I was eight.

Au Before you were eight, OK. But did those kinds of experiences ever happen again after that first time?

A   I've had somebody try it, but no way. I will defend myself.

Au O.K., let's forget that for a moment. Not that I don't want to discuss it; that's not the issue, but I'd like to follow along the school experiences for a minute, then we can come back to that a little later on, if you'd like. I wonder if you can remember when you were with us and your interest in the Civil War?

A   Yes, for sure. I'm still a Civil War freak.

Au Do you remember how that happened, how that interest of your's developed.

A   I was getting to look at the freedoms and rights for everybody.

Au But not when you were nine or eight . . .

A   Well, I was looking into it because I was fascinated by it.

Au Did you have a grandfather living back in those days?

A   Yes, I had. My great-grandfather and grandfather lived back then.

Au Your great grandfather lived near or with you when you were eight or nine years old.

A   My grandfather did, but he wasn't into the Civil War. It was the great-grandfather.

Au Yes, but was it your grandfather that told you these stories, do you remember?

A   Yeah. He was a good man.

Au Well, now tell me. Do you remember what the impact of those Civil War stories was on you, and how you reacted or what you did about them?

A   The Battle of Gettysburg and a lot of other battles got me.

Au Oh, I know that. I'm not asking you to talk about the Civil War necessarily, but how you felt about it. What you did about it.

A   Oh, I felt that people were dying, you know.

Au Yes. Do you remember? This is just a kind of fun experience to recall, because the Civil War got in your way a lot back in those days, Andy, whether you remember now or not. Do you recall your own behavior which involves the Civil War?

A   I'll admit that it did, 'cause I had a lota things to do with it.

Au You used to come into my office after you got out of the taxicab, and I never would talk to you until I knew what I was that day. You would turn me into a sergeant or a captain or a corporal. Or, if you didn't like me, I was a private.

A   [laughs] OK. I'll rate you up with the generals now.

Au   [laughs] I wouldn't think that was necessary. But nevertheless, you had a
      rank for us all, your teacher, Mrs. S., you had a rank for her every day,
      and for the boys that were in the class. And you used to get very angry if
      we didn't understand what roles we were playing.

A   I see, OK.

Au   Do you remember any of that?

A   Sort of, yes.

Au   Fortunately, those memories fade out, don't they.

A   After a while they certainly do.

Au   Well, it was so extreme on your part that we spent a lot of time with you
      trying to work through your whole Civil War concept, and why it was
      so difficult for you to deal with anything unless it was in a Civil War
      setting.

> There is some confusion in Andy's remembrance of who was sig-
> nificant in this Civil War episode. It was actually the grandfather, not
> the great-grandfather. The grandfather constantly told stories to Andy
> with the War being the central content. By the time Andy entered the
> clinical teaching program these stories had taken on a perseverative tone
> which colored his total adjustment to teachers, peers, and to family. Lit-
> tle or nothing could be accomplished with him unless the War setting
> was taken into account. Teachers for more than a year played into his
> perseverative fantasy in an effort to establish success experiences in
> school activities. The perseveration constituted a significant hurdle to
> his achievement, but more so to his overall social adjustment. It is obvi-
> ous now that this trying experience has faded in his memory even when
> the interviewer recalls for him significant details. This is seen as good.
>   It is perhaps well to obtain a glimpse into the family which reared
> Andy during his early years and which today still plays a significant role
> in his life. The social worker's comments from 1962 give us insight into
> this aspect of Andy's background: "Andy was an unplanned and at first
> unwanted child. He was born when his mother was 43 years old. Mrs.
> Roberts stated that 'at first I was really upset, but when the other kids
> were so excited that everything worked OK.' She stated that the preg-
> nancy and delivery were both very difficult as she was going through her
> menopause. She remained in the hospital for one month after Andy was
> born suffering from a gall bladder attack; and her daughter, Andy's
> older sister, took care of the newborn child. At the time Andy was born
> the natural grandfather 'was partially deaf' and the natural grandmother
> 'was dying of cancer.' This grandmother, in fact, did die the following
> January after Andy's birth. They were living in the home of the maternal
> grandparents. Composition of the home when Andy was nine years old:

*Mrs. Roberts, age 53. She is primarily a housewife, but does sell Avon
products to supplement family income. She seems in reasonably good
health, but has gall bladder and hernia problems. Andy's father, Mr.
Roberts, age 60. He works different shifts as a boiler engineer. Andy's
grandfather, age 92, is almost entirely deaf and blind, and requires constant watching and care. Andy's brother, Stuart, age 26, is a material
handler. Andy, age 9.*

Au   Well now, let's turn to your junior high school experience. Did you have
big problems or little problems there? Any that you can remember?

A   Just general problems, like kids trying to beat up on you and everything.

Au   Why did they try to beat up on you particularly?

A   Everybody tries to show himself well; how much better he is.

Au   Were you trying to show how good you were?

A   Not really. Some guys I was afraid of; some guys I wasn't. But I had figured that there is no need to fight—why fight them, 'cause the man might
kill me, you know. They could do that.

Au   You really felt sometimes you might be killed?

A   Yeah, actually.

Au   This was at Smith Junior High School?

A   True.

Au   That is in a pretty good neighborhood, isn't it?

A   Yes, but it doesn't matter what school you go to. People are always out
to get you. There are fights in just about every school there is. Somebody doesn't like somebody, they try to tear them apart or mess 'em up
for life.

*Stuart, the older brother, was described by Mrs. Roberts as "a
good kid and all that, but he never went to High School and is a little
backward." He does not date at all and never has bothered too much
with girls and does not care to. "He is more interested in hunting, fishing,
and that sort of thing." Mrs. Roberts stated that Stuart is a home boy and
enjoys it a lot. He does the ironing, mops the floors, "because I have a
hernia." She mentioned that he has a continuing speech impediment, despite the fact that he has attended several classes for this as a child, and
she often helps him write letters. Stuart was in the navy for 9 months and
was honorably discharged because he was so nervous, had many head-
aches, and was not considered good navy material. As a child he had
very unsatisfactory experiences with a school psychiatrist and seemed
unable to make progress in special classes for speech and mental retardation. He followed his sister, Sara, 5 years his senior, in school, and as the
mother recalls could never live up to Sara who was always very smart.*

Sara expressed a desire to keep Andy and bring him up with her own children. Mrs. Roberts' response to this was: "My husband thinks he is our responsibility. Andy is a lot of fun." Mr. Roberts: "He has a good heart. We would never let him go, he belongs here."

Their marriage was described by Mrs. Roberts as a good one. She said, "Mr. Roberts is a good man, affectionate" and mentioned that when they were first married they did not have much money, but things are better now. The home in which they live belongs to the grandfather.

It would appear that Andy had multiple mothering parental persons both in terms of age and sex and everyone tended to baby him. There was evidence of overprotection.

This family is attuned to a somewhat noisy atmosphere. This could be disturbing to an outsider, but to Andy this would be consistent with his home environment. To all appearances the Robertses are an upper-lower class family with the style of living in keeping with the working class group. It appears that Mr. Roberts is the most effective member of this family.

Parental response was that of protectiveness concern with no significance of physical or affectionate contact. The patterns of this family indicate multiple parental figures and experiences.

The over-protectiveness mentioned by the social worker is obvious from time to time in the remarks which Andy himself makes. He lives with his parents, seeks a relationship with them, is dependent on his wife, and seeks a dependency relationship with friends who indeed may not actually be friends in a true sense. There is much wishful thinking in many of Andy's comments, if one chooses to interpret them as such.

Au   Yeah, I understand what you are telling me, but at the same time, did you have friends?

A   I had very good friends, not too many, but enough, a few. I didn't fight anybody, most of the time.

Au   Well, let's not worry about the fighting for a moment, but did you have friends that would invite you to their houses?

A   Not around the general area, because I lived over on the west side. Once in awhile I'd go to their houses, not very often.

Au   And did you ever invite the kids to your home?

A   Very often.

Au   And did they come?

A   Some of them.

Au   So, you did have some friends. Can you remember any of their names?

A   Not from about fifteen on back. From fifteen up, I can.

Au   And would that be while you were still in the city or after you were out in the suburbs?

A   While I was in the city.

Au   How old were you when you moved from the city; do you recall?

A   I was sixteen, because it was the day my brother died, the day before I was sixteen [this is Stuart mentioned earlier]. And he had bought the house my parents are living in right now.

Au   He must have been much older than you are.

A   Fifteen years, exactly.

Au   So he was thirty then.

A   He was thirty when he died, and I was just turning sixteen.

Au   But you were still in junior high school when you were in the city. You moved from the city right into the senior high school in your new town?

A   No, I was in junior high school still for just about six months.

Au   Six months still in the ninth grade. And then you had really just one year in the high school in the suburbs. You said you left at the end of the tenth grade?

A   Out there they start at nine, ten, eleven, and twelve. Two years in high school.

Au   I see. And then how did you get along in the high school?

A   I was OK. I had my friends. Lots of friends back then, still have them.

Au   Both boys and girls friends?

A   Both boys and girls, I still have the friends.

Au   Good, that's great.

A   A few of them still go up there yet, because I was much older when I went up there. When I went, I was like, I'd say, I was slow on learning. So, when I got up there I was about eighteen and most of the other kids were under me. So I didn't want to fight, 'cause if I fought anybody under me, then I would be liable for, you know, going to jail.

Au   At eighteen you are an adult, aren't you?

A   So I know if I fought somebody I'd have to, you know, pay the penalty.

Au   Some place along the line I guess I'm a little confused, because you were eighteen years old and in the tenth grade, is that what you are telling me?

A   Eighteen and in the tenth.

Au   So just let me move back from there without making a big issue of this. Did you repeat any grades before the tenth grade.

A   Yes, I have repeated grades.

Au   What grades did you repeat?

A   Kindergarten.

Au   Oh, way back.

A   I was a rotten little devil when I was in kindergarten, so they put me back a year. I didn't like that. I failed, I think it was fourth grade and one other, if I'm thinking right. It was seventh grade, I think. So I was a ruffian when I was younger.

Au   No, you did not fail the fourth grade. But you think you failed the seventh after you left us?

A   I'm not sure if I did or not. I'd have to check my records to make sure.

Au   Well, that's not too important. I'm just trying to get a picture of how easily you moved through school after we saw you. [School records indicate he did not fail the seventh grade, although his achievement that year was quite variable.] Generally speaking, you are telling me that you got along pretty well in your classes.

A   Pretty well, yes. My teachers liked me.

Au   Good, that's great. And so you didn't have any serious run-ins with the teachers?

A   Not that much, no. The principal didn't like me too well.

Au   Where? In the suburbs or at Smith School in the city?

A   Mostly out there. They all thought 'cause I was eighteen, you know, they thought I would do everything in the book, and I never did that.

Au   What were some of the things you didn't do?

A   Well, didn't smoke or anything. I smoked cigarettes, yes, but I didn't smoke any other things.

Au   Uh-huh. Have you ever tried marijuana or hash?

A   I've tried marijuana. There is nothing wrong with it.

Au   I'll accept your feelings about that.

A   Once in awhile won't kill you.

Au   What about hash?

A   Hashish in the navy.

Au   In the navy. Have you ever gone further than that—with speed, heroin?

A   When I was in the navy, yes, and I asked for some help when I was in there. I was using everything to get out of the navy.

Au   Help from what?

A   From the navy. 'Cause I was messing my life up when I was in there. So I was on the road to hell in Spain, and I asked the "man" if he could somehow give me some help. He wouldn't give me any. He wouldn't send me to a psychiatrist or whichever. So I finally says, then let me out of here. So I finally got out.

Au   You got out of the navy.

A   I got out of the navy, and I'm home and I'm fine now.

Au   How did you get out of the navy? On a medical discharge?

A   A general discharge, unable to adapt to the service. [The pattern followed here was used by his older brother as well.]

Au   How long had you been in the navy?

A   About a year and eight days exactly.

Au   And where were you? You said you were in Spain?

A   I was in Spain for awhile. That is before I got out, I was in Spain. Let's see, Spain, England, mostly in the Mediterranean. I didn't go that far past the Mediterranean.

Au   And you were going to tell me something about the Chief.

A   He was, I was working on this medical supply at the time; they had me there. They had to have us doing something, so they put me in medical supply. And, I enjoyed that. We'd get off like about two o'clock in the afternoon, and the Chief always thought I was lazyin' off because I had come back to the barracks instead of going someplace else. And, I'd wash and I'd shower and everything, and they thought I was lazyin' off. He started getting me every job he could to keep me working, and that didn't set too well. So I just went AWOL for a week on the base.

Au   Oh, did you? On base?

A   On the base. Hell, I went riding horses and everything.

Au   Where was this? In Spain?

A   In Spain. The "man" was trying to mess me up, and I said, well, I'm going to mess you up, so I took off for a week.

Au   How do you look back on the navy experience now?

A   It was fun. I should've stayed in, but it was OK when I was in there, when I look back at it.

Au   Why were you asking if you could get some help from the navy psychiatric department?

A   I was taking about anything I could take in front of me just to get out of there. I didn't like it too well. It was too hard of a hassle.

Au   You were taking drugs?

A   At the time. Some drugs, not all of them.

Au   Taking what else?

A   I experienced most with what I could find. Mostly speed. Coke once in a while. That's about it. I don't shoot up. I don't pop pills. These pills, I know they can kill me now, you know.

Au   So that it was basically a concern about needing drugs that caused you to seek help?

A   Well-being. Needing and well-being of getting out of there, also.

Au   What were some of the other reasons you wanted to get out of there?

A   They had operated on my ear back in '72 when I first got in. By the end of the year they wouldn't help me at all. I had pain in my ear. They'd've put a PE tube in my ear, and every place I went they thought it was a ruptured eardrum, 'cause it was nice and round and they could look through it, and they'd say, "Gee, that's a punctured eardrum," and I'd say, "No, it is not. It is a PE tube." And they wouldn't believe me.

Au   What is a PE tube?

A   I'm not sure. It is something to drain the wax from my ears more rapidly. And it was plugged, and they wouldn't help me at all on it, and the pain was just tremendous.

Au   Do you now feel that there are people who don't understand you and are trying to get you, or something?

A   There are a lot of people out there.

Au   Out where?

A   In the world. There are some crazy people, but there are a lot of good people.

Au   And you are concerned about the crazy people trying to get you? Is that the idea?

A   I'm concerned about them plus regular people out there. I have my friends. I see them every time. I watch everybody though.

Au   What was the best experience you ever had in the navy?

A   The day I went in. It was a good experience.

Au   What was good about that?

A   I don't know. It was an experience of joining the service and, like a dummy, I should have stayed in, but I didn't. I'm out now.

Au   Could you get back in if you wished?

A   Not if I wished, no. I'd have to talk to the, write a letter to Washington and find out first.

Au   But the discharge you have, does that prohibit you from ever getting back into the service?

A   Not necessarily. I have an RE-4, and I have to have an RE-1. So I'd have to write, it prevents me from getting back in on my own, you know without going through certain steps.

Au   What was the worst experience you ever had in the navy?

A   When I was in the deck department, they put me in this, with this First-Class there, and he was a crazy. He didn't like me at all, and this other colored guy that was actually worse than he was. He would do everything in his power to get rid of me. He didn't like me for some reason or other. I wouldn't fight anybody on the ship, 'cause I figured what-the-hell! If I have to, if I'm backed up in a corner I'll fight, but if I'm not, I won't fight. I'd rather talk my way out of it. And this colored guy couldn't see that. So I just took care of him in my own way.

Au   Andy, how do you feel about blacks?

A   They are super-cool people. They are human like the rest of us.

Au   But apparently you feel that you have had less than favorable treatment by blacks. Is that right? You've mentioned it so often.

A   I have met some very few good colored people that are really super-cool people. But, in the navy they are out to make money one way or another, like everybody is in the navy. Everybody sells drugs in the navy. Ninety percent of the navy nowadays is nothing but drugs.

Au   Is that right?

A   Really. Officers are into it and, uh, that is like it is. Officers are into it. First Class and on down.

Au   When did you first experience any kind of a drug?

A   When I was in the navy.

Au   That was the first time? Not in high school?

A   No, in the navy.

Au   Do you remember how that first experience took place?

A   Yeah, we were sitting down in the . . . in our cruise lounge there. This guy comes in and says, "Who wants to go get high?" He brings in a big old pipe and starts getting down with us. I said, "All right, I'll try it." He just come in for friendship. Wanted to get high with somebody.

Au   How much did you spend out of a month's pay for drugs back in those days?

A   Oh, I might have spent as high as about $30.00 to $35.00 from one month to the next.

Au   Did that seem to be a lot in comparison with the other men, to your friends who were spending on drugs, or not so much?

A   Yeah, I didn't want to spend that much on it, because I knew it was expensive and I had to send money home, and my parents, so I tried my best.

Au   Have you always helped support your parents?

A   No, I'm trying to, but it is hard to do with jobs nowadays.

Au   When you were in high school, you mentioned that you had both boy and girlfriends. Did you have a steady girlfriend when you were in high school?

A   Oh, a couple. When I was in high school I met my wife.

Au   Oh, did you? What's her name, her first name?

A   Rachel.

Au   So that would have been when you were about eighteen or younger when you met Rachel.

A   Eighteen exactly when I first met her.

Au   And, is she from your town also?

A   No, she is from South City. Way up about eleven miles north of us.

Au   How did you happen to meet her?

A   Well, I met her at the beach. There was a little place called the "Brown Hat" up there, and it's not too big. We got together ever since.

Au   Did she finish high school?

A   She finished high school. She's two years older than me.

Au   Oh, I see. Has she ever done any work? Is she working?

A   She's working now.

Au   What does she do?

A   She's a custodian for the school district.

Au   How long has she had that job?

A   About two years and a half.

Au   Did she go beyond high school, Andy?

A   She took two years of nursing school.

Au   Really. Then she is turning now to become a custodian?

A   Yeah. She never followed up on nursing.

Au   Where did she take the nursing training?

A   Up north.

Au   At a community college?

A   Um, I think so.

Au   Or a hospital?

A   She worked for nursing homes up there.

Au   I see. As a regular nurse or a nurse's aide?

A   Nurse's aide.

Au   Well, that's great, and how long have you been married?

A   One year and nine months.

Au   Any children?

A   We had one, but she lost it at 4½ months. Her blood had mixed with the baby's, and I heard on the news the other day that RH negative has to have a certain shot or something before the baby. So we both heard it and were freaking out, and now I got to check out with my doctor what's going on.

Au   That's too bad. You can obviously check those things out. Was it an RH problem?

A   Yes, she's RH negative.

Au   I see. Well, I'm not going to go into those problems here, but you certainly should be very cautious and check very thoroughly with your physician, if you're going to try to have a child at some point along the way.

A   We hope to.

Au   Yeah, that is great. If you wish a child, you should certainly try to have it
     under the best circumstances, which means being awfully careful on a
     genetic and medical basis.

A   Hmmmmm.

Au   Now you said you had more than one girlfriend. There was one in high
     school was there?

A   This was before Rachel. Then my wife and I, before we got married,
     were split up for two years. So I was on my own. During them two years
     it was my thing and hers. I got around and experienced girls really often.

Au   You went out with other girls. Going back to that one experience, you
     said you had with boys and one time somebody attempted, some other
     boy or man tried to have sexual relationships with you. That didn't ap-
     peal to you, that turned you off?

A   No way.

Au   So that the second time . . .

A   I'm a man, not a woman.

Au   Right. So it didn't succeed.

A   Right.

Au   About how old were you then?

A   Oh, I'd say I was about 5 to 7. Something like that.

Au   Oh, a long while ago. The second time, were you that young?

A   The second time was when I was in the navy.

Au   I see.

A   Some dude did try it, and he didn't make it.

Au   Some who?

A   Some black gentleman had tried it. He got me drunk, and tried, but I
     said, "no way."

Au   Do you drink much?

A   Once in awhile; I'm not a heavy drinker.

Au   When did you first have sexual relations with girls before you were mar-
     ried? Or did you ever have sexual affairs?

A   Not really, no. I had fantasized through it, but I had never done it until it
     was done with my wife.

Au   When did you first begin to learn how to go about having sexual rela-
     tions?

A   Oh, when I was sixteen.

Au   Can you tell me how you learned this? Did it come from your friends or
     your parents or what?

A   Mostly about everything. From the television, from my parents. My
     mother and I are super-good people. We love each other.

Au   Well, I talked with your mother on the phone recently. She certainly feels very good about you, and as I recall, years ago she always was a very good friend of yours, too.

A   True.

Au   You always maintained that close relationship?

A   Mmmm-hum.

Au   She has not been hesitant about talking to you about problems dealing with your own growth, sexual problems, and other similar problems.

A   Now that I'm eighteen and older, we can talk what we feel. And I just tell her like it is. She'll tell me. Like I told her, like I was listening to the radio this morning and Bill Jones, the reporter, has all these women call him up and asks them all sorts of questions. He has the weirdest vocabulary, but he gets away with it over the air.

Au   Uh-huh.

A   And he's super-good. He was asking questions to this girl who called him up and said she is sick of people coming around with gossiping. She says, "Why don't they come straight to the source and ask the source?" So I told my mother that. I said, "If you have a grievance, bring it to me."

Au   Well, that's a good point of view. Tell me other things that you remember about school that specifically trained you for a job, or did you get all of your job training after you left school?

A   Mostly high school.

Au   You had some job training in high school?

A   Job training in high school.

Au   What did you hope to do? You left and went into the navy, but what did you hope to do?

A   I was hoping to get into certified public accounting.

Au   Do you still have those hopes or what?

A   It pays, it has its, I can do, like I was talking to my wife, I said I'd like to open a truck stop or something.

Au   A truck stop?

A   Yes, they do make their money at a truck stop. If you have good mechanics and everything else.

Au   Is that what certified public accountants do?

A   Well, they keep books for anybody.

Au   I see.

A   Keep for colleges, universities.

Au   A truck stop, though, would be for doing accounting or for taking care of the maintenance of trucks?

A   Doing it all, generally. I would have somebody else do my truck repairs. I wouldn't do it myself.

Au How are you in math?

A I'm fairly good in it yet. I got all A's, mostly.

Au Did you really, in arithmetic?

A In arithmetic, yes, and business.

Au Business courses in high school?

A I've taken business courses.

Au Because when you came to us, you know, you could hardly read.

A True, I—what I do now, is I read for what it is. Read anything.

Au What kinds of things do you read?

A Anything. I read magazines, books.

Au What magazines do you read?

A *Time* magaine once in awhile, but have you ever seen a book called the *National Lampoon*?

Au Do you read that?

A It's a crazy magazine and it's okay. I like to read it once in awhile.

Au What other things do you read?

A The newspaper.

Au Yeah. Sports page, editorials?

A The comics first, 'cause I like to brighten my day up. Then I read the rest of the paper.

Au Uh-huh. Are there things about the newspaper that you sometimes don't understand?

A Um. If there's a word I don't understand, I usually ask my parents or else I'll go into the dictionary.

Au Your father is living?

A My father is living, yes.

Au You're living with your parents, you and your wife? She's living with you?

A Yes. My father is 73 and my mother is 67. So, I'm actually taking care of my parents.

Au Yeah, I didn't realize that your father was that old now. I doubt that I ever met your father. I met your mother, although I'm not sure she remembers me. Well now tell me, how did you get along with your reading experiences in school?

A Reading. I picked up very fast afterwards.

Au So you didn't ever fail an English or reading course?

A I didn't fail English, no. I might have been behind once in awhile, but after that I'd catch my mistakes.

Au Did you ever need a tutor or anything of that sort in school, after you got through with us in the clinical teaching program?

A   Once in awhile. If I needed some help I'd ask the teacher, and the teacher would say, well this is how it is, and she'd look at it and explain it to me. I'd take it from there.

Au   Now, you said you left high school when you were eighteen, went directly into the navy, and were in the navy for a little more than a year. What did you do, or what have you done, after coming out of the navy, other than getting married?

A   Try and hold down a job.

Au   What kinds of jobs have you tried to hold down, Andy?

A   Well, I've tried taxi-driving for awhile.

Au   Taxi-driving. Where?

A   In the city.

Au   And why did you leave the taxi-driving?

A   Ah, they had an instance where I think they didn't like me. The dispatcher didn't like me, and she tried, they asked me if I was drinking the last day on the job. She asked me, she says, have been drinking? I says no, I'm out here at Burger King getting a hamburger. She had a car follow me the whole day, and every mistake he caught me making, he'd write it down.

Au   You know that really; there was an unmarked car?

A   And they never gave me a ticket. They finally stopped me and never gave me a ticket; took me off the road, and that was it.

Au   You think it was the police or somebody else?

A   It was the police.

Au   Who had asked the unmarked car to follow you, do you think?

A   I don't know; I wouldn't know. I cannot actually make statements saying it was—the police.

> The psychologist reported: "Andy's drawings of a woman suggest that his feelings toward women are highly ambivalent. He appears to distrust women, expecting undue domination and intrusiveness. At the same time, sexual features are emphasized in the drawings." (C.A. 11-11)

Au   So, you got your driver's license when you were about how old?

A   I got that when I was eighteen.

Au   Eighteen?

A   My father wouldn't give it to me until I was eighteen.

Au   Why?

A   He didn't trust me.

Au   I see. Did you pass the license exam on one try?

A   It took after the fourth try.

Au	The fourth try!
A	Four tries it took me to get it.
Au	What was the problem, the written part of the driver's exam?
A	Mostly, the driving.
Au	The road exam.
A	The road exam, yes.
Au	What happened?
A	Well, the first time I failed it; I'd taken a left-hand turn on a one-way street from the farthest lane.
Au	That's not so good!
A	And he says "automatic failure."
Au	Right.
A	I couldn't get into parallel parking. I couldn't do that too good.
Au	Then, what was wrong the third time?
A	Just, I don't remember what was wrong the third time. I can't remember that.
Au	And the fourth time you passed.
A	The fourth I finally passed.
Au	Now did you have a big celebration after that?
A	Yes, I'm on my own now.
Au	No, I mean after you passed the exam?
A	Oh, I had great confidence in myself for passing.
Au	Good.
A	For some reason or another, I just couldn't get into driving at the time.
Au	Do you think that parallel bit had anything—was related to any of the kinds of learning problems you had had when you were a little boy?
A	No, I don't think so. I outgrew all those troubles.

At this point the interviewer was interested to learn if Andy recalled some of the learning difficulties which he had as a child which might have been related to his problems with the driving examination. He apparently remembered little. The records, however, are interesting. His teacher said: "Andy has great difficulty in targeting. The afternoon at the bowling alley was a disaster from start to finish. Using the lightest ball in the house, he collected a score of 18 in the first game; 22 in the second" (C.A. 11-0). "He reproduces figures (Bender) in a tightly knit, orderly fashion, in a hyper-neat manner. Compulsive counting on the dots and many erasures marked his performance" (C.A. 11-0). "Judgment of distance is faulty. There is a gross visual-motor problem. His performance on the large tricycle in maneuvering three positioned bowling pins was comparable to Jerry who is four years his junior" (C.A. 10-2).

Au   Do you remember some of the problems you had when you were a kid?

A   I would stick on one thing and wouldn't get off of it; I know that.

Au   Like what?

A   Civil War.

Au   That's exactly right.

A   Right now, I'm stuck on trucking, and I'm trying to get into it. It's hard.

Au   What else? Then after you left the taxi-driving, did you have to get a chauffeur's license, too, to be a taxi driver in this state?

A   Mmm, you have to have a class 4.

Au   Class 4? Do you have to have a special examination for that?

A   No, I just went down to City Hall.

Au   And applied.

A   Told them I wanted to apply for taxi driver, and they just gave it to me.

Au   I see.

A   Took me three days.

Au   How long did you work for the taxi company?

A   For about a year.

Au   A year. Then what did you do?

A   Well, just about nothing.

Au   Just about nothing. How long ago was that when you left the taxi company?

A   Back in '74.

Au   '74. That was after you came out of the navy? Tell me some of the things that you've done since the taxi bit.

A   Ah, cooking out at the Inn.

Au   Cooking in what kind of outfit?

A   It was a bar, racetrack, country music place.

Au   And what kinds of things did you cook?

A   Hamburgers, steaks, chicken, whatever come in front of me.

Au   How did you happen to become a cook?

A   My father's been cooking all his life, and my mother and father both taught me how to cook.

Au   Did you have to remember orders and read recipes out there?

A   Just short-order cooking.

Au   I see. How long did that last?

A   It was like on the week-ends.

Au   For how long?

A   He'd open his kitchen up. For about a half-a-year.

Au   About six months, and why did you leave that? You didn't leave because
     he was dissatisfied with your cooking?

A   No, my cooking is still up there.

Au   Mmm hum. And did you ever make any mistakes in cooking?

A   The only mistake that I remember is that I had this Joe Johnson—he's like
     a brother to me—his brother's family is just like my family, really. He
     was in there cooking with me, and I had six hamburgs on the grill and six
     buns on the counter, and he was cooking chicken for me. He says put in
     some chicken, so he grabbed some chicken. We got it wrapped in cello-
     phane with rubber bands around it. He was flicking rubber bands off in
     the air instead of putting them in the garbage cans, and two of them
     landed on the hamburg buns. So I just, you know, put the hamburgs on
     and took off. Chef came out and says, "We got a complaint. We got a
     lady out here with hamburg trouble." I says, "Is it cooked or uncooked?"
     She say, "It's got a rubber band in it." I says, "Oh, really! Is it rare?" She
     says, "No, it's not rare." I says, "Good. Pour it out and eat it." Says, "I'll
     make her another one if she want it."

Au   The rubber band bit didn't go so well with the . . .

A   Ah, no, but mostly it was his kids. It's like, it's his restaurant, and he has
     his kids coming down to the kitchen.

Au   I understand.

A   And they'd all come in my way.

Au   I see. It wasn't that you forgot orders or that you didn't cook things
     properly.

A   No, I didn't forget any of my orders. We used to have some good size
     crowds come out there.

Au   So, you left the cooking business at about six months, and then what did
     you try?

A   Nothing, really, just odd jobs and custodial work.

Au   Custodial work. Where?

A   I like custodial work. At North City in the public schools.

Au   Ah, a regular job or . . .

A   I worked for twenty-nine days. During the twenty-nine days they had
     misplaced $24,000 in their budget, so they got rid of anybody they
     could. It's not my fault.

Au   Mmmm hum. Did you enjoy the work?

A   Yeah, I'm still into it.

Au   What do you do?

A   I'm working for Allentown schools, part-time right now.

Au   As a custodian?

A   Custodian. Their benefits are good, and they're paying $3.75 an hour.

Au How long have you been working for the Allentown Public Schools?

A   For about—actually about a year.

Au Really, how often do you work?

A   I'm on substitute work and they haven't called me in full-time yet.

Au I see, when was the last time that you worked out there as a substitute?

A   Yesterday. I have a job tomorrow and Monday.

Au Well, good for you.

A   I'm getting in full-time finally.

Au Wonderful!

A   Like yesterday, I asked to go to Hill Elementary School.

Au Yes.

A   This guy named Toby—I don't even know the guy—and he tells his fore-
    man, he says, "I've known him for five years." So we were sitting there
    talking, and he says, "How'd you like to work my shift Monday?" I says,
    "Heck yeah, I'll work it."

Au Now, is that temporary still or . . .

A   This will be temporary, but I'm gonna talk to Mr. Brown, and I wanna
    wear my shirt in for him. I have a shirt. One says "Bills" in front of it, and
    when I walk out, if the man doesn't want to hire me, it says, "Still Unem-
    ployed" on the back.

Au Don't be insulting to him, now.

A   Yeah, but it's not insulting, but, I mean, I've been unemployed for the
    last two years, really just odd jobs.

Au What does the "Bills" mean in the front of it?

A   "Bills" means I have bills to pay. And if he doesn't want to hire me, "Still
    Unemployed" on the back when I leave.

Au You have bills to pay.

*The psychiatrist commented during the staffing just prior to
Andy's transfer to the public schools at C.A. 12-3: "Andy has shown remarkable growth in school achievement during the time he has been
here. His motor development has improved. However, he still is a pre-
adolescent with problems which could eventually get in his way, i.e., the
perception of his own sex role; his dependency on parents or other adults
for support in many areas; his fears (hostilities) of what he imagines people try to do to him. In a final interview Andy again, or still, depicts females as castrating and seductive while men seem to be fatally caught in
the middle between these seductive and threatening women. There appears to be a constant concern for the relationships between individuals
and their roles. Andy expresses undue concern about his relationship
with people and this is a pervading concern."*

Au   But you'll continue working in the school system on a temporary basis?

A   Yeah, naturally.

Au   Mmmm hum.

A   But there is, was, three full-time positions open, and I called 'em up and asked 'em for one, you know, put my name down for 'em, and he went on vacation the following Monday.

Au   I see.

A   Nobody gave me a call at any time.

Au   So, how long ago was that?

A   That was about four months ago, and I'm still working part-time.

Au   Do you feel that you've gotten a square deal?

A   Ah, no, most of the time.

Au   Mmmm hum.

A   Most of the time—a lot of times—it's my mistake for, you know, firing myself and quitting, rather, or whatever.

Au   Hum. You've never been fired?

A   Except for the taxi company, no.

Au   Oh yes, that's right. What does your wife think about living at home with your father and mother?

A   Well, my parents are old and her parents are also in their sixties, so we like to stick around the house mostly, like my mother-in-law lives about ten miles north of us. We try to stay close to our parents, so in case they do go, we can be there. And take it from there.

Au   Sometimes when two families are living under one roof there are tensions.

A   Oh, there are tensions, yes, naturally.

Au   Do you get along 50 percent of the time as good friends, or is it less than that or more?

A   We sit there and play cards most of the time. We get along. I need my parents, I guess.

Au   Do you?

A   We get into cards and like I told my Father, my Father came up to me one day and says, "I got a bone to pick with you." I says, "pick it. Y'know," I says, "tell me what your troubles is and I'll try to help out." My Father once in awhile—don't tell him this, he'll get back—he gets back on his taxes. He has an entire dream of winning the New York State Lottery. When it was up to $1,000,000. Never did it, so he let his taxes go and a few bills and stuff and couldn't come up with it. He finally come up with it with his insurance policy to pay his taxes off. But the last batch of taxes my wife and I paid off.

Au   So you help out?

A   We help out as much as possible.

Au   Do you have a social life, you and your wife, outside of your home?

A   Mmm hum. We're down at the Inn mostly. It's a bar, restaurant and country music.

Au   Where you worked?

A   Where I worked, yes.

Au   You're into country music?

A   Well, I've had Ernest Tubb come out and ask me for a second hamburg, and Tex Ritter asked me for a second cup of coffee.

Au   Well, good for you.

A   I make my own.

Au   Ah-ha and ah, tell me now, have you ever sung?

A   Ah, once in awhile I do. I'm a country music freak.

Au   Mmm hum. You told me you sang in the church choir.

A   I used to when I was younger, yes.

Au   Do you have a social life at the church?

A   Ah, we haven't been in the church.

Au   Ah-ha, well, I'm not making a judgment; I'm just trying to understand what you are telling me. So you don't have friends in the church, but do you have friends that also go to the Inn?

A   Uh-huh.

Au   Ah, do you see some of those friends outside of the restaurant?

A   Oh, all the time. Like this morning, I stopped in and used my ah, one that's teaching me how to play the steel—this Ronnie, I can't remember his last name; he's new to me. Like he's been going with this chick that bought my trailer; I used to go to high school with her, and she bought my trailer and ah, he's new. He's come in since I've been gone.

Au   Mmm hum.

A   I was down in Florida for about three weeks.

Au   Who is your best friend?

A   Joe Johnson. He . . .

Au   He's the guy that was cooking along side of you.

A   Cooking along side of me. We're brothers.

Au   He's where, did you say?

A   He's in Florida.

Au   Oh, he's not around here now.

A   I never got the chance to get down to see him.

Au   Who is your best friend around where you live?

A   That would be Laura and Ronnie, mostly.

Au   And you see them how often?

A   About every other day or every day, whichever.

Au   You have social engagements with them?

A   Mmm-hum. We're invited out this Saturday.

Au   Well, that's good. Your wife works days or nights?

A   Nights, she works from 3:30, from 3 in the afternoon to 11 at night.

Au   Well, that interferes with your social life a little bit, doesn't it?

A   All except on the week-ends.

Au   And your temporary work is usually also in the evening, or is that sometimes during the day?

A   Like I usually work from, mostly from 1 till 9:00. From 9:00 I'm free and up.

Au   Mmm-hum. How much money did you earn last year? Did you pay taxes on how much, about?

A   I paid taxes on about $2,800, somewhere around there.

Au $2,800 and how much did . . .

A   My wife earned more than me.

Au   About how much did she earn?

A   About $4,700.

Au $4,700. So, together you earned over $7,000?

A   Mmm-hum.

Au   Do you own a car yourself?

A   No, don't own one. At the present time, like my wife and I were talking last night, and I asked her, I says, "Why don't we get one big loan, pay off everything we've got?" 'Cause I figured we're only about $600 to $800 in debt. I've got to get all my bills together. And I says just pay everything off at once and it would be better for credit rating.

Au   Mmm hum. Then pay back the one big loan.

A   One big loan. Plus borrow enough to get a car, too. I have to use my parents'.

Au   So, you'd have a big, big loan before you got through?

A   Really. Gonna have to.

Au   You're dressed very neatly, Andy.

A   Well, I try to, yeah.

Au   You have plenty of clothes, do you?

A   Not too many, but when I go out I like to look nice. I'll buy a new shirt once in awhile to get with my clothes.

Au   Mmm-hum. Well you certainly look nice today.

A   Thank you, sir.

Au   You weren't sporting sideburns and a mustache at the age of eleven, when I last saw you.

A   No, I wasn't sporting them but I, my wife says if I shaved them off, she'll leave me.

Au   She will?

A   So, I've got to leave them; I had 'em trimmed up today. My mother trimmed 'em up for me, and I trimmed up my mustache.

Au   Well, good for you. Has your wife seen you since they've been trimmed up?

A   She hasn't seen my hair. I stopped down to Ronnie's today; he's got one of them hairblowers.

Au   Yeah.

A   And I says, let me use it. He says, OK, so I put it on, and it's messed up in front, but it's OK.

Au   Ah, you look very, very good. Really very good. Well, Andy, this has been very nice . . . having the opportunity to talk with you.

A   It's been very nice here.

Au   It's been a pretty *good* ten years, and I hope it won't be that long again before we see each other.

A   Okay, I hope so. We'll keep in touch. I'd like to.

Andy sees the world as hostile, as threatening, and as "full of crazy people out there." If he can obtain a full-time job as a custodian, he will probably do well, for the routine of the work will provide him the structure he needs; he will not be threatened by the children of the school. His wife will provide him with work cues to make him succeed. Whether his wife can provide the dominant guidance he needs after his parents are gone is a matter to be judged later. He needs what his father and mother have provided for so long. Andy is not a pleasant person, nor is he physically attractive. His relationships and successful social adjustment will have to be developed within a pattern of external controls. There is insufficient internal strength.

Andy is one whose academic needs were met through clinical teaching. He exemplifies, however, those who need much more in-depth therapy than the schools can usually provide.

7

John: Unequipped for Life

John's early records are equivocal insofar as a specific diagnosis is concerned, but in retrospect most of the pieces in the puzzle called dyslexia are to be observed in his behavior and neuropsychological data. His severe reading problem continued throughout high school

The youngest of the five young men included here, John represents many of the needs of adolescents which ought to be the focus of a good secondary program: sports, sex education, drug education, and driver education, in addition to the more traditional academic emphases.

John is a handsome young man, who obviously has observed and learned from observation how to make friends and to control people. He is not brash, but he is no wall flower. He exudes sexuality, and he employs his virility to his own preconceived needs. His sexual values, however, are still relatively superficial and immature.

Through sports John has found a high degree of satisfaction and personal salvation. Contact sports assuage his energies. His sport-minded friends provide him behavior models which his parents have not. But where did this clumsy, hyperactive boy learn the control and coordination required to move quickly in football, to shoot pool, to handle a lacrosse stick with finesse? Certainly not totally in the thirty minutes per day of gross motor training he received in the special clinical teaching program. We have often stated that exceptional children do cease to be exceptional. This is true of John at least in the motor sphere. But how did it happen? What took place neurologicaly other than the normal growth of adolescence? Nerve regeneration? Response to structure? Conditioning? We do not know. We do know that other than the three or four years of special clinical teaching—perhaps sufficient—John grew up more or less like Topsy in a junior and senior high school program which until recently was little concerned for his total development. John can tell us better.

Author   Well, John, it has been a long time since we have seen each other and visited together.

J   At least ten years, and I am really glad to see you. I would have recognized you. I remember you very well and all about that class we were in with Mrs. S.

Au   You do really remember the class, the room?

J   Sure, I think it was on the third floor facing east.

Au   Right, but on the second floor. What was in that room? Have you any idea what made it different? Or was there anything different?

J   Well, there were five or six cubicles. That was different from anything I'd had before.

Au   Right. One for each of you kids. Eight cubicles.

J   On the north wall four, and three or four on the east wall. We called them our offices.

Au   You do remember pretty accurately. Do you remember which cubicle you had?

J   I think it was on the north side, about the second one in.

Au   You are exactly right. I have a picture of you at my office at home, and there is where you sit. North wall, the second from the left—the second from the window. Do you remember the name of the guys that sat next to you on either side?

J   No, not really.

Au   Where had you gone to school before you went to the clinical teaching program?

J   St. Jerome parish school.

Au   How did you get along there, do you recall?

J   Ah, I didn't get along with the nuns very well, Nuns didn't like me too good.

Au   They didn't, did they?

J   I don't get along with nuns very well.

> Both of John's parents showed concern about his hyperactivity and lack of success in school. Mr. Larson, especially, seemed to identify strongly with John's problems stating, "If John continues to fail he will feel like he is a 'nothing.'"
>
> John was described as "overactive and into everything" from the time he began to walk. In kindergarten, he was described as overactive, irritable, prone to temper tantrums and hostile to other children. His first grade teacher at St. Jerome Parochial School reported to the Clinic that John's attention span was very short and he didn't want to learn with the class. She stated that he displayed irritability, temper tantrums and dislike of group activity.

Mr. and Mrs. Larson traced John's problems to the age of four months at which time Mrs. L. had a hysterectomy. John was cared for by a paternal aunt and uncle. When John returned home at 6½ months, he slept poorly and cried whenever his sister and brother approached him. He cried a great deal and constantly wanted to be held and rocked. Mrs. L. said she carried him around most of the time, adding rather apologetically, "anything to shut him up." Mrs. L. said she had a difficult time with the hysterectomy, as there were "complications" and she did not feel well for two years following the operation. A tumor described as "pre-cancerous" was removed, and she did not believe the doctor's statement that she did not actually have cancer. She felt ill and failed to gain weight and for 1½ years thought she had been sent home to die. The doctor finally convinced her by showing her the lab reports.

From the time John began to walk, he was very active and aggressive and rather destructive. Mr. L. described him as "like a spring unwound." He would arise at 5:30 in the morning and begin taking things out of the kitchen cabinets. He would often wander into neighbors' yards and houses and pick things up to the extent that neighbors had ordered him out of their yards.

Although they found him a rather difficult child, John's parents were not aware that he had a problem until he entered kindergarten and they received complaints from his teacher at St. Jerome Parochial School. The teacher punished him by making him sit in the wastebasket and by sending him to the first grade teacher, who was a nun. John would react to this by putting his head down on the desk and falling asleep. He has since this associated nuns with punishment. John failed the first grade at St. Jerome. His teacher stated that he didn't want to learn with the class, had a short attention span and disliked participating in group activity. She said he displayed irritability in mood and mannerisms toward others. "During temper tantrums his choice of words are not becoming to a five-year old; words he has never heard from anyone in the class."

Mr. and Mrs. L. implied that both teachers at St. Jerome were rather negative in attitude toward John, but defended this by adding that there were over 50 children in each class. In first grade at Van Dyke School, there were only 25 in the class and John was able to do some work, but even here there was too much pressure.

Au   When you were at St. Jerome, you must have been about seven years old. I think you were about that age when you came to us; maybe a young eight. Had you failed any grades at St. Jerome?

J   No, but almost. They had taken me out of St. Jerome and put me into Van Dyke, and from Van Dyke I went up to the clinical teaching program.

Au   Why did they take you out of St. Jerome?

J   My reading level wasn't up to first grade standards, I guess. They
       thought I'd have a more relaxed atmosphere in a public school than I
       would in a parochial.

Au   You said you didn't get along with nuns, but actually how did you get
       along with the nuns at St. Jerome? Do you remember any unpleasant ex-
       periences that you had at St. Jerome?

J   The nuns have a tendency to put you down when you are a little kid.
       They can, and they do. For some reason I didn't like that. I didn't get
       along with them too well.

Au   But how did you behave at St. Jerome? Do you recall? This was a long
       while ago.

J   Not really.

    *John had some extremely difficult adjustment problems when he
was at St. Jerome's. He was hyperactive on a motoric basis to the extent
that the teachers were really unable to control him physically. On the occasion which led to his transfer to the Van Dyke School, he had almost
literally been carried to the front door of the church from the catechismal
class by one nun on each extremity. There he was more or less deposited
with one nun standing "guard" until his parents came to get him following an urgent summons. His stay in Van Dyke School was very short, for
he was admitted to the clinical teaching program in the public school system within a few days of his departure from the parochial school.*

Au   You had some real troubles, I think, when you were at St. Jerome, as I
       recall, from conversations I had with your mother before you came to
       us. Perhaps, fortunately, you don't recall them now. They were a bit
       messy. How did you get along at Van Dyke?

J   Pretty good.

Au   But, do you have any idea why you were eventually enrolled in the clini-
       cal teaching program?

J   I think it was because of my reading, and also because I was pretty hy-
       per. Reading has always been a problem for me. I've heard the words
       "poor reader" a million times for as long as I can remember. I was hyper
       too.

Au   We didn't have any trouble with you, as far as your behavior was con-
       cerned, as I recall, when you were with us in the program. Do you have
       any remembrances of being disciplined or being controlled too much up
       there?

J   No, not really. It was a good time for me for the most.

Au   You're correct. The times were better for you then. Let's skip the special
       education years for now. You were in the program for about three years

with us, and when that program stopped, you were approximately nine years of age—a little older than that, I guess. You still at that point weren't ready to go back to the neighborhood school to Van Dyke or to any other school. You went to Hazelton Center later. Do you know why you went there?

J   No, not really.

Au   The teacher you had at the clinical program, since it was closing, also went to Hazelton Center. As a matter of fact, she asked to have you go with her there. She liked you and because you were making some very good progress at that point with her. The Hazelton Center program was for kids who were having quite serious learning problems, and so you went along. Do you have any recollections of what went on at the Center?

J   Not really. It was a long time ago; it's kinda hard to remember.

Au   It is kind of long, isn't it? Do you know how long you were at the Hazelton Center?

J   I think for about a year, a year or two, I think.

Au   What happened after that?

J   Then I went to Postill School for the fifth and sixth grades.

Au   And after Postill, what?

J   Then I went to Clinton Junior High School.

Au   You were at Clinton for how many years?

J   For three years.

Au   Then you went to . . .

J   Coughlin High School.

Au   You were in the tenth grade when you started there?

J   Right.

Au   How old were you when you started at Coughlin?

J   Seventeen.

Au   And now you're nineteen?

J   Right.

Au   So that from the time you got into Postill, you didn't fail any grades at all?

J   No, a course or two in high school only.

Au   Things went along pretty well?

J   To an extent, yeah.

Au   What do you mean, "to an extent"?

J   Well, as normal as you do in school. You just do your thing, and everybody is happy.

Au   So what was the "thing" you were doing?

J   Well, just trying to get through school.

Au   What were the most difficult programs or courses or classes that you had in, let's say, junior high school?

J   Just trying to keep up with the reading—it was the hardest thing. I had learned to calm down a lot and to control myself. I got along better. I can do better in a verbal class than I can when there is a lot of reading involved, because I can pick up better from what somebody says, better than if I had to read it in a book. I'd probably read it in a book four times, but if you explained it verbally I could pick up on it the first time and probably repeat it for you word for word.

Au   How about your handwriting? Do you write reasonably well, legibly, so people can understand it?

J   Yeah.

Au   So it's essentially the reading part of things where you have trouble? You've taken courses in English in high school?

J   Yes.

Au   What have been your biggest problems there, other than reading? Do you have to write themes?

J   Themes aren't hard to write; it's prefixes and things like that which are hard for me. Things like that; it's mostly generally reading.

Au   What about a prefix? That's difficult for you?

J   Well, I had to break a word up into three parts and figure it out. Put it on paper on three different parts, stuff like that. It is hard.

How was John perceived by his teacher when he was enrolled in the clinical teaching program at the age of 7 years? The following are the educator's comments:

1. **Motor Coordination:** *He was able to perform all the tasks. His movements were characterized by a degree of rigidity. Rigidity was also noted in his cursive writing. His manuscript writing was jerky. His drawing of himself was adequate in terms of identification of parts, but it did indicate a rigid self-concept.*

Summary statement: *All of his body movements were characterized by a degree of rigidity and, conversely, nonfluency. Motor training should be structured toward achievement of fluency.*

2. **Visual Perception:** *He indicated some confusion in discriminating between blue and purple. His form discrimination was fairly adequate, but limits were quickly reached in terms of complex and fine discrimination, i.e., (1) he could not perceive form relationships in #2 figure background puzzle, (2) he could not perceive the relationships of interlocking geometric forms, (3) he dissociated in #6 block design, (4) he did not have closure on the drawing of the diamond. He has difficulty in perceiving patterns and compositions. Laterality seems to be a problem.*

(5) His horizontal line was slanted, (6) he tended to rotate as he drew horizontal lines. He needs help with left-right discrimination; reversals in "h" and "b."

3. **Auditory Perception:** *He was able to reproduce environmental sounds adequately and was able to identify the locality of the source of the sound.*

4. **Oral Expressive Language:** *He appeared restricted in oral expression. He did not use complete sentences. He tended to answer questions asked by the teacher. He was not free to be spontaneous. He needed the external structure presented by the teacher. The content was relevant and coherent. He needs consistent support and guidance in more adequate oral expression.*

5. **Reading:** *He was fair in comprehension of beginning consonants. Rhyming was no problem. He was able to structure a logical sequence of events with the pictures. He was weak in recall. He appears to be functioning at the level of reading readiness, although his capacity level appears to be at a higher level. There are some evidences of dyslexia-type characteristics.*

6. **Arithmetic:** *He was able to relate pictures (dominoes) to arithmetic numbers. He was unable to relate to words, e.g., "one," "two," etc. He was able to count from 1 to 50, but this appeared to be rote. He appeared weak in real number concepts. He cannot work word problems. He cannot add or subtract. He needs concrete experiences with quantities as a basis for adequate abstractions. Some of his problems here may relate to aforementioned comments relative to dyslexia.*

John's high school reading problems quite obviously are related to the "dyslexic-type" behavior his teacher noted 12 years earlier. This problem is an abiding one, and is a concern to John as a young adult. He refers to this frequently during his interview.

Au	John, what courses did you take last year?
J	Well, American History II, American History I . . .
Au	All right, stop there. What grades did you get in American History I and II? Do you recall?
J	I failed it. Up until last June, before the end of the marking period and the summer began, was the first time they realized in high school that I had a reading problem. They never knew it.
Au	In high school?
J	In high school. They never realized that, so I just had to go along by what I could get myself, and up until then, 'til now, I'm doing well. But before that, let's say in 10th and 11th, all my 10th grade year and half my 11th grade year, I had trouble. I had to go to summer school in 10th grade for American History I, or Social I and II, 'cause I failed it.

Au   You passed it in the summer?

J   I passed it in summer school. I took it over again, and passed it in sum-
      mer school. Then, the other half of 11th grade I passed that, but it was
      hard. From the end of June, well, the beginning of the semester last year
      until now I've been doing very well, because they realized I have a read-
      ing problem, and they helped me or at least had a different opinion about
      me. I took my exams verbally, and I scored well; I was in the 90s on some
      of those exams.

Au   Really?

J   In social science exams, yeah.

Au   Well, that's wonderful.

J   Like today I got my, well, tomorrow I get my Regents' Scholarship Test,
      and I'm in a special reading program at Coughlin. It is called Creative
      Reading, and I was sitting there reading while the teacher was reading
      the questions to me, associations. Like one of them today was what is
      blue to green? Y' know, how you have to associate like that?

Au   Mmmm-hmm.

J   Some of them I did know, and I was getting 'em before she was, because I
      can associate. If you read it to me, I can give you the answer.

Au   That's great!

J   I was just trying to figure out.

Au   Was this part of a Regents' Exam that she was giving you?

J   It was the State Regents' Exam. I read a lot of the pamphlets you get, and
      then you have to go; tomorrow it is for six hours.

Au   Tomorrow it is for good, for real. Today was for practice, is that right?

J   Just to see how I, just to see how I did.

Au   Sure. What about tomorrow? Will she do it orally again?

J   I guess I got to take it regular; I got to read it myself, but I'd like to figure
      if I could just for my own benefit, I'd like to just take the test orally. Just
      for my own benefit, just to figure out how well I'd do, 'cause I know I
      could get at least a $1,500 scholarship. I know I could!

Au   Mmmm-hmm.

J   The reading comprehension is the part where I'm lost, right there, be-
      cause I can't read it. Whereas, if somebody read it to me verbally, I know
      I could get at least $1,500 to go to college.

Au   You know, when you first came to us at the program, you couldn't read
      anything. You just weren't reading, and your writing was impossible.
      Back in my office I have a number of folders which include a lot of the
      reading, writing, drawings, and arithmetic lessons that you completed
      when you were with us.

J   Mmmm-hmm.

Au   I can't say completed, because they just weren't very good. Your writing was poorly formed and illegible, and your reading and math papers when you were 8 years old show less than a first grade achievement level. Your learning abilities and your present reading problem may well have been related to some suspected neurophysical problems which were pointed out when you were about eight years old, and which for the most part you have now overcome.

> *The neurological findings on John are inconsistent among the diagnosticians. The program neurologist states that a "complete neurological examination is negative." The report of the EEG Laboratory, however, reads in its conclusion: "Mild abnormality due to: (1) diffuse background slowing, (2) focal sharp activity from right parietal area. This record could correlate with organic brain involvement." At the same evaluation period the staff psychologist reports a continuation of earlier noted difficulties in visual-motor integration as well as characteristics of "perseveration," "reversals," and "dissociation."*

Au   But if you are now at the point where you can read even partially the Regents' scholarship examinations, you've made a tremendous amount of growth. That's wonderful! Have you ever asked the principal over at the high school, or anybody else, if you might take the scholarship examination or other exams by having someone read them to you, and give it to you orally?

J   I was wondering that today, and then I had a lot of things to do when I left school today. I just didn't think about it; I left. I thought that since it is a Regents' Test, and it is given all over the state the same day, that the reading comprehension is important, that I'd have to do it like all the others.

Au   Mmmm-hmm.

J   That is the way I thought, so I said it wasn't doing me any good to go down and talk to them. But the only reason why I'm doing well now is because of you today. Last year you explained me to them. You explained to these people that I've got a real reading problem, and I got a reading waiver. I got a waiver, so I don't have to pass the 8th grade reading competency to graduate.

Au   Well now, tell me about that, because you may think I did more than I actually have.

J   No, see what it was, was my records. They never followed me so they never knew. They thought I just didn't go to class; I just failed because I just didn't feel like doing it. Then when they finally realized that I did have a reading problem and there was a reason why, they all stood there looking at each other wondering why, where they missed it somewhere along the line. There was a big gap between 10th, 11th, and now. I'm a senior, and now they finally realize what was really going on all along.

Au Mmmm-hmm.

J That they're more than happy to help me now.

Au They are?

J Oh yeah, they're more than that; they bend over backwards, as a matter of fact.

Au Well now, what happened? Your father wrote me awhile back, asking for some of our records when you were a little boy. What happened? What prompted him to write me? I did not send your records since they were at least ten years old and not relevant.

J I don't know; I couldn't tell you. I never asked him why.

Au Well—

J Was it—I finally said it to myself that if I could take these exams orally, that's probably what started it. Because I know I could pass the exam if I took it orally. *I know I could pass it!*

Au The school was asking your dad and mother for records on you from way back.

J Ah-ha.

Au What prompted the school to ask for these records? Have you any idea?

J I think my mother called up and asked if I could take my tests orally and a couple other things, but I can't remember now what the reason was behind it.

Au Mmmm-hmm. But there were no hang-ups as far as you know about you getting in the 12th grade this fall?

J No. I passed all my classes last semester.

Au Ah-ha. Except American History?

J No, I passed American History. That was second half . . . no, first half I failed.

Au You retook that, did you?

J Yeah.

Au So, now in the 12th grade, John, what classes are you taking?

J I got four classes. I've got gym first period, Creative Reading, which is a reading class, second period, wood shop and American History III for my history elective.

Au Mmmm-hmm. Have you ever taken chemistry or physics or algebra or any math courses in high school?

J I took the 8th grade math competency; I passed that.

Au Mmmm-hmm.

J After that I never took any more math.

Au   Mmmm-hmm. The phys. ed.—let's go back to that. Is this something you enjoy?

J   Yeah, I played football up until last year. Well, until . . .

Au   On the high school team?

J   I played varsity when I was a junior.

Au   Really? What position?

J   Defensive end. Until my parents decided that it was the end of that. They didn't want me playing anymore; I got hurt one too many times. I broke six ribs and had a cerebral concussion.

Au   Did you really? So, did they withdraw you, or did you decide that it was a good idea to withdraw?

J   Oh, I got a little mad over that. I've been hurt. I've played football since 7th, 8th, 9th, for five years I played. Every single year I've played, I've gotten hurt. See, when I played first I was twelve, I think. I broke my arm in three places. At Clinton, I broke my ribs twice, then I tore the cartilage in my knee in the 9th grade year. Then my 10th grade year I tore the cartilage in my knee again, and up until last fall, my junior year, beginning of the junior year, it was at Coughlin and the Mayor's cup, because Coughlin is named after a mayor. In the game, I got a concussion, and I was in the hospital. I was out for an hour and 45 minutes. And the only reason they knew who I was . . . when I woke up and told them who I was. See, the coach didn't have enough brains to tell them who I was or what my parents' phone number was, because they cannot give you any emergency treatment, 'cause they didn't know how old I was. They weren't about to put themselves on the line for me, so I just had to lay there until they decided, until I came to, and they were gonna do the rest of the work on me. Then I just got so mad and fed up that I quit and went to work.

Au   How much do you weigh now?

J   160.

Au   Really! You don't look that heavy?

J   I'm tall.

Au   You are tall . . . You were a pretty tall boy as I knew you, too. Now how did you and the coach get along before you got teed-off for this last experience?

J   Oh, we got along fine.

Au   How do you and the guys on the team get along?

J   Fine.

Au   Do you have lots of friends?

J   Yeah. Three-fourths of them play on the football team now. See, the way that I made my friends, and the way I was playing in sports, I was a jock, was what I was.

Au   Mmmm-hmm.

J   You know. If you want to have a lot of friends, just play in a sport.
       Don't matter if you are black or white, as long as you can play together,
       you all stay together. That's one thing that kept me out of trouble, why I
       never got busted.

Au   Mmmm-hmm.

J   Because I played sports and I just never got into breaking windows and
       robbing cars and stuff like that. I could never figure out why people I
       know now always got busted and I never got busted. Now I started
       thinking about it one time. It was because I played sports with every-
       body, and I hung around a different crowd of people that did totally dif-
       ferent things.

Au   Well, I think that's a very good point of view. I think you're correct.
       What kind of crowd are you hanging around with now that you are not
       on the football team?

J   Well, I hang around with the same kids.

Au   The same kids, mmmm-hmm.

J   Well, I also hang around with people I work with.

Au   You work with, where?

J   I work at the Senior Citizens Home, and I've worked there for a year and
       nine months.

Au   Oh. What do you do?

J   I mop floors and stuff.

Au   Do you?

J   Well, I need the money.

Au   Sure, of course. Why do you need the money?

J   Now, I have to pay car insurance. I got a high standard of living; I like to
       party. Like to buy clothes, and it costs a little money.

Au   You've got a good-looking suit on right now.

J   Thank you.

Au   Tell me, what kind of a car do you own?

J   I own a '65 Ford. I know a couple people who helped me work on it. I
       painted it and got chrome wheels on it and stuff. It looks nice.

Au   Mmmm-hmm.

J   It's an older car, but what are you gonna do? Things are expensive these
       days.

Au   You betcha. How much do you have to pay for insurance?

J   Well, I haven't got the premium. They said to me three weeks ago the
       premium was coming up, and it's not gonna be too good either. I guess I
       was paying like $240 when it was still in Mom's name, cuz I can't afford

it. Because I haven't got drivers' ed. I never took drivers' ed. I went and looked at insurance. Even if you can get insurance, it will cost me almost $600 a year. I haven't got no points on my license, never gotten any speeding tickets or anything. It would still be $600.

Au   Why didn't you take drivers' education?

J   I just never decided to take it; I never had it in school. I never took it.

Au   It was available for you?

J   Right. But I never took it.

Au   Why didn't you take it?

J   I just didn't think about it. I was working at the time. I was thinking I'll just wait until I'm twenty-five. I'll pay the extra couple bucks.

Au   Was it because you couldn't read well?

J   No. It was after school, and I was working, too, and it cut into that.

Au   I understand. Tell me then, how old were you when you got your driver's license?

J   Seventeen.

Au   Did you pass it on the first attempt?

J   What, the written test? Yeah, my first time around.

Au   The first time around, uh huh.

J   Yeah, my brother went over the questions with me, and got the test and went over the questions with me.

Au   There's a written and a road test . . .?

J   Right.

Au   When you went to get your examination, were you able to handle the written test satisfactorily, even though you have trouble with reading?

J   Mmmm-hmm. It's common sense questions. You come to a stop sign, what do you do? Go? Come to a rolling stop? Or stop? Just questions like that, general common sense questions.

Au   How old is your brother?

J   Twenty.

Au   I didn't realize . . . I guess I did know you had an older brother, but I didn't realize that, twenty, he's just a year older than you are?

J   Mmmm-hmm. About 18 months.

Au   I never met him. Tell me then, the road test . . . how did you get along with that?

J   I passed it. I had to use my sister's car; she's got a Vega. I used her car. It's a small car; it's easy to parallel park.

Au   Mmmm-hmm.

J   It's not hard to do. With a bigger car, it's so much harder to see over the back of it when you're parallel parking.

Au   Yeah.

J   It's easier to maneuver with a small car.

Au   But you passed it on the first attempt?

J   Right.

Au   That's very good. Have you had any run-ins with the cops since you got your license?

J   No, I've gotten parking tickets; that's about it.

Au   But not speeding?

J   No. It costs too much. There's no reason for it; it's just a waste of time. If you're gonna do it, you're gonna get caught, especially around here.

Au   Yeah, that's true. Now, tell me, how long have you worked at the Senior Citizens Center? Is that what it's called?

J   Yeah, it's up on the top of the hill.

Au   I know where it is, but I never knew it was called that. How long have you worked there?

J   A year and nine months.

Au   When do you work? What hours?

J   I work 3:30 P.M. to 12:00 at night. It's a full-time job.

Au   Are we interrupting your work this afternoon?

J   Oh, I had to take a day off from work to come here.

Au   Oh, I'm sorry about that—but I appreciate your . . .

J   No, that's okay.

Au   Very appreciative. Do you work alone, or do you have a foreman?

J   I work with a kid that's, well, he's twenty-three. He's my supervisor; I work with him. I used to work with a kid from school who quit yesterday. Got sick and tired of the boss and quit.

Au   How do you get along with the boss?

J   I get along with him fine, because I need the paycheck. So, I just go, "Yeah, yeah, sure, sure," and walk up the hall. I don't let him bother me.

Au   You tolerate it?

J   Yeah, well, that's all you can do. That's what he's paying me to do. He wants to run his mouth off, let him run his mouth. I don't get any more or less for it, so I just let him talk and walk up the hall.

This relatively mature adjustment technique was not typical of John during his early school years. Aggression was a commonplace attempt to control in any social situation, and when this failed, as earlier noted, he put his head down and fell asleep. John has overcome many serious adjustment problems, some of which are noted by the program psychiatrist who worked with him for a two-year period beginning in

1964. An excerpt from a periodic report is illustrative: "Counterphobic activity is an attempt to gain mastery over his feelings of being destroyed if he is aggressive. He turns destructive impulses inward, and attempts to master them by mastering a threatening external situation that he sets up or provokes. This could be consistent with his depressive feelings and sensitivity over failure. Also, his school failures and his experiences with severe discipline in school meted out by the nuns in overcrowded schools have reinforced the notion that females are threatening and have to be manipulated. Activity also is a way to overcome anxiety by being preoccupied with activity rather than internal stress." His technique of turning "destructive impulses inward" appears to be a present continuing method of adjustment to tension. The program psychologist also noted this tendency in anticipating heavy demands for nurturing in the early months of John's participation in the clinical teaching program. "Psychological appraisal of John indicated that he is a child of average measured intelligence and impaired visual-motor development. He also displayed a high degree of anxiety and fear of failure, particularly in an academic setting. He should respond well to perceptual training, reduction of stimuli, structure, and frequent reinforcement. Some caution is indicated by John's tendency to withdraw, to cry, and his adjustment and history of sleeping in school. One can predict that, during his initial adjustment to the class, John will make exceptionally heavy demands upon the teacher for a nurturant relationship."

Au   What kind of work do you do at the Senior Citizens Center?

J   General housekeeping.

Au   Well, that's great! Do you ever have a vacation?

J   Yeah, I got . . . I went up to the mountains for two weeks. I got a two-weeks' paid vacation. It's a pretty good job. Like today, I got three floating holidays a year. After three months, you get three floating holidays a year to do what you want with.

Au   Mmmm-hmm.

J   One sick day a month that's allotted to you and two weeks' paid vacation every six months. Me and a couple kids from school went to the mountains for two weeks. That was a good time.

Au   Who went with you?

J   A couple kids from the football team—friends of mine. Just pitched a tent.

Au   Pitched a tent?

J   Had a good time there for awhile.

Au   Cooked out.

J   Yeah.

Au   Good. Have you got a girlfriend?

J   Yeah.

Au   Steady?

J   Well, she's a little mad at me since Friday night, but she'll come around.

Au   What happened Friday night?

J   I got in a fight with her. I was talking to some other girl, and she got all bent out of shape. Like I told her I'd meet her at 9:00, and I didn't get there until 9:30. When I walked into the door, I bought a drink and I was sitting there talking to a girl I haven't seen in awhile. She used to be a waitress up at work, so I was sitting there talking to her for awhile. My girl was standing over at the other end of the bar, and I didn't know where she was. I was talking to her for about half an hour, and she thought I was trying to pick her up. So she got all bent out of shape and left. Ah, she'll come around.

Au   You haven't seen her since Friday night?

J   I haven't talked to her since Friday night. She's mad at me.

Au   Is she in school with you?

J   No, she's a secretary.

Au   I see. So, Friday night, and today's what, Tuesday? So, it's three or four long days, is it?

J   Well, she'll come around. I didn't do anything, so I'm not gonna worry about it. She just gets bent; she just gets mad and thinks I'm gonna come running back to her, and I'm not gonna. I didn't do anything, so I'm not gonna run back to her.

Au   How long have you gone with her?

J   Eight months.

Au   Have you had a lot of girlfriends?

J   Yeah, on and off. Usual.

Au   When did you first start going with girls?

J   Seventh grade, 6th or 7th grade.

Au   You serious about this one?

J   Not really.

Au   Good friends?

J   No. I mean she's got her own ideas, I got mine. I don't know, I'm just gonna have a good time for awhile. I'm not going anywhere.

Au   What do you mean, "She's got her ideas, you've got yours?"

J   Well, she wants to get really serious and I don't. If I'm gonna get serious, I've got a long time before I'm gonna be married; a long, long time. I'm just gonna enjoy myself while I can, because when I get older you can't. You're tied down to work and responsibility, and right now I just want to relax and have a good time while I'm young.

Au   Mmmm-hmm. You go all the way with her; do you have sexual relations with her?

J   Mmmm-hmm.

Au   How frequently?

J   Twice a week.

Au   How long has that been going on?

J   About eight months.

Au   And you've had relations with other girls?

J   Mmmm-hmm.

Au   Do you remember how old you were the first time you had sexual relationships with a girl?

J   Probably about fourteen.

Au   Ah, I don't mean to pry into your private life anymore than I already am, which is quite a bit . . .

J   Mmmm-hmm.

Au   But how did you know about having sexual relations with girls? Where did you begin to get some understanding of what was involved?

J   Probably the garbage going around the locker room?

Au   Fourteen. You were in the locker room?

J   While I was playing junior league football.

Au   Oh yes, uh huh. Did you ever have any good discussions about girls, sex, going with girls, your own personal behavior with girls with your dad and mother?

J   Yeah, my father explained it to me once or twice.

Au   Once or twice. About how old was that? How old were you then? You have any idea? Do you remember? Was it before or after your first experience with a girl?

J   Probably before, I think about twelve or thirteen.

Au   How do you protect yourself? Do you know something about contraceptives? Did you then?

J   Well, she's on the pill. She has been since I started going out with her.

Au   Have you, to your knowledge, have you ever gotten a girl pregnant?

J   No. There's no reason for it today. You can put her on the pill, or I can use a rubber or one of the two. It's better than having a kid, because right then you're bringing a third responsibility into the world, when all you want to do is have a good time. So, it's a lot easier to, and it's better to be safe than sorry, I think.

Au   Righto! What about drinking? What about drugs? Have you ever tried either? You said you tried it, I believe. You have a drink occasionally or frequently?

J   Yeah, I drink. Socially like everybody else does.

Au   You ever get drunk?

J   All the time. Friday, Saturday nights go out and have a good time.

Au   Can you remember the first time you were ever stewed?

J   Not really.

Au   In high school with the football team?

J   Probably a dance at Clinton, when I was in 7th or 8th grade.

Au   Mmmm-hmm.

J   Go to the dance and get drunk. Split a six-pack or something with somebody. Start from there.

Au   Start from there? What . . . how do your parents feel about that, or how did they feel about it?

J   Oh, my father knows. He gets uptight because his father was an alcoholic, so he gets all hyper and bent out of shape about that. But if you handle things in moderation, you're not gonna hurt anybody. What's good for somebody isn't good for me; what's good for me isn't good for somebody else. What's good for somebody else isn't good for me necessarily either.

Au   What about drugs? How about marijuana? Hash?

J   I smoke pot all the time.

Au   How frequently?

J   Probably every day.

Au   Do you? Are you on it right now?

J   No, I didn't get high before I came here.

Au   Thanks. How about hash?

J   I've smoked hash before.

Au   How frequently?

J   Hash is expensive.

Au   When was the last time?

J   Probably Friday night.

Au   Friday night. When was the last time before that? Any recollection?

J   I don't remember.

Au   A long while ago?

J   Not really.

Au   As much as a week, two weeks?

J   Probably a week, two weeks.

Au   How about speed?

J   No, no speed.

Au   Any other . . . LSD?

J   No, never done LSD, cocaine.

Au   Mmmm-hmm. Where do you get the marijuana?

J   Everybody smokes. You can get . . .

Au   Where can you buy it?

J   School.

Au   Guys at school? Are there pushers who come around?

J   Friends. Everybody's got dope. Everybody's got pot. All ya gotta do at Coughlin is just walk around the hall. Nine out of ten people you talk to got it, either are gonna get high or know who's got pot. Dope, nobody cares about pot anymore. Just pot; big deal. Just go out and get high.

Au   Can you buy it outside school?

J   Yeah.

Au   Do you have a regular guy or guys as source?

J   Yeah, I know a couple people that always got pot.

Au   So you can always get it?

J   Right. Free access to it. Yeah.

Au   Free access, meaning they don't give it to you, you buy it?

J   Right, it's there. If I want it bad enough I can go get it. Just make a few phone calls. I go look for a few people and I can find it. It's not hard to do.

Au   Mmmm-hmm. Your dad and mother know about this, too?

J   Yeah. My brother got busted.

Au   How did they know about you? You didn't get busted?

J   No, but he thought it was me.

Au   Who, the cops?

J   No, my pa.

Au   Were you talking about it afterward with your dad?

J   Yeah. He said that he just doesn't want me getting arrested. You just have to be careful.

Au   How much do you pay for an ounce?

J   For pot? Twenty bucks.

Au   Is that about the going rate through the area here?

J   Yeah. That's about it: twenty bucks.

Au   How much do you pay for hash?

J   Probably about $15.00 a gram. Depends on how good it is.

Au   How big is a gram?

J   About that wide.

Au   Where do you see yourself going after you finish high school?

J   Well, this summer I want to work at a ceramic factory up north. And I want to try to get a job there because I like working with my hands, and I love to work with clay. And I thought if I want to make good ceramics, that I could take a 4-year apprenticeship and sometime maybe in a small shop or something like that. But automation beat me out. Anything I can do with my own free hands, a machine can do faster. So, that's that. Now I have to find something else I want to do. But I'm glad that I found out while I still have a year of high school left—that I might be able to find something that I might want to do.

Au   Have you sought any advice from anybody as to the kinds of things you might do?

J   I really don't know what I want to do.

Au   Mmmm-hmm. Let me back up just a bit. You indicated that you had a reading problem. Ah, I don't think I'm telling you all about the school, but one of the problems that your mother and father spoke to me about was that the high school people weren't particularly excited about giving you a diploma.

J   The principal doesn't like me at all.

Au   And why doesn't he like you at all?

J   Because me and him just don't get along. Ah, was it last year, 3 years ago, I got into a big hassle up there. And ever since then he hasn't enjoyed my presence up there too much.

Au   Was it on that basis, or was it on the basis that you were having very unique reading problems?

J   It was my grades, generally. They were really low.

Au   How did that work out?

J   What?

Au   What did you finally agree to? Have there been any decisions about your graduating?

J   Right. I got fourteen and a half credits now, and at the end of the year, I'll have 17 and I'll have enough to graduate. I'll have my four years of English, my history elective this semester. And my sequence, which is wood shop. So I have enough credits, and I have my sequence so I can graduate.

Au   So you'll get what kind of diploma? A Regents' diploma? General diploma?

J   General diploma.

Au   And will there be any hanky-panky about that general diploma? It will be a regular general diploma?

J   It will be a regular general diploma. What I want to make sure on is that he don't put down on there that reading was waivered. If he puts that on there, he's making another one. Because when I go for a job, I want to just hand the guy the diploma, the same as the normal diploma that everybody gets. The waiver is in my record, but it's not on the diploma.

Au   Has he threatened, or has he said that he was going to write this on the diploma?

J   No, I just made sure before he had a chance to, so he didn't make a clerical error against me. I made sure that he didn't do that.

Au   How did you get a feeling that he might put something on the diploma?

J   I just think that . . . well, OK, maybe because I had to wait for it, that they just might have it printed on there that there was a waiver on the bottom in small print: "WAIVER." You know, for some reason, when there's no reason to have it on there.

Au   Mmmm-hmm. Well, you're quite correct. Now I suspect that it's probably illegal to put anything on the diploma, but you don't know that this was actually going to happen.

J   No, he won't do that.

Au   Yeah, I would doubt that that would happen, too. So, let's pick up again then on other possibilities of working in a ceramic shop. What other kinds of things might interest you?

J   Ah, I was thinking maybe I could get into general carpentry, something like that. Then I was thinking maybe I'll just go to community college for two years and see how that is. You know I've got the brains to do things. It just doesn't all get together sometimes.

John's reference to his ability level is of interest. He does have ability, and he obviously uses it rather well. His early intellectual function, however, fell into a very typical pattern common to children with perceptual processing deficits.

A WISC administered when he was 7-3 years of age resulted, insofar as gross results were concerned, in a Verbal IQ of 100, a Performance IQ of 87, and a Full Scale IQ of 94. The lower performance quotient is typical. The same processing factors which serve to depress school achievement will lower psychological test results.

Following a year of highly structured learning experience, perceptual and motor training, the same psychologist on the same test reported John's levels as Verbal IQ of 101, Performance IQ of 101, and a Full Scale IQ of 101. A year later these figures were Verbal IQ of 108, Performance IQ of 103 and a Full Scale IQ of 105. At 18 years of age, John volunteered as a subject for a doctoral student who was doing a practicum in clinical psychology. On the Wechsler Adult Scale only a total IQ score was available in the school records. This was 114, probably quite representative of his level of functioning intellectually.

Au   And you would be eligible to get into the community college?

J   I imagine I could.

Au   What might you do there? What attracts you to want to go there?

J   After two years of college, maybe I could find something that I could build on for four years and go on to a 4-year college after two years.

Au   I see. Did your dad or mother go to college?

J   No.

Au   Are they pushing you to go to college?

J   No. All my parents want me to do is just find something that I like to do that's constructive. That's why I want to get into that ceramic thing. To make custom ceramics is what I really want to do. But custom ceramics are too expensive, and you can buy them at the store cheaper than have somebody make it for you. Because if you want a special centerpiece, then you could go to a department store, and they could do it for you. So, that's all. The openings are scarce for new people.

Au   Have you thought of the army or navy, marines?

J   No. I could never get into that rap; I've heard too much about that. No way!

Au   What have you heard about it that turns you off?

J   Well, I think I did say that before. I just don't think I could adjust to four years of somebody telling me what to do. It's not worth it. It's a volunteer army now. I just don't like the idea at all. Because if you don't do what you're told, tough. I talked with a lot of people . . . and you go to the recruiting office, and they tell you all this stuff, that you get this, and this and this. And once you get in boot camp, and then you're at your orientation for what position you're qualified for. If you can't qualify for it, then you have to go and dig a ditch for four years. It says that right in the contract that if you're not qualified to pass the test. So that's where you stay, and there's nothing you can do about it. And I'd get so frustrated that I'd get a dishonorable discharge. These days you might as well be a criminal. Because that's just as bad as that, because nobody will trust you. Because it's right down in your record. If you were in military service, you have to show your discharge papers. And on your discharge papers, if you get a whatever, an H-4, H-5 or something like that—that's more important than the date. Because I'm better off staying in what I'm doing than get myself into a position where I got, where it's gonna be detrimental to me. And there was never anything in it that really interests me anyways.

Au   OK, let's move away from the army or the navy or anything else related to the military. I think that you're dead set against that. But I'm trying to get you to think with me just a little bit more specifically about future jobs other than the ceramic activities. What do you think, and other than going to the community college now?

J	Huh! I really don't know.
Au	Do you really get along well with your dad and mother?
J	Yeah.
Au	You said you didn't like the regimentation concept of the armed forces. Do your parents try to tell you what to do?
J	No. They're very liberal, but they are, well, like my mother said to me, and I can still remember her saying that to me, "If you want to drink, don't drink behind my back." Like my mother knows I smoke pot; she finds it all the time, you know. And she just gets mad, because she's afraid I'm going to get arrested. She doesn't see anything wrong with it, but she doesn't want to see me in jail either.
Au	Does she know that you were also going with girls; sleeping with girls?
J	Yes, I mean . . .
Au	Does your dad know it specifically, or is he guessing, too?
J	I imagine he knows, too.
Au	You imagine, but you never actually discussed it with him?
J	No.
Au	Mmmm-hmm. You're over 18 now and officially an adult. Has that made a difference between you and your dad and mother?
J	Yeah, I think it has a lot.
Au	Do they treat you as an adult?
J	Yeah.
Au	They expect you to be in on time?
J	No.
Au	Do they ever set hours for you?
J	She gets mad because I miss those early classes, because they think that I've been out all night. I'll go out after work with a bunch of guys and stay out partying all night, then come home. And she doesn't like that too much. She just wants me to graduate from high school.
Au	Sure. Well, you can understand that, don't you?
J	Yeah.
Au	But there are no sisters. There are just the two of you . . .
J	No, I have an older sister.
Au	How old is your older sister?
J	Twenty-seven.
Au	Is she living at home, also?
J	Yeah.
Au	How do you get along with her?
J	Great!

Au   Is she employed?

J   Yeah, she's a school teacher.

Au   Oh, really!

J   Yeah, she teaches at the Head Start Program, I think.

Au   She's a teacher or teacher's aide?

J   I think she's a teacher's aide.

Au   That's great! Has that sort of thing, working with little kids, ever appealed to you?

J   I was thinking about maybe trying to teach kids about the problem I have, because I can understand how they feel. There's nothing I hate more than somebody going and saying, "I know how you feel." How do they know how I feel? You know, when people do that, I really hate that. That really makes me mad when somebody says that, because they don't, and they can't even imagine how I feel. It's so ridiculous. At least *I* think it is.

Au   Are there other activities involving skills and motor activities in which you participate? For example, do you play golf?

J   Yeah. I like to go fishing.

Au   Yeah, that's not quite what I was thinking of. You play football, that's for sure. And you can pass the ball and catch it, I suspect. But what I am thinking about now are things you may do which require skills and require hitting a target, targeting, fine skills.

J   I've played lacrosse before.

Au   Really? So that you can handle a lacrosse ball? You can handle the lacrosse ball accurately?

J   Mmmm-hmm.

Au   Ah, where do you play lacrosse?

J   Coughlin High School.

Au   I didn't realize that they had a lacrosse team. Were you on the team itself?

J   Yeah.

Au   How many guys are on the team?

J   Eight.

Au   And what position did you play there?

J   Backfield.

Au   And why did you stop?

J   Went back to work.

Au   I see. But your skills in terms of seeing where you were going to put that ball and actually getting it there were relatively well developed, so that you could actually assist the team. You were on the first team?

J   Mmmm-hmm.

Au   What other kinds of specific physical skills do you have? How about basketball? Do you play basketball? You're tall.

J   Yeah. I played basketball in ninth grade. I don't like it. I like contact sports better. I get so mad that . . . I get into the game too much, and basketball . . . I get too mad.

Au   What about bowling?

J   Yeah, I like to bowl.

Au   What's your average?

J   I don't know. I just do it once in awhile. If anybody wants to go bowling.

Au   So you have a score of 90 or 120, or . . .?

J   I don't know. I couldn't tell you.

Au   Do you know what your highest score was?

J   Not really.

Au   But you feel that you could compete with the other guys who bowl with you? They don't make fun of you when you bowl?

J   No.

Au   OK, but you *can* get that ball down there and make a few strikes?

J   Oh sure. Oh, I know what you're trying to do, get an association or idea of how I can hit the ball or not. I can play pool.

Au   You can play pool?!

J   I can play pool pretty good. And I can bowl on a bowling team. I can do well. I can get it together now in almost all motor activities. I love golf, but it's too expensive. No good at skiing.

Au   You know that there was once upon a time when you couldn't put a puzzle together?

J   Well, . . .

Au   Do you know what a pegboard is?

J   Mmmm-hmm.

Au   Well, you couldn't make lines with pegs?

J   Huh???

Au   Yeah, really. This was before you began reading. We had more trouble with you trying to put red pegs in a line in a pegboard. You just couldn't seem to get it, couldn't get the idea. But now you're shooting pool, you're bowling, you're playing lacrosse. That's great! I think we're about finished. I can't think of anything else to ask you. Can you think of anything you want to tell me or ask me?

J   No. It's just been good to talk with you again. Hope it can happen another time soon.

We must ask ourselves, what in reality has the secondary school provided John other than sports and an outlet for excessive energy? One might even ask whether or not the school *used* John and his abilities in sports. As a youth who will be nearly twenty when he graduates, is it right that ceramics is his only perceived vocational outlet? He has stuck it out, and will finish high school. John has kept his cool throughout several years of secondary school in spite of his reading problems and some failures. How long can this continue in the face of no realistic prevocational preparation? He has a clean police record; he is socially effective. These characteristics alone will not support him in the post-high school years.

This is a good example of the failure of secondary education to prepare for post-school living for those other than college-bound pupils. Is it revolutionary to expect that secondary schools and teachers will address the unique needs of adolescents with learning disabilities? When will this group of educators come to understand and effectively respond to the long-standing concept of individual differences in youths? Their failure to do so in John's case may be demonstrated in the next few years.

8

Tom: A Social and Educational Failure

Tom REPRESENTS A DIFFERENT ORDER of learning problems as compared with the other young men who are included here. He also, however, experienced the same clinical teaching program as had four of the others, but utilized it in ways different than his school friends. For Tom the experience was a "holding period" which, if continued longer, might have changed his life. It did not continue. Each of the other four had either a specific diagnosis of neurophysiological impairment or was functioning as if he did. If not a specific diagnosis of such a physical impairment, then there was a diagnostic picture which, while not specific, was highly suspect of neurophysiological dysfunction.

Tom's problems stem from a variety of etiological factors, chief among them environmental deprivation and environmental disorganization (home, for example), poor teaching in the early home and school years, emotional problems relating to school entrance, divorce, and a myriad of other similar external presses on the developing child (see Figure 2).

Within the total population of learning impaired, individuals with specific learning disabilities represent a large but generally unknown population insofar as size is concerned. Included in this group one would find Scott, John, Ronald, and Andy, each with basic deficits of perceptual processing.

John, for example, could be placed in the section of the learning disabilities subset (Figure 2) of accurately defined dyslexia. As a child he also had serious emotional problems; hence for him the schema might have been drawn to indicate an overlap of the dyslexia subset with that of emotional impairment. Scott could have been found in the learning disability/emotional impairment overlap area. Andy would join him there, but in opposition to Scott, Andy has been unable fully to deal with

127

his emotional problems. Ron, with his learning disabilities coupled with a potential for convulsive disorders, would fall into the learning disability/epilepsy subsets and overlap.

We debated considerably about including Tom in this discussion, because he may appear as an extreme example. We have come to the conclusion that he is not extreme within the social and economic culture which produced him. There are thousands more like him, and they deserve to be heard. We do not agree that learning disabilities and delinquency necessarily go together, and the data to the contrary are far from clean. Tom is one of those where the link has been firmly, if not irrevocably, forged. What Tom forcefully says reminds us of the necessity of a total community attack on the environmental factors which directly and indirectly produce learning impairments in children—childhood problems which may eventuate in a succession of affronts against society. This is Tom.

Tom's learning problems were often seen as identical in their manifestations to those of the others as boys, but their etiology and origins were quite different. In his young adult years, psychiatrists would undoubtedly classify Tom as "constitutional psychopathic inferiority," unable to profit from his exposures to good teaching, learning, and counseling. Not all children with environmentally produced problems of learning by any means follow in Tom's path, fortunately. In order to understand this in his adolescence and young adulthood, a more detailed picture of his childhood will be presented than has been the case with the other young men. The reader should be alert for issues of social and familial disorganization, failure of mother-child and father-child relations, and the lack of any adequate value system leading Tom to the development of even a minimal internal locus of control.

Three complete neurological examinations, EEG studies, numerous psychological and pediatric evaluations, and endless periods of observation declare Tom's neurophysiological growth to be negative and of no consequence to his problems of learning. "No neurological abnormality," states one neurologist. "No abnormalities were noted on neurological examination," writes another. The electroencephalography laboratory reports "Impression: within normal limits."

The social worker's report on Tom sheds light on his background as a child, and from this his present state can be evaluated more adequately.

Presenting Problem. *Tom, age 8, was referred to the clinical teaching program from the public schools and more directly from the Clinton School, because of acting-out, aggressive, provocative behavior which disrupted the classroom and served as an inhibiting factor in his ability* to learn. Problems cited in the report from the school included aggressive behavior, clowning in class, verbal sexual overtures to his teacher and several little girls, and some truancy and tardiness in addition to academic problems.

Onset and Development of Problem. Tom was described by his mother as an active child, into everything, curious, and full of questions. He was observed taking things from coat pockets at the Youth Center when he was three years old. There were minor neighborhood thefts of candy bars, etc., and a good deal of aggressive fighting in peer relationships. Mrs. Jones went to the Child Guidance Clinic with Tom several times, but discontinued as she felt she was not getting help with her problems and the worker was "only curious to know about me." There were several occasions when Tom got terribly angry and would hold his breath until he passed out. Although Mrs. Jones was unaware of any similar incidents occurring during the past few years, Tom has had one episode in the clinical teaching class in the early fall when he ripped off his shirt.

According to Mrs. S., Tom's present teacher, Tom has shown improvement both in his behavior and in school work since the beginning of this school year.

According to his mother, he has shown improvement in the home, especially during the last two months. She has had no difficulty with him in the neighborhood; and he has begun to read and play better with the other children as well as demonstrating a cooperative attitude toward sharing responsibilities in the home. He persists in asking questions continually, and has a "very glib tongue." However, a problem of enuresis persists.

Family. Mother: Mrs. Jones is an attractive woman in her early twenties. She lives in Green Housing Project with her children, and has been receiving an ADC monthly grant from the Department of Social Welfare ever since the birth of Tom. Housekeeping standards appear to be quite good.

Mrs. Jones is the oldest of six children, has four sisters, and one brother who is currently in the Austin Penitentiary. She recalls, with no apparent trace of bitterness, having many responsibilities as a child, such as caring for the other children, washing the family clothes by hand, cooking and sewing. She appears to be very handy. Her father is a trucker and had worked whenever he could get a job. Her mother worked on and off also; and the family appears to have been on and off of the welfare rolls. Her parents separated when Mrs. Jones was fifteen years old, and while they are not legally divorced, both "keep company" with other persons. Mrs. Jones's mother is working and there appears to be a feeling of family cohesiveness among the women.

Mrs. Jones completed the seventh grade in school, and she never had the ability to grasp the school work. School learning was never *linked in a meaningful way to future job possibilities, or the realities of life; thus, incentive and motivation were minimal.*

Her first child was born out-of-wedlock when she was fourteen. She became pregnant with Tom when she was sixteen and subsequently married Mr. Jones when she was eight months' pregnant. She married him because of her mother's insistence and threat to send her away from the home unless she complied. She felt at the time that one thing was about the same as another and agreed to do this.

She and her husband shared a room in her mother's house until the time of Tom's birth. During the period that Mrs. Jones was hospitalized, Mr. Jones got into "trouble" and was sentenced for a period of fifteen to thirty years in Austin Prison. Mrs. Jones remained in her mother's home with her two children for three years. She cited mother-daughter conflict over child-rearing and disciplining as the principal reason for getting an apartment of her own. Mr. Jones was released from prison and was in the home for a period of only three months, when he "got into trouble" again. He has not been in the home since. Mrs. Jones visits him once or twice a month and seems to have some feeling for him although she professes indifference. She is willing to take him back into the home when he is released if he "is willing to change his way," although she recognizes the unlikelihood of his being able to do so.

Mrs. Jones does have boyfriends at present. She sees these men as long as they stay with her, and emphasized the social, companionship aspects of these relationships including the material and emotional gratifications. She is quite frank about the fact that she does not want to "fall in love" with anyone, but wants to be with "someone who will be nice to her and good to the children." Her dependency needs have been accentuated; her self-reliance undermined by the fact that she became pregnant at an early age; and she has seen Welfare as an accepted way of life for people during her lifetime. Mrs. Jones viewed herself as "a sinner," and has had little in her life which would contribute toward self-worth or a sense of values. She is motivated to take care of and do the best she can for her children, and she has been able to establish a consistent relationship with the social worker. There has been an attempt to reach her through Tom by pointing out the repercussions that her attitude, feelings, and behavior have upon him. Mrs. Jones has been attending 7th grade classes twice a week at a vocational high school for the past eight weeks, and is anxious to involve herself in some vocational training program. She has been drifting, somewhat resourceful, but unaccustomed to thinking things through or planning ahead.

Father: *Mr. Jones, age 32, completed the 10th grade. He is currently serving a fifteen- to thirty-year sentence at the Austin Prison. He is originally from Iowa and was in New York for several months at the time Mrs. Jones met him. From Mrs. Jones's description he is not a bad, drinking man, but "gets mixed up in the wrong company and gambles a* lot." Although there was some reprisal when he re-entered the home, over the fact that Mrs. Jones had had two daughters by another man, she stated that he was always good and fair to the children, treated them well, and showed no favoritism. She "respects" him a great deal for this, and is somehow aware of the fact that he can't seem to avoid getting into trouble. Tom saw him for only three months at the age of three.

Half Brothers and Sisters: *Donald, age 9, Tom's older half brother, attends Clinton School, and was born out of wedlock. Geraldine, age 7, attends Clinton School, and was born out of wedlock. Rose, age 5, attends Clinton School, and was born out of wedlock. Tom is the only child of Mr. and Mrs. Jones; the last two children have the same father.*

Developmental History. *Tom was born October 24, 1955. The pregnancy and birth were uneventful and normal as described by Mrs. Jones, but this was a period of great emotional stress for her. The first three years of Tom's life were spent in the home of his maternal grandmother, where there was conflict over mother-daughter role responsibilities and child-rearing practices. Tom was described as a "very loving, average baby."*

Tom was nursed for three and a half months, had no eating problems, but is described as having a ravenous appetite at present. Tom was toilet trained at 18 months, but has had a severe nocturnal enuresis problem which has persisted since the birth of Rose. He is the only child in the family with this problem, and Mrs. Jones is aware of the emotional implications. She has tried to waken him at night, but this has been unsuccessful. She prefers to accept this as something he will grow out of in time and feels that punishment for this would be fruitless and undesirable.

Tom started to walk at about a year and a half, has been active, and has appeared to have good motor coordination. Tom started talking at about two years and from what Mrs. Jones says, once he learned how to talk "he never stopped." He has been a little quieter in the home recently. Tom usually gets to bed between eight and nine o'clock but all four children share the same room; and they often do not get to sleep before ten, sometimes eleven. Once asleep, he usually sleeps soundly.

The principal methods of discipline have been beating, more recently taking away desired privileges or rewards. Punishment appears inconsistent at times, and when the mother is uncertain as to who is responsible, she will punish those whom she feels most likely to be responsible. There is rivalry and the children's relationships conflict within the home. Tom is described as "free, sharing," but there is much fighting between Tom and his half brother, with Tom usually getting the worse end of it physically. Tom has usually mixed with a group of boys slightly older than he, and Mrs. Jones has been unhappy about this, yet feels that she cannot choose his friends for him. She feels that these past friend-

ships have contributed substantially to his minor delinquent behavior and that at times he might be used by the group. She seems to be keeping closer tabs on him, and he has been in the home a good deal more of late. The fact that he is delivered home from school has been very helpful.

The Medical Report submitted by Dr. S. in October of 1963 reveals that Tom is a well-developed, fairly well nourished boy who is in good health. The neurologic examination performed by Dr. H. in December of 1963 indicated that Tom is well-coordinated, with good muscle tone. His reflexes were generally hyperactive, but symmetrical, and no abnormalities were noted.

Evaluation: Cultural factors would appear to be significant in this family and related to Tom's learning impairments. The father is out of the home, and the predominant figure is the mother. There have been boyfriends of Mrs. Jones with whom Tom has had some limited contact, but there has been little opportunity for the children even to develop a healthy relationship with a male person. "Marriage" or "parents," as understood from a middle-class perspective, do not mean anything to Tom in terms of what he sees and experiences. Tom appears to have a relationship with his mother which is proving to be one of frustrated dependency, hostility, and acting-out. The enuretic condition (which may be a manifestation of regression) may also be an expression of resentment against his mother for lack of attention and emotional sustenance. This in turn leads to difficulty in relating to females and authority figures. There appear to be some sado-masochistic elements in Tom's need to punish himself in order to punish others, and much of his clowning, aggressive, and hyperactive behavior is seen as a defense against feelings of inadequacy.

Mrs. Jones appears to be inadequate in her role as wife and mother, but her present functioning and attitudes seem to be consistent with the behavior in her own family of origin. She does meet the physical needs of the children. Mrs. Jones has been seen by the social worker once a week on a regular basis for the past three months. She has been consistent in keeping appointments, and is motivated principally by a desire to see that the children "keep out of trouble." This could be a reflection of the fact that in this family a sense of right and wrong is largely externalized, and there is the need for controls outside of the individual himself. Mrs. Jones appears to be grateful for the consistent communication and support she has received from Mrs. S., and feels a link with the school.

She is realistic and has appraised the realities of her life in a practical, naive way. She is a woman who shows warmth, is frank, and direct in a manner that a child would be. She understands what she "should do," but fails to see that this would bring her any personal happiness. She is fairly immature, wary of most authority figures but evidences some potentials for growth and awareness of her family situation.

Tom agreed to an extended interview, and was visited in the conference room of the penitentiary where he was confined on the latest of a long series of arrests:

Date	Charge	Disposition or Status
4/19/67	Criminal Receiving	Closed 4/25/67
5/2/67	Malicious Mischief	Closed 5/4/67
5/4/67	Petty Larceny	8/30/67 Lowland Training School
5/17/67	Malicious Mischief	Closed 5/24/67
6/6/67	Criminal Receiving	8/30/67 dismissed
6/26/67	Malicious Mischief	8/30/67
4/14/69	Petty Larceny	Closed 5/2/69
5/9/69	Criminal Possession of Stolen Property	5/9/69 Susp. Judgment
8/30/73	Petty Larceny	9/10/73 170.55 CPL
2/12/74	Petty Larceny	3/12/74 $50 fine and 1 year conditional discharge
10/24/74	Public Intoxication	10/25/74 $50 or ten days
11/13/74	Stolen Property 3rd	2/14/75 60 days; 3 yrs. probation
6/18/75	Possession of Controlled Substance 7th	10/16/75 1 year
	Possession of a dangerous instrument 4th	1 year consecutive

(This is apparently the double charge on which he was released from the penitentiary on 11/15/76)

10/16/75	Federal Petty Larceny	Pending
2/2/76	Attempted sodomy 1st and Attempted sexual abuse 1st	Report indicates that the action was pending, but when visited, he had been cleared of that charge, although it is still on his record.
9/3/76	Arson 4th degree	At the time of the record it was noted to be still in the county court, but on 9/3/76 he was acquitted of that. However, it should be noted that that charge was an intrahouse charge, where it was thought that he along with others had attempted to set fire to the institution.

Author   Hello, Tom. It is good to see you again.

T   I'm very surprised. I was stunned that you'd come to see me. I'm gonna be honest with you. I've had *problems* from day one when I walked through this penitentiary door. Which isn't really so unusual because I've been having problems all my life, ten years now off-and-on. I had twelve arrests prior to the one I'm here on now. I've been here thirteen months, and I'm here for fifteen.

Au   You're going out soon?

T   Yeah.

Au   Good.

T   But I've been down; I've been down constantly, thirteen months here and three months at the Public Safety Building. I've been charged, had formal charges lodged against me while I've been in here too. Maybe all this might not be relevant to your thing, but I somewhat see it relevant to give you a better outlook of me and my, oh, ya know . . .

Au   Where you're coming from?

T   Where I've been, and you know before the end of the interview I would like to let you know where I'm going too.

Au   I'd like to hear that from you, Tom. Why don't you light your cigarette?

T   I don't have matches.

Au   Let me see if I can get some for you. Do you remember some of the boys who were in school with you and me?

T   This little, short, plumpy dude, right? Like I forget the guy's name. [He starts to reminisce about his time in the clinical teaching program.] One name was Andy, I forget the name of which one was plumpy and which one hit me in the face. Oh, I know who hit me in the face with a chair, he was kinda narrow faced.

Au   Scott?

T   I think it was Scott. I'm not sure. He hit me in the face with a chair, we got into something, and I ran up on that platform in the classroom.

Au   You remember, don't you?

T   Sure I remember, he left me with a scar that will be with me the rest of my life.

Au   Oh no, really? I didn't know that. I think I have a picture, is this the one? But he wasn't plump.

T   No, no, no. He, I didn't. Let me see. Scott was nice.

Au   Oh, he was a fine boy. He's married now, and has a little baby boy.

T   Really?

Au   Hmmm mmmm.

T   Scott. Now Scott was nice. That I remember now. Only one that stuck out like a sore thumb, along with me that I remember was the plump one.

Au	No, we didn't have too many problems with you. Remember your teacher, Mrs. S.?
T	Sure. Mrs. S., and Mrs. McC. I remember. Wow. I forgot all that.
Au	It's like going-home week, isn't it, all of a sudden?
T	Yeah. If you can show me this guy because I have to look him up.
Au	I don't think I have his picture.
T	Y' know over the years I've had to think a lot. Over the years, I've laxed and it's [his memory of the thrown chair] been eased an awful lot.
Au	I'm sure it is.
T	I would like to see him again anyway. Just to show him my scar. I guess we all were problems.
Au	You all had lots of problems in learning.
T	I was very, very disturbed. I was very disturbed when I found out that my third year with you it would be my last. I don't think I had any run-ins with the law while I was with you. Yes, I had. Yes, I've lived on the west coast. I left in '66, right? How old was I when I started with you?
Au	You were eight. You were with us for almost three years. So you were an old ten or a young eleven, a young eleven, I think.
T	I was an old ten.
Au	The end of 1965 you left us at the program.

Because of the extensive social work statement included earlier in this chapter, details of Tom's behavior in the clinical teaching program are not further included. Suffice to say his aberrant behavior continued, although progress in better social adjustment was observed during the time he was in the structured program. There was not enough home and community support, the duration of the program too short, and his separation from the program coincided with additional family upheaval to insure his progress. His academic achievement was less than any of the boys in the program. The long academic achievement plateau on which he functioned prevented sufficient stimulus and motivation to constitute a genuine success experience which might have offset some of his community presses. Tom's achievement record is recorded as follows:

Date	Grade placement in:			
	Reading	Arithmetic	Language	Total Grade Placement
10-15-63	2.3	2.8	1.8	2.2
6-12-64	2.3	2.7	2.3	2.6
11-24-64	2.9	2.9	2.4	2.7
6-2-65	2.5	3.6	2.8	2.9
9-24-65	2.6	4.2	2.9	3.2

On May 15–16, 1964, his intelligence levels were registered on the WISC as Verbal IQ, 91; Performance IQ, 92; Full Scale IQ, 91. This is a slight,

*but an insignificant improvement over seven months earlier when, in Oc-
tober 1963, the three IQ scores were 81, 96, and 87 respectively. Consistency is observed in the comparison of these scores with those recorded
seven months earlier—92, 83, and 87. Tom is probably functioning as an
adult at a low average range, but he is highly sophisticated insofar as
street language, learning, and concepts are concerned.*

Au   Where did you go after you left us?

T   That's what I was getting to. I left there, wished I had them dates downpacked [down pat], and I'd like to get them downpacked. I left there like
you said, an old ten. I been in and out of trouble with the law, right? But
I've been in and out of trouble with the law even before I even came
there.

Au   Oh yes?

T   You see, eight years old, right? I remember when I first, my mother first
told me I'd be going to school there, right? Remember the drug store that
used to sit right on the corner?

Au   Yes.

T   The building is still there?

Au   Sure.

T   I've been there once looking for Mrs. S.

Au   Yeah, she's a teacher here in the city. I don't know where, but she's a
teacher still.

T   I would ask for you to find out. One time I called there, like in '73 after I
got out.

Au   Hmmm mmmm.

T   I come back here, I come back here in '73 until now. Okay, I called her,
right, and oh that woman. I don't think she really realized what, what at
the time she really meant to me. Now that I look back that I'm older I
can, I forgive nothing. I really don't believe I've forgiven anything. I
never had a father; my father lived the type of life that I've lived so far.
Right now he's out; he's managing an apartment building. He and my
mother are separated.

Au   You know him, do you?

T   Sure I know him, hmmm mmmm. I can't think; I don't really know him.
I know of him.

Au   Has he ever lived at home with you?

T   Yeah.

Au   Here?

T   Yeah. But it was only momentarily. Like I had just got out of an institu-
tion. My mother was going with one man, and she dropped him and got

back together with my father. Then we lived three months with them together, less than three months. She was forced to go bankrupt; she owned
one house on Mainland Ave., and at the present time we were living in
the house that, up on Handley Drive. I forget the address.

Au   Hmmm mmmm.

T   She was the first one when I was eleven years that signed a paper for me
to be sent to Lowland State School for boys and girls, right? Now, I'm
eleven years old, and my mother's sending me away, and now I'm a kid
eleven years old, how am I suppose to think of my mother, right? I don't
know how I was suppose to react to that, me being a kid and all that. But
I know how I did react—if I forget to go back into that you let me know.
But to get back on the subject 'cause I have a tendency to once I start
talking.

Au   I'll tell you when to come back.

T   Okay, so, what happened was when I left I was very, very disturbed, my
leaving that school [clinical teaching program] affected me mentally.

Au   Really?

T   Right. Because prior to coming there, which was almost three years, you
said I come there at eight. So I come there when I was what, almost
seven, right?

Au   No, you came to us when you were eight and you left at ten.

T   Eight. Right. I remember Jefferson grade school. I remember . . .

Au   That was before you came to us?

T   Right. I remember me living with my grandmother, with all my cousins
on Wilson Street.

Au   Yeah.

T   Also, remember my brother being a year older than me. It was his job to
pick us from school and cross the streets and this type of thing. I remember one time he wasn't there and I was very, very young, the age I
couldn't recall but I'm talking about grade school, talking about Jefferson School. I know it wasn't over second grade, second or third grade.
I'm on the street corner. My grandmother lived on Wilson. [During the
interview Tom was extremely tense. His comments have been reported
here practically verbatim with a minimum of editing. As the reader will
note, his ideas are often not coordinated, his language flow is sometimes
alogical, and it is difficult to follow.]

Au   Hmmm mmm. I didn't realize your grandmother lived there.

T   Oh she plays a very important part in my life. Um, so I remember one
day my brother wasn't there to pick me up, I'm very young, right. So,
I'm standing on that corner Wilson St. and whatever the cross street is.
She stays there. There was a corner store here, a laundromat here on the
same side of the street at the end of the block of the school. That corner

store, there was something else there but right next to it was the corner store which was out of business at the time. There was another corner store which was in grocery business. The grown-ups used to go there all the time, and buy collard greens and stuff. On this corner there was nothing but houses but she stayed second, possibly house from the corner and I only had one street to cross, right?

Au   Yes.

T   I'm standing there and they had a light up, right? I remember, I didn't know, but I remembered one way or the other, vaguely that you cross on the green or the red. Now I knew yellow; ya know yellow didn't mean much.

Au   Hmmm mmmm.

T   But I knew somebody making it very clear to me that on red or green you go, one or the other. I crossed the street, right? I come home by myself, right? My brother got chewed out for it, but I didn't get no type of recognition for me making it home safe.

Au   Ah yes.

T   I look back on that and other times in my life when I didn't get the proper attention. I was the type of child that, I don't go along with this now but evidently it must be true. At the time when I was growing up, I was the kind of child that was very selfish when it came to attention, and when I didn't get what I thought was my proper share, I would stand out. I would make it my business to be noticed.

Au   Hmmm mmm.

T   I've always had problems at school. At one time, I got, no, I can't say that. I can't say at one time it was worse. I always had problems with little things, smaller things when I was younger, ya know. But it was always something, and I just don't believe that I had the proper attention, love, and affection. Okay, now from childhood up until five, four, you know what? I think I was only in kindergarten or first grade when I crossed that street. Because when we moved from our grandmother's house on Wilson Street, my mother moved into Greenbriar Court. The Court runs right into a street across from the park. And going this way you could go straight down make a right down Wilson, and you're at my grandmother's house and I remembered that. That's why I remembered when I moved out of my grandmother's, I don't remember moving but I remember leaving, thinking I had to leave. It was just moving houses and I was very young—eight or nine years.

Au   Your mother was a beautiful woman.

T   Oh! Back to what I was saying, I don't think I had been neglected when I was a child. As a result, being a child I don't think I was well aware of a lot of things, but by the same token I must give myself credit. I was very intelligent when I was young. I've always been, I've always been good in my mind. Y' know, you have a problem. I always thought it out thoroughly and y' know. The times I got into trouble, even when before I couldn't help, but think that I, y'know I use my head a lot, y'know? And verbally I've never had a problem.

Au   You were always a leader of the boys at the clinical teaching program. They looked up to you.

T   I never had a problem of getting my point across or sitting down with anybody that I can remember in my entire life. I've always been able to hold a conversation.

Au   Hmmm mmmm.

T   If not more. So I used to look forward to going to school in the morning. That blue cab come picking me up.

Au   That's right.

T   And bringing me home. I remember the very last day I left with a grudge. I left with a grudge for a guy that stayed on Davis Street. A little short, fat, plumpy guy, and that's why I mentioned him earlier. Now, he, I forget exactly what he done, but like I say over a time and a time is the best healer. I've never forgotten him. Remember how you would get in a conversation about my history which I can get into quite a bit, y' know my schooling and all that? I think about him, y' know, y'can almost imagine how much I think about this guy. All the applications I filled out in jobs and this type of thing. But the hatred and the "to get him" was gone a long time ago, I don't even know when it left. But y' know, it's no problem. I'd like to see him again and sit and have a beer with him, y' know.

Au   I really don't recall whom you're speaking of.

T   George! He used to live on Davis St. with his mother and I think he was the only child with his mother was a type of woman.

Au   I don't remember.

T   But I'm telling ya! I gathered that his mother, 'cause I'd seen his mother a couple of times [certain ones rode home together], me and him riding home together. I remember his mother being the type of woman that was, y' know, aggressive, and he was the type that we called a mother's boy, right?

Au   You're right. That is the right boy. I don't see how he had enough nerve to hit you.

T   No, he wasn't the one that hit me.

Au   Oh.

T   He wasn't the one that hit me.

Au   I see.

T   He was mouthing off, he had been mouthing off, right? He used to talk a lot about, he used to sell a lot of wolf tickets, right? He always talked a lot of garbage, right? Me, I'm, y' know, I've always had a lot of hard times. It wasn't until I was about eleven years that I started hanging around with guys older than me. That I got scared of somebody.

Au   Hmmm mmmm.

T   As a result, I think in my life I was put up to do things when I was a child. But I can't have tried. I've thought about it. I sorted it out. I cannot lay one something on the reason for my life being the way it is. There's no major reason. There's a whole lot of things—compound.

Au   Let me ask you a few questions, will you?

T   Okay. Oh, wait.

Au   Go ahead.

T   Before you get back to any questions, I want to clear up something. You mentioned that my mother was a very beautiful woman. She signed the papers first for me to be sent away, right? I'm eleven years old, I'm at Lowland State School for boys and girls. At that time, I did not hold it against my mother. I had been in and out of family courts a few times before she signed papers. She come down, and the first time I went to Stoneybrook [a county home] I don't know; there was something in me. I didn't have to go to Stoneybrook 'cause a couple times prior to that they had released me in her custody, and this particular time I said I didn't want to go home or something like this or something to that effect. It's on my record.

Au   Yes.

T   So, she says, "all right sweetheart," but she said it in a sarcastic way, you know. "Okay, if that's what you want, sweetheart, fine." Something to that effect. They were signing the papers from day one after, right? I've never in my life held it against her. I've always thought like when I first went I stayed 13 months, got out. Stayed out 8 months before I was sent back away to Industry [a state correctional facility for delinquents]. I stayed 10 months and got out, right?

Au   Let me get this straight now. After you left us you went to Lowbrook?

T   Right.

Au   For a while?

T   One time.

Au   One time. For about how long was that, Tom?

T   I went to Lowbrook for at least a week.

Au   Yeah, a very short time.

T   Right.

Au   Generally speaking. After that is when your mother signed the papers?

T   Well, I'd been to Lowbrook by that time. Maybe one time before, yeah she did sign the papers after my going to Lowbrook. I had already been in trouble with the law as far as getting blue tickets. Remember the little

things they used to give out? Blue tickets? I got one blue ticket for stealing at that drugstore. That's why I said when I first went to the drugstore, when I first went to the clinic school, the drug store was there.
They used to have a thing that looked like this. We used to run up it and
slide down.

Au   Mmmm mmm.

T   Being kids, y' know. So we're into mischief. So I'm very shaky when my
mother, I think she came up to me the first time. She came up to me and
talked to me and I was scared to death. It was just before I'd been busted,
and my mother didn't know where the store was. As soon as I seen the
building, I seen the store, I took a defensive attitude which later I
smoothed it out. I went to Lowland; I stayed 11 months, I come back, I
think I was on parole. Yeah, right, I was on parole.

Au   That's upstate New York or downstate New York?

T   Close to New York City. Lowland State School for Boys and Girls, it
was called at the time. We're talking about '66.

Au   Well, or early '67, somewhere in there. The exact time doesn't make too
much difference. After Lowland, then what?

T   I got out, I stay . . .

Au   You were out on parole?

T   Right.

Au   For how long?

T   In the final analysis of me being on parole, I was violating. I'd been, I de-
served to be violated because I had skipped school a couple times.

Au   You violated your parole, is that what you're telling me?

T   Right.

Au   I'm not gonna make any judgments on who was right and who was
wrong at this moment. When you violated parole, then what happened?
Were you sent up again?

T   Yeah, I was sent to a place called Industry.

Au   Yeah, I know. Then how long were you at Industry?

T   Ten months.

Au   Ten months. By now you must be in your teens?

T   Oh yeah, I'm . . .

Au   Because Industry is for youths.

T   Y' gotta be at least thirteen to go there.

Au   Yeah.

T   I was just thirteen.

Au   You were there ten months?

T   Yeah.

Au   Then you came back to here?

T   When I went there I was fourteen, excuse me. I come out and went back here to town. My father had just come out of prison and it was in '68. I was living with my mother. I was going to Charles School. I had a teacher in sixth grade there that now is a reverend.

Au   Oh.

T   I think at the time he was a reverend, but he was told to quit school for his health. Right to the day, we've never lost contact.

Au   Do you get to see him? Does he come here and visit you?

T   That's what I'm getting to, right? We had a big riot here, maybe you heard about it. Anyway as a result of that, in which I was active, I must say against the administration here and the way they handle things. I'm usually the one that did anything about it on our block. Y'know, I'm well respected 'cause I've been in so long. I got him appointed here at the time. We were all sitting in the messhall, grievances all up in the air, everybody's ready to fight. I'm not pushing, it, but, you know how it is.

Au   Hmmm mmmm.

T   So, they says, it's on a Sunday night, I'll never forget it. As a result of that I was charged with six counts of, five felonies, seven charges altogether. Stuff I never even done, but because of the administration the way it was. I'm sure you probably know. Right? Okay. The administration out to get me as a result of me being so active down on the block, getting things in an uproar, and through them being in turmoil and through them being in that state of mind, a major fire was set.

Au   Oh?

T   Who was charged with setting the fire? Tom Jones, right? But I had knowledge of the fire, that it was going to be set, but I didn't go near where it was to be set. I'm too, I got too much on the head to do that, right? I'm thinking all the time downstairs. But I'm opposed to this administration. I had written things, rather submitted things to them and it never got to them. It would never get to them. I was very, very disturbed, I'm looking at fifteen months to do here I was sentenced to. Two years consecutively, do one and the other and that's very unusual time here 'cause usually the majority of people are doing years or under, right? I've gotta make my stay as pleasant as possible, right? I'm here on thirty, I'm here thirty days before they label me as a troublemaker. I can't get nothing. Tom Jones, my name is one with the guards. I'm a loser, right? I had already been charged with extortion three times by . . .

Au   Here or outside?

T   Here. I just come here on thirty days. I wasn't here six days before I was charged with extortion three times.

Institutional records show a constant inability to adjust. On 12/8/75 there is noted an in-house violation of cutting phone wires, destructive of institutional property, and inciting a riot. For that he was given fourteen days in the lock-up, fourteen days of loss of all privileges, five days loss of good time. On 12/13/75 he again committed an institutional violation—"a refusal to obey orders of an officer to turn down the radio after 1:45 A.M." For this he was given a loss of radio privileges for seven days and a loss of all privileges for ten days. On 12/20/75 another institutional violation is recorded: "forced your cell door open and released yourself without authorization." For this the punishment was to be determined by the superintendent. On 12/14/75 an institutional violation involving a verbal abuse and threatening to interfere with procedures. For this he was given five days in the lock-up and five days of lost privileges. On 12/14/75 the cell block officer wrote to his supervisor, "I am continually having to take abuse from Resident Jones when attempting to deal with the population with R Gallery. Resident Jones is a constant agitator and problem; becuase of this I am requesting at least ten days lock-up with no privileges to start 12/22/75, the day Jones is supposed to un-lock. I feel this request to be fair and just in view of Jones's constant abuse." On 1/4/76 an institutional violation—refused to lock-in when ordered. Continued harassment of officers. The penalty was fourteen days in the "keep-lock," in his own housing area, fourteen days of loss of privileges. On 1/5/76 another institutional violation—harassment of other residents, making threats against residents; the penalty again was fourteen days lock-up, loss of privileges, and loss of ten days of lost good time. On 1/7/76 an institutional violation—refused to be locked in. Again, the penalty was fourteen days lock-up, fourteen days of lost privileges, and ten more days of lost good time. On 1/6/76 there is an institutional violation regarding an unauthorized use of the telephone, disobeying an order when told to stop. The penalty was fourteen days of lock-up and fourteen days of loss of privileges. During the week of 11/17/75 there is an institutional violation involving the soliciting of items from various residents in his living area illegally and he was informed this was a misconduct violation. He was given at that time up to fourteen days in the lock-up and loss of all privileges during the period of the lock-up. On 11/22/75 he was accused of taking a container of deodorant belonging to a resident and appropriating it for his own use. For this he was given fourteen days of loss of privileges. On 11/18/75 there is a verbal reprimand becuase he refused to return to his own area after leaving the mess hall.

T   I had so many charges and the way they got me, which I'll tell you. This is all pertaining to my stay here, this is all what I'm facing and what I'm going through, basically now at the age of 21. By me being inconsemated [incarcerated], OK? Like I said, I was a legal troublemaker. I came here on October 16, I had three months jail time in the Public Safety Building. I came here October 16, of '75, they had it out front, my term, I would leave March 15, '77. So, it was gonna be tough, so I said well, just make it as sweet as possible. I already knew this place was a day care center, I'd been here twice—once for a few hours and once for 27 days. But they were trying to crack down. They wanted, which I can't blame 'em, they wanted power, and authority in the hands of the administration, which it should be. But when they decided to crack down they went about it entirely wrong. At the time I came, I come in the middle of something. I came here when the place was already in turmoil, there was a couple of brothers that have state bids [wanted on state criminal charges] and were still minors. A religion called Five Percent Nation. Are you familiar with that?

Au   I just know the term. [The following monologue is included as an example of Tom's alogical, "word salad," and non-directional language and conversational patterns.]

T   Okay, now that particular religion is affiliated with the Moslems. The only difference is that they have Five Percent Nations. They have the Moslems—then the people who are deaf, dumb, and blind do not have true reality of their self, right? Which now in their eyes would be considered the same way, but at one time I was in their religion when I first came. There's a lot of studying and it's a lot of mental work, that's what held my interest enough to even get into it. Now the difference between Five Percent Nation and Moslems is the, the only difference is because the Five Percent Nation believe that they, each and everyone of them, they. Now the Moslems believe that Elijah Mohammed, the guy that died. He was God.

Au   Hmmm mmm.

T   Which he projected that image. The man got a lot coming, and I give it to him, but he projected an image that I honestly believe is wrong. Because over in Mecca, I don't wanna get into all that. But anyway I have to say he's wrong, because he led the Moslems to believe that they weren't God and I honestly believe every man is God himself. I'm not a, I forget the word, but one of those people who don't believe in a religion. My mother was one at the time. Right now she's saved and sanctified, filled with the holy ghost. She had this since sixty, since she left here.

Au   So, the Five Percent Nation was strong when you came here with your brothers?

T   Yeah. Like you say, I know something about it, and I'm willing to bet that you know what you know about it through a prison system.

Au   No, I don't. I don't know anything about it except I heard the title.

T   Oh. But it's very, very, very popular in prison. In prison if it's not Moslems it's the Five Percent. The people that aren't in either, both Moslems and the Five Percent consider themselves 85 Percenters.

Au   Hmmm mmmm.

T   People like preachers and . . .

Au   Chaplains.

T   Chaplains and stuff like that they call 10 Percenters. They say, the reason they call them 10 Percenters is because in their. I used to have all that stuff memorized, I used to have it on. They live off the sweat of others, and they pushed that stuff and they live off the sweat of others. In looking through these people's eyes they consider them 10 Percenters, but you can't consider a preacher a Ten Percenter without considering Elijah Mohammed, a prophet, I'm giving him all that's due him, maybe a little bit too much. To consider him God and everyone else, he wouldn't teach the Muslims that they were God. The Five Percent Nations believe that each and everyone of them were God and that three hundred and sixty degrees was a complete cycle, and that with all them together they'd make one, dig it?

Au   Hmmm mmm.

T   In other words, if there was like five of us in this room and we're all together and one was in the Five Percent Nation but he wasn't active we do not have a circle. We're suppose to teach him and these guys here, they were tough. I can't help but think . . .

Au   Here at the penitentiary?

T   Yeah. I can't but think if I ever went up the river [prison], by which it was very likely I would get into this thing, simply because, not only because I was there . . .

Au   For your own protection?

T   Right. For my own protection to have back-up security. I will have became addicted to it. That's the type of stuff we're talking about, which any religion can be that way if you get into it head-over-heels, like my mother she's in that and she's sanctified. You might as well forget about Arlene Jones because she's gonna be there until she dies and no one is gonna change her, right? So anyway I . . .

Au   Now hold it; let's back up a few minutes, Tom. You were at Industry. You went back there just as your dad got out of prison.

T   He had been out when I went back.

Au   Then how long did you stay in town after you got out of Industry?

T   That's a nice way of putting it, or before I got right back into something else.

Au   I'm trying to get a picture where my friend, Tom Jones, has been all these years. So you were out of Industry, and back in town for how long?

T   I think it was like four months.

Au   Then what happened?

T   My mother left.

Au   Then your mother left and went out to Los Angeles?

T   Right.

Au   Did you go with her?

T   Well, this is the way it was. She went bankrupt, she had gone on a shopping spree, everything she had good credit for fifteen years and she can go anywhere and say "charge it." She was forced to obtain a lawyer and he told her to go bankrupt. So she had to sell the present house she was living in and the house she owned on Potter Avenue she gave to the man she had been with for five or six years. A man who was dedicated to her, devoted to her, and dropped that check and moved down south for Thanksgiving, but he finally came back and said that somebody, that he had to go. She don't know till today why. But anyway we're talking about '68 when I got out and she cut this relationship off, which at the time she left it up to all her kids. We played a major part in her decision. We had to consider a man that we been living with but wasn't too fond of, her boyfriend, especially my sisters. My brother didn't have no problem with him and I didn't have any problem with the guy. My sister, it was just my oldest sister and she had problems with, not only him, but anybody in the household who had authority. She just had a nasty attitude and she's changed somewhat today but she's become irresponsible. She's the only sister I have here in town and she's very close to me. She [mother] talked to all of us together then she talked to me separately and my mother has told me many a times things that I don't think mother tells their kids at certain ages. My mother told me when I was very young, she says, "y'know you're Tom, you're the most intelligent one of the four." It was unusual for her to say it, but she did say it at times. Through her work that way, she never showed me more consideration, time, love or affection than the others. 'Cause when she was home, she was home and she was sleeping. When she got home she'd just sleep and eat. My mother has always through the years always been a hard worker. Two and three jobs, she's always had two jobs as long as I've known her and then three. She talked to me and she asked me she says Tom. I just come out of Industry, right? By me just coming out of Industry had a lot to do with her up and leaving. It was one thing for her to go bankrupt, it was another thing for her to leave the state and go to almost another country, right? But she was concerned with the type of future, what the future held for me, considering my past. She told me, at the time, "look I'm gonna leave." At the time we were already aware she was going bankrupt. She tells me, she didn't tell the other kids that she was gonna leave, but we're in her bedroom now. She tells me, "Tom, I'm gonna leave and any of you kids that want to come with me, I'll send back for you." That's just how she said it. So, I said, "Mama where you going?" She tells me, "I'll write." She says Los Angeles, so I'm talking and later I find out, 'cause it was nothing for me to go through my mother's pocketbook. When I was very young I used to take money out of there. It wasn't no problem taking money from her, I did it. As I was a kid I used to go in and take money, so it was nothing for me to go through her pocketbook. I think you're aware of this, if not I'll tell you remind me to tell you about the household chores. I went through her pocketbook and I found an American Express airline ticket and it said California. The only thing I could read on the thing was California so I'm thinking, I'm thinking, I'm thinking. She already told me she was leaving, but she said she told me, "I'll write you." So I don't know, I really don't know and I'm—So what happened she still, I didn't find that ticket until after she got through talking to me. She went downstairs so she wanted to say that "Tom, I'll send for anyone of you that want to come," but I told her right then and there I said, "Look Mama, you don't think you can go anywhere without me going." Because the way she put the question was if I want to come now fine and I said, "Yeah, I'm coming." At the time I just got out of Industry, I think I was 15, yeah I was, I was going with a girl that was eighteen and I was what I thought was really involved in a relationship. Never had sex with her. I was bumping every other young girl out there, but this here one I thought she was really something special. I can't help but to smile when I think about it because then I wasn't dedicated to the life. When I say the life I mean the limelight, the fast life.

Au   Hmmm mmmm.

T   Then I was squared up in that respect when it came to girls. But this one particular girl she was special. I just come out of Industry and I'm going to, I'd already been to Charles School and she's going to Smith School. My father told me, "Aw, it ain't nothing. Once you get your dick wet you'll forget her, if that's all you want to do. You don't want to marry her, no." Which I think he was right in telling me that I shouldn't because I was ready, "Hey, baby, let's get married," y' know. I think he was right in discouraging me in which he, my mother left, me and her did leave together, 'cause I told her I wasn't gonna let her go without letting me go.

Au   How long did you stay in Los Angeles with her?

T   I stayed with her all the time I was there. From '69 to '73.

Au   You went to school out there?

T   Yeah, I went to school. I was still a confused, mixed up person.

Au   Hmmm mmm.

T   Education. Believe it or not, everything I know in the different fields I learned in places like this [prison].

Au   I'm sure that's true, Tom. Let me just ask this quickly. You were out there from about '73 to . . .

T   June of '73.

Au   And then what, did you come back here?

T   I came back here . . .

Au   Were you in trouble with the law out there?

T   Yeah.

Au   Were you put away?

T   Yeah, I done time, I done 21 months up there.

Au   Where? In one of the juvenile homes?

T   No, I was a juvenile at the time but they don't consider you an adult until you're eighteen. I was sent to a place called CYA, California Youth Authority. They have the Youth Authority. If you ever get into trouble and go to the youth authority they have jurisdiction over you until you're 21.

Au   Hmmm mmmm.

T   So, in '73 my uncle died. My father's only living brother, my father's only brother, right? I had just come out of the joint and I'm laying up home and I get a call from my aunt. At the time I'm working, I get right out of the joint and I have good intentions. I mean I had very good intentions, I went down 21 months. I had one furlough and I been active in the educational program there. I'm really active more than any place else which I think the only reason for that is because I was a little older, a little smarter. Because opportunity has always been wide open to Tom, right? I took advantage of the educational program to the extent. I didn't get all I could get out of it, but I got a lot out of it. I could have done a lot more than I did. What I did do, in completions, I got a completion. I got a certificate of completion of my high school equivalency.

Au   Good.

T   I did come out with that certificate. Well, they sent it to me, it was engraved and all. Me, I know how I went about to get that, it didn't mean nothing to me, because I know I was still a dummy, as far as education goes. I knew I needed a lot of help, so my parole officer when I got out of there was black. I don't know, I'm not prejudiced, and the reason I'm not, I have good reason to be, but the reason I'm not is because it was the way my mother raised me. All through my life I have a lot of reason why I should be prejudiced, y' know. I'm not. My best friend down in the block is white.

Au   Oh?

T   He hasn't always been my best friend, but through people leaving and me and him getting closer, and his friend leaving. Here in jail we—and what started out as a game on my part turned into true friendship. I mean dedicated, when I say dedicated you can take it to the bank. I mean it, when I say it started out as a game, I mean it in the sense that I, when I first told him I come up to his cell and says "look, just between me and you I smoke marijuana and I drop pills."

Au   Here?

T   Yeah. So me and him. I come up to his cell and says, "Look, be my partner," which when I came on the adult side at 18th of May.

Au   Adults, huh?

T   Right, I just turned 21. Been moved from the minor side to the adult side.

Au   I see.

T   See . . .

Au   Here?

T   Right. May 18 I turned 21, but prior to all that I was isolated for three months. I was isolated until two months after my 21st birthday. They had me isolated for a crime, a charge that had been lodged against me while I was here, right?

Au   What was that?

T   First degree attempt to commit a crime and first degree attempt of sodomy.

Au   Hmmm mmmm.

T   Okay. Soon as I was charged with that, or as soon as they were in the process of charging me with it, 'cause it happened like the second, right? They didn't tell me nothing at all until the 25th. Then they cornered me and my buddy coming out of the mess hall, about thirteen of 'em and said we're going to solitary, and I told them we're not going anywhere and blah, blah, blah. So they forced us, I told 'em, at the time I tried to reason with them, I said look, I wanna see the Commissioner because I knew how the administration run. Guards would take it upon themselves to do things the way they felt it should be done, y' know. They didn't have no authority to do it. They would lock up people and leave them locked up two or three days and let 'em out which was dead wrong. A guy had have an incident, he's going be locked up immediately. If they also feel it's serious enough he will be written up, and they have procedural steps to take, right? Right. To today, it still depends on who you are and what you do if you get the same thing as the guys on the black list, dig it? Nothing has changed, I mean I doubt if it ever will. But I'm saying this is something that really gets up underneath my skin, right? But I've learned since I've been here. Them white people upstairs taught me this, and it's very valuable to me.

     Like I say December 6th was a major uproar in the messhall here, I'll get you newspaper clippings and everything so you can read over my past history. I want to tell you, y' know. So, it was a major uproar here. There was guards manhandling the inmate that had been locked in not by the procedural steps. He was black. He was in the Five Percent Nation. I was in it, and we had people who were dedicated, but I was the one of the bunch not to use my head more but thought different. Because all of 'em were intelligent everyone of 'em. I've learned something from

all of them, but I was the one that took the other outlook of the situation, y' know. Because I usually—generally 99 times out of 100—I view both sides before I do something, and I got into something that taught me here. It was called—I forget. But anyway a man started it. It was a program. What I got out of the program was you have control of yourself regardless of where you were at and this type of thing. It was long and drawn out, a lot of avenues for that subject and I got a lot out of it. This here was in the latter part of '75, no I'm sorry this was the first of the year, in January. Through that big major incident jumping off in the messhall, an officer grabbing this guy, physically grabbing him and they're not suppose to put their hands on you for no reason. State law. Unless you swing on them, put your hands on them, or you refusing a direct order, and they try to coach [coax] you in, this type of thing. They must seek the time to talk you in, and that's the state law, right?

Au   Hmmm mmm.

T   They went in that messhall. Anyway, they were dead wrong when they put their hands on 'em, and everybody including myself got highly upset. There was a lot of people which took vows and made, in otherwords till death do us part. That's how dedicated I was, y' know. I told him, no I felt when they grabbed him we should have tore his face right to the ground dead. Because I was already fed, already fed up and already submitted all this stuff, like I told you. They had labeled me, we couldn't get nothing. No programs and this type of thing. And I had a counselor at the time, and if I'd tell them I'd want to see him on a Monday, if I seen him Wednesday, I was lucky. I was really and truly lucky. It was nothing for him not to see me until the next week. Wasn't only me, it was everybody.

Au   That's the way it was, eh?

T   Yeah, yeah that's the way it was. So, at that time, since then they taught me a valuable thing, but at that time I was ready to go physically. But we're at the back and I couldn't win. Worse than that, possibly I could be charged again which nine times out of ten would have been a felony. Also it was that I couldn't win. I'd be the loser, and I was also worried about by March 15th I wouldn't be in their life no more. But they could put a permanent scar on me, that could last for years. I just thought of all that, I'm fed up, they put their hands on him and I said let's tear this down. Everyone was excited and in an uproar. So my cousin, in the outcome of that he got his leg broke. I mean almost in half. He's walking again, but he had a lawsuit out and I'm a witness and I'm glad. I hope he gets all the money he can 'cause of the way the thing went down. This all really irrelevant but it gets you an idea of what type of activities is going on while I was here and what type of conditions I was subjected to when I first came, this type of thing. Afterwards I was acquitted of all this stuff they said I'd done.

Au You were acquitted for the sodomy too?

T   No.

Au That was a real fact?

T   No.

Au Oh, it wasn't?

T   No. I'll tell you, I have nothing to lose and nothing to be ashamed of but . . .

Au I understand, I think.

T   Me and my partner was down in the shower. There was a white dude down in the shower. I told him, I said, "look, when can I get my cigarettes." He says, "well, you have to be kidding." He says, "Tim was playing cards all the way. He's on your side." Now, me and my cousin was partners and him and someone else. Got him up to eight or nine packs or seven or eight packs.

Au Poker?

T   Spades.

Au Spades.

T   Right. Partnership, anyway. His partner that was gambling with my partner ran out of money and he had to give up the game. So, this dude [Tom] said, "I got him now." Once I get somebody, once I get advantage of somebody, I'm not gonna let him go, if I can help it.

Au So you guys were in the shower and you were talking about . . .

T   About the cigarettes, and he said he didn't think that he owed them to me. So, he wasn't gonna pay me so I, so we all start screwing around. So I walked over to his stall, which he was on the end. He wasn't in it when I first came down, but two black guys come down and he moved to the end. I'm talking to him, and he says he's not gonna pay me, so I said, "like hell you're not. You gonna pay me my stuff, or I'm gonna take it out in blood." So he goes on trying to show me he wasn't afraid, and I was upset and excited at the time. I didn't care, I was aware of the situation, I had witness. He's the only one and this type of thing. I pushed him and he fell up against the wall. It was kinda rough the way it was painted. So he scratched his elbow and shoulder. So anyway Tim grabbed him and said go on and leave him alone. Tim trying to keep it down so . . .

Au Tim is your cousin?

T   Tim's my partner. Tim with my cousin here, and Tim was the one that did one to three on whatever he copped out to but he was promised a year and I told him at the time. I was facing all these charges, three counts of arson, disturbing and inciting to violence as a result of the riot. That was an outside charge; institutionally I was charged inciting a riot and sodomy. But institutionally those were the five charges of that event. Those, they were already in the process of the grand jury and I

Au   So how did the sodomy thing get hung on you?

T   It got hung on me because when I come up out of the shower I'm expected to get locked in for a fight or assault. Me and Tim come out of the shower we didn't hear nothing, dig it? From nobody, I even went upstairs to ask one time. The dude made an accusation, indirect to that effect that I tried to fuck him down in the shower room, but it was only an accusation. No one came to me, no formal charges, no written report, nothing, this is the 2nd of February so like three weeks going on. We come out the mess hall, and they cornered us out there, guards coming out. They got a lot of hallways, they were coming out of the woodwork, there were about thirteen of them. They said, "you guys going to W Block?" He was out for me from the word go, stealing all they could. Anyway so I told him, I says, "no, but somebody tell me something 'cause I know how you guys are." I says, "you white folks have a tendency of," you know. I go on, you very seldom hear me say "you white motherfucker," and I don't go that way. I say, "you white folks this and you gotta stop doing this," and you know. "If you continue to do this,"I says, "you have to look in the mirror every morning," this type of stuff. I cussed out the guard, and they denied me a furlough just last week. They denied me a furlough for the same reason I was acquitted for, right? Just happened to deny me the furlough for the same reason I was acquitted for. Only person I can take is that they're playing second judge and jury. The law of the land has made their decision. I look at it like that and this is the same way I told them. Sitting right there I told them I said, "look, if you deny me a furlough," which I was something like eighteen days or twenty days short of going home anyway. What did I care about a furlough, I'd been down eighteen months already, you know. But its just the point, the point of principle. Anyway, back to that sodomy thing.

Tom was acquitted of the sodomy charge. At this point Tom's conversation roamed over many subjects. About 20 minutes of recorded interview is omitted as he flashed back in his memories to a variety of barely related topics.

Au   Just generally speaking before you came here did you have friends, good close friends? You talk about a close buddy here.

T   A few.

Au   A few. Black, white?

T   Both.

Au   Both. Hmmm mmmm. But most of the time you kind of feel you've gone your own way?

T   Alone? Yea.

Au   You have a lot of girl friends, you say.

T   Yeah.

Au   When did you start going with girls?

T   Oh God, I started when I was very young. Me and my sisters used to play around.

Au   How old would you have been?

T   I was about five. But we, but my mother used to put us in bed together when I was younger, right? By me having a bed wetting problem, that's was always a reason, a horrible reason for putting you in bed with the girls.

Au   Right.

T   I think a couple years passed, I think I was about five or six. We used to screw, but it wasn't like now. I used to just play with her. I wouldn't go that far into her. We used to just get in bed and screw. I stopped that when I was eight, nine.

Au   Your sister is older than you, isn't she?

T   No, I'm second oldest.

Au   Oh really. How much younger is she?

T   Well, the way it used to go, me and my younger sister and my brother and the oldest sister, but me and my younger sister, we were more involved in this type of activity than the other two.

Au   Were they involved together?

T   Yeah, like I said I remember them having sex. When my mother first caught wind of it, I was, I think I was nine, 'cause she was crying driving a car, going toward grandmother's house coming down the hill. But prior to all of this me and my first cousins we used to screw around. My oldest first cousin and my youngest first cousin, yeah, I screwed her too.

Au   So, you really learned about sex within your own family to begin with, isn't that right?

T   Right.

Au   Hmmm mmmm. Was your mother mad at you?

T   She was really mentally disturbed about the whole thing.

Au   Right.

T   She was so disturbed that she didn't whip me! She was that upset about it.

Au   Right.

T   But she never held anything against me.

Au   After your mother learned about this, did you continue having relations with your sisters?

T   No, I had stopped by the time she had learned, right?

Au   Why did you stop?

T   Because it got so that I was afraid of my mother finding out and it would hurt her, y'know? Because, like I said, prior to this my cousins and I used to mess around, right?

Au   Hmmm mmmm.

T   I remember my aunt, my cousins' mother—my mother's sister, somebody told my mother. I think my aunt told my mother, right? But my mother didn't lay too much on it. My mother was—I couldn't detect that she was really worried about it. I mean she didn't say much. I didn't take that impression that she was really mad very long. But I knew that it was wrong, right? At a very, very young age. Screwing, in general, I guess is wrong, and I, my aunt, she was more upset about it than my mother.

Au   Then when did you start going with girls and having relations with them outside the family?

T   Well, just before I came to the school, I think it was. 'Cause I was going to Colton School, right.

Au   So, you've been sexually active for a long, long while, haven't you?

T   Yeah. But you know. I've got to have it.

Au   How do you take care of that here? When you're inside?

T   I do mess around with weaker guys here. I have guys that already turned out this way.

Au   How do you get them?

T   How do I get them?

Au   Where do you get them?

T   Making a way and a time and a place is no problem here.

Au   Hmmm mmmm.

T   But um . . .

Au   How often?

T   It's not too often because of the consequences.

Au   Once a week?

T   Oh no. Maybe yes.

Au   When the last time?

T   I'll tell ya, the last time was in August. A homosexual came through here in August. He was gay from the word go. I say, y' know, I can't tell you how many times in, how many times I've engaged in homosexual activity while I've been here. But for me, I'm very, very active sexually and as a result, I took it, y' know, a way of alleviate all this would be to get my mind into something else and I got into weight lifting, right? I noticed that when I jack off, like the night before, and it's my day to work out I'm very weak. So you know, I've went in here, y' know, two weeks—two weeks and a half at a time without masturbating, ya know. But always wake with a hard-on, y' know. It'd get right up and it go to school with me. This time, I have a lot of, lot to be let loose, a whole lot and I'm aware of that. So this gay guy comes along.

Au There have been homosexual experiences here in prison, and I suspect that there probably were also in Industry and in other places too?

T Right.

Au Always with weaker guys? Younger or older?

T Joey was my first piece. Now I remember a guy, he was meek. Yes, weaker and younger.

Au These are all guys that you forced into the thing, or did they willingly give in?

T Well, not physically.

Au Well, not physically forced, but psychologically forced.

T Conned, yeah.

Au Conned into it! What do they get out of it in return? So you conned them.

T Well, sure. Many times I promised them things, ya know.

Au Such as?

T Well, I gave a guy a bag of potato chips and cigarettes, y' know, and a radio. Which I asked him to leave, he's back here now again. Which I'm not the kind of person who'd put it out 'cause I know he's gotta have his sexual but he did jack me off because I disappointed him in that relationship. I know he don't, he don't go to sleep, so I'm not the type of guy that would make things hard for him. But he wanted these things, like he had asked me for it. I told him OK, but prior to all that I had been crapping on him anyway, right? He says ah, he won't, I seen a chance, so I shot into his cell.

Au How many different guys have you had sex with on the inside?

T Maybe 30–40. I don't know.

Au How about outside, when you're out. Did you have experiences there too with men?

T Right. But I—

Au Gay men too?

T No. On the street, like if I met a person of this nature, and it was to my advantage, financially, I would get involved.

Au Hmmm mmm.

T On the streets, that would be the only way.

Au Did you use to hustle downtown, hustle men?

T I used to, when you say downtown are you talking about the bars and stuff like like, no, you see when I was on the street, right? No. I didn't hustle on the streets.

Au   You said financially favorably to you.

T   Right. Well, see . . .

Au   Where would you pick the man up?

T   Well see, it wouldn't be no problem, I mean the few men that I've had any relations with here in town. I met one in a bar and the woman at the bar told me he was gay, right? He was digging on me so I go into the bathroom until he came. But not that it was prearranged with us, so he comes in. So he talks, he was about 49, and when he was younger he was in the drag, the dressing up, but now he was just for men, just physically right. He come in, and he asked me, so I take control of the conversation, I says, I don't how I get it started but I take control. I was the aggressive one in the conversation to the extent not that I'm doing more talking. But to the extent that it's make my values clear, once I had established that and get an understanding. After I did with him I, we went home, to his home. But there has been times when prior to when we'd get in the restaurant I had long hair down to my shoulders.

Au   Oh yes?

T   That's unusual for a black person. It had a permanent in other words; it was straight. Like I used to go to this shop once a week, and all my life I don't know where I picked up but I been very attached, very, very attached to clothes. Everyone has something to hold on to. Clothes is my thing.

Au   Right.

T   Everything has to be perfect in clothes. Like I've been busted more times in town where I picked up petty larceny than anything else. I been busted matter of fact in my life more for petty larceny stealing clothes than anything else.

Au   How many times have you been busted all together?

T   Whew! Yeah, a guy came up here to talk to me from federal parole, probational officer and he had all the info. It was about seventeen times.

Au   How much did that guy pay you when he took you to his house?

T   Well, I stipulated $50 in the bathroom. He agreed upon that, but he gave it to me when we got to the house. But I also seen a lot more money, right, so I . . .

Au   How much did you take?

T   Well, in the final analysis of that day, I only took $50 but I, before I left I made sure he would continue on this type of thing, y' know. As time went on, I moved in with him and, he dressed like a man. I never, I went with one homosexual here that is very well known. He's about 32 now, been in drag since he's been about sixteen, right? And still just like a woman.

Au   Do you consider yourself a homosexual?

T   I've been hit with that so many times by people in institutions because of my activity, and I've been told that if you engage, you're are considered.

Au   I'm asking, do you consider yourself a homosexual?

T   I'm getting to that. No. I don't consider myself a homosexual. There are limitations in a homosexual relationship, right? There are limitations. Like I've been offered a lot, a lot of money, I mean 2, 3, 4, $500 to go all the way with a very important man that's staying here in town, right. But I wouldn't. No, I need the money, but it's something that deep down that I hold on to. To have another man de-fuck me, I can't see it. I can't imagine, but I do entertain the thought. But to carry it out, no.

Au   So, if you had a choice between a woman and a man, you'd go for the . . .

T   Woman.

Au   Let's turn to another issue, Tom. What are you going to do when you get out of here?

Au   Um, when I leave I'll be in worse. I've thought about it, and I'd like to, and I do want to tell you what I plan to do and what I would like to do. Those are two different things.

Au   Have you ever had a job? What kind of work have you done?

T   I don't have any skills, do not take in training. Let's see, oh in my job history.

Au   What's one thing you've worked at?

T   I worked in GE here.

Au   Doing what?

T   Assembly line, a boob tuber. A guy that works on a assembly line taking a big rotating thing every so many seconds it comes around, and when the tube comes in front of you in this tray, you grab it and first you hit this to release. Rub it here, rub it here, and ya know, the heaviest one, the biggest one. It's about 40 or 50 lbs. right?

Au   What other kinds of jobs have you had?

T   I worked in a convalescent hospital twice, when I first went to L.A.

Au   How long is the longest job you've held? Six months? Three years? More?

T   No, six months sounds right and no, no, no. I worked at Toni's Kitchen but I didn't really consider that a job.

Au   What did you do at his kitchen?

T   Wash dishes, pick up the trays . . .

Au   Ah, ha. Bus boy type of thing.

T   I worked there longer than anywhere else. Only because . . .

Au   You never tried to get in the service? The Army?

T   The thought, I went down to the place. Only thing that motivated me to go there was 'cause I had a prior charge in court, which was a misdemeanor. I could have left the state, and nothing would have been said. They're not gonna come after me for a misdemeanor; a felony, yeah. At the time I didn't have any felonies, and at this time I don't have any. I would like to go into the service, only because it would make me financially secure when I'm older.

Au Hmmm mmmm.

T   I know I'm gonna get old, and I'd like to look out for it now.

Au So, you're really gonna be looking for a job aren't you?

T   Yeah. I'm not looking for any help. Ya know, I would like to get into some type of training program, something that would almost guarantee me a job afterwards. I'm willing to sacrifice at first, and that type of thing. But college is, I'm not likely to get involved in a college program because of my lack of education. I must tell you my plans.

Au You already thinking of going back to California?

T   I had planned to leave here immediately after I got out. Stop in New York, I have a brother Donald, he's been in college. He graduated in June of this year. Now he's continuing on. And spend a few days with him then go to L.A. That is expected of me, that's what my people want me to do. Now, what I want to do or what I like to do or what I'm gonna do are all different things. That's what they want me to do, right? I want to see, I want to go both places, right? But also I would like to stop in Chicago, 'cause I have a woman friend that I was very, very close to here in town. She was 35, and we're both two years older now. I was eighteen then. I like the type of life she lives, ya know. She runs the con game, flim-flam stuff, drugs, this type of life. She's been in drag nineteen years and I like this type of life. I know what it does.

Au She's in drag, you say?

T   She's been in drag nineteen years.

Au What do you mean by that?

T   In that respect, when I say she's been drag and she's been in this con game and this stuff, she's been turned out she's been in the life nineteen years, that life. I'm using drag in that terminology would mean, dope, and stuff.

Au Like homosexual drag?

T   No.

Au Okay.

T   But I like the money.

Au Can you stay out of trouble, if you go there?

T   When I was here working, I was working at Tom's, right, and she told me "yeck, yeck." She wanted me to quit the job. I held onto the job three months after I met her. It was a month before I found out what she actually done. She'd become very, very fond of me, y' know.

Au   So, you think she might be able to get you a job there with her?

T   Oh—

Au   Or just live with her, and let her keep you?

T   Yeah. The way that life go is good to you and bad to you. When it's good to ya, ya must look out for bad times coming, and she does that right. So, nine times out of ten, if I went there she would, she would automatic take care of me, but her financial situation has a lot to do with it. If I went there at a bad time, I couldn't expect nothing from her. If I went there during good, that's speaking for itself. So, it depends, and she told me I was the only man she ever went with, that had never done no type of wrong. Every man, if you didn't juggle dope, he boosted, hustled. And the only thing I was doing then was playing women who were on welfare and stealing downtown. Stealing leather coats and selling them. Stuff like this, y' know.

Au   You said you had a son?

T   I have a son.

Au   How old is he?

T   He's 17 months, 16 months.

Au   You have a son by this girl?

T   No. My son's mother; my son is her fifth kid. So, when I met her there wasn't nothing to our relationship.

Au   Where was that, here in town?

T   Yeah. When I met her I was getting her welfare check, y' know. I would take care of business, buy food and this type of things, just bare necessities, and the rest money was for me. But there is nothing there. She had my son, and that's the only thing that keeps me communicating with her, because that little money is up to no value to me when I get out.

Au   Hmmm mmmm. What's your son's name?

T   Ronny. Right, his mother named him. I didn't have no say in it because during her pregnancy she go very, very, y' know—

Au   Do you see the boy? Do you see the baby?

T   I seen him, yeah, but not like I want to.

Au   Hmmm mmmm.

T   He was, like he was taken away from his mother in February of this year.

Au   Hmmm mmmm.

T   Him and all the rest of her kids are presently in a foster home, right next door to my grandmother. Now, drugs like I mentioned, I want to clarify this I think it's terribly important because drugs play a major part in people's lives. I don't care who they are. Marijuana I've been smoking since I went to L.A., before I left.

Au   How did you get started on marijuana?

T   The first, we moved into a apartment, a man, I was standing on the porch. A man sitting there and he pulled out a cigarette, a marijuana cigarette. He put it toward me so I took it.

Au   What other drugs have you been on? Have you tried them all?

T   No. Yeah, Well . . .

Au   Hash?

T   I tried hash before.

Au   How about LSD?

T   No.

Au   Heroin?

T   Yes. Now heroin—

Au   Speed?

T   Yeah. Everything, downer, upper, I tried those. Valiums, I like 'em. Heroin, I tried acid once, but I liked it too much to take it again.

Au   Mmmm hm. How much have you been into heroin?

T   That's what I'm getting to, I was introduced to heroin by the 35-year-old woman. She is an ex-addict, there's a difference between a dope fiend, an addict, and a junkie. She was an ex-addict, right? She had two marks right here and when I met her. She was just up in the penitentiary for nine weeks. She was in prison in Detroit. She had three months on paper, right? I didn't find all this out until later on, but anyway I was introduced [to heroin]. I read about it in jail and seen what it done to people. But ran in contact with it, never. Matter of fact, I had it all made up in my mind that I wouldn't even touch it, right? Okay, I'm involved in a relationship with a woman that she tells me. Y' know, I learned a lot from her. Good and bad, I learned a lot from her. She's telling me about her background and her use of drugs and I said well, I couldn't tell by looking at you. She said, "Oh yeah, baby." I really must stay away from a drug, heroin, right? So, through an ex-pimp schooling me 'cause whenever I had a problem I go to him. He told me, he says keep away from that drug scene, he says if you don't you're gonna blow your woman, right?

The interview was brought to an abrupt halt when Tom was called to go to his noon meal. Following that, he asked to return to the interviewer, and somewhat more than two hours of additional interview were recorded. This added information sheds no new light on his thought processes, adjustment patterns, goals, or realistic plans for the future. In reality these latter do not exist for him. He was released from the penitentiary on November 15, 1976, was returned there November 18, 1976, charged with possession of a controlled substance, and was held until December 26, 1976. Penitentiary officials fully expect this to be a continuing life pattern for Tom, and this conclusion is certainly supported by twelve years of discordant behavior since the clinical teaching program experience.

In early adulthood, Tom represents an emotionally disturbed adult who had severe learning impairments. He was not a child with specific learning disabilities in an accurately defined sense of the term. Although, as a child some of his psychological characteristics were similar to those of Scott, Ron, Andy, and the others, they were essentially the result of disorganized life environment, not of neurophysiological malfunction. Twelve years ago this young man should have been described as a *learning impaired child; etiology: environmental deprivation and disorganization.*

9

Scott: Order Out of Chaos

SCOTT IS THE SUCCESS STORY of the five young men presented here. He has "made it," as he so frequently told us. Making it on his terms was a rough, and often horrible experience. Childhood was horrendous, adolescence was worse.

Scott always indicated a certain amount of inner control, not enough to provide him the adjustment mechanisms he needed, but control was occasionally there. Where did it come from in the face of the awful family life he experienced? On one occasion when his classroom was in a state of relative calm, Scott all of a sudden screamed: "Mrs. S., Mrs. S., come and hold me quick. I'm going to explode." And explode he did. Mrs. S. did quickly grab him, and she held him tightly until his violent behavior subsided. Where did he learn to use an adult in this appropriate way? Out of what mold was Scott formed? He could have been among the "ten most wanted." The potentials were there.

Did the structured program he received as a young child provide him a "cooling off period," as he has once stated to one of the authors? Did he begin to realize he could succeed as his reading and number skills improved? Was his teacher, Mrs. S., a behavioral model for him later? We believe that each of these things happened, although the answer is qualitative. We believe that the clinical teaching program provided him pause and structure, permitting him to more thoughtfully integrate his skills and emotions. It provided him a knowledge that he could succeed; this founded a base on which he could build his life under the traumatic conditions which were yet ahead.

Author   Scott, I want to start off by talking with you about where you are now in your life, but in a few moments I'd like to jump back and pick up when

	you were a little kid, so just keep that in mind as we talk. You are working now for a dealership in industrial equipment repair. Tell me a little bit about what you do, will you?
S	I've got an eight-to-five job. I work on transmission repair at a dealership down on First Street. I'm working up to be a master tech, which is a—it is not an assembly line, but you do a lot of, like, warranty work, like repair and rebuild engines and carburetors and things like this—mostly major overhauls, something that goes wrong. Like, we take care of people's needs; like, they buy a new machine of any type, we take care of the warranty work on it.
Au	How much do you work independently, right now?
S	Independent—well, most of it is independent, like, it is fifty-fifty—I work on a flat rate basis.
Au	I didn't mean money-wise. Do you have a supervisor or a boss who stands over your shoulder?
S	A foreman?
Au	Yes, foreman. How many of you are working in this particular department?
S	Yes, there's a foreman. There is pretty close to about ten of us.
Au	Ten of you who are doing approximately the same job?
S	Yeah, right.
Au	And then there is a foreman over the ten of you?
S	Yeah, right. Well, he more or less assigns the work and divvies the work out. You know, he kind of separates the work.
Au	And he checks your work every step of the way, does he?
S	Yeah, more or less.
Au	Scott, of the ten men—I presume they are men, are they?—that are working there?
S	Yeah.
Au	Of the ten men that are working on this kind of a job, if you were to rank them one to ten, from best to worst, or from best to least qualified, where would put yourself?
S	Probably around four.
Au	Four from the top or from the bottom?
S	From the top.
Au	How long have you been on that job, Scott?
S	Close to two years, now.
Au	And how long do you think you will have to work on that job in order to achieve the master technician rating?
S	Well, probably I'd say a couple of more years. A lot of the guys that are

	working there, though, have been there pretty close to twelve to fifteen years. So they got the experience on me. It is going to take a little while.
Au	There are promotional possibilities for you, though.
S	Oh, yeah. Well like, a lot of the work that comes down, more or less like the higher paying job, goes to the guy with the most time in there and then it comes down the line like that.
Au	You are unionized, are you?
S	No. The union would kill us.
Au	Well, I don't want to go into that, but I was just wondering whether you had a union.
S	No, we are not really that big of a firm to have a union.
Au	I see, and tell me, how much do you earn? Do you get paid by the hour?
S	No, by the job.
Au	Do you mind if I ask you, approximately how much money you paid income tax on last year?
S	I'd say pretty close to $10,000 to $11,000.
Au	That is pretty good.
S	I am probably capable of doing a little better; I was new, though. Like I say, you gotta kinda fight, 'cause you have all these other guys. You gotta get your fair share of the work.
Au	Your wife works. How much does she get paid a year? Do you know?
S	Well, she just now went on a full-time basis. She was working part-time and she was getting paid, I think it was somewhere between $5,000 and $6,000. That is when she was working part-time. I don't know; we haven't figured it up since she has been working full-time.
Au	So, the two of you now really are earning together something a little better than $20,000?
S	A little less.
Au	A little less than $20,000? Well, I think that is pretty good for where you are in your life. There will be a time when Wendy probably won't have to work, and you will be making that much yourself.
S	I hope.
Au	You know you will. Let's jump way back. Do you remember the experience that you had with us when you were at the clinical teaching program?
S	I remember quite well.
Au	About how old were you then? Do you recall that?
S	I was in about second grade, so I must have been about eight or nine?
Au	Yes, I think so. You were voted the one least likely to succeed at that point. I believe also you had failed at least once by then.

S   I can believe it.

Au   Now, why do you say that?

S   I was full of hell.

Au   Yes, that is one way of putting it.

   Scott was an adopted child. While he appears to have had temper tantrums from the time that the first child was born into the family, mother thought this to be fairly natural and associated his problems with the beginning of his school experience. She has complained about his excessive nervousness, fidgeting, and nailbiting, and feels that there has been a tremendous change in Scott in the past two years in terms of his cooperativeness in the home, and the relative lack of temper tantrums; especially this year. Scott has had only one temper tantrum in early November which occurred when his mother left the children with a babysitter in order to work. At this time, he was highly destructive, smashed the lunch dishes, threw everything off of the table, and things against the wall, and his mother was called home.

   Scott was referred to the special project because of this provocative behavior, short attention span, and acting-out behavior in the form of lying, temper tantrums, and attention-getting mannerisms. This behavior was disruptive to the regular classroom and was a serious impediment to Scott's ability to learn. According to a psychological report submitted by Dr. R. in June of 1962, Scott had a "psychoneurotic disorder." Dr. Y.'s psychiatric evaluation in May of 1963, suggested that Scott represented a "psycho-neurotic pattern with acting-out and aggressive tendencies probably related to moderate non-specific MBD etiological factors."

   The neurological report submitted by Dr. B., the neurologist, in April 1963, indicated possible presence of "organic neurological features." An EEG, taken on April 16, 1963, indicated positive choppy record which was indeterminate in relation to complaints. There appears to be more than a possible neurological basis to some of the behavior Scott showed.

Au   You had been in Adams School, I think before you came to us. Do you have any recollections at all of Adams School?

S   I remember. As a matter of fact I do. I probably remember Adams School more than any other. Probably because they tore it down right after I left. I remember quite a bit about kindergarten and first grade.

Au   What do you remember about it?

S   Well, I remember a lot of fights and other stuff we got into. I was a mess.

Au   You and the other kids, or you and the teacher, or—?

S   Mostly me and other kids. I don't know. It's weird, but I remember it. I remember nothing but trouble—at school and at home too. I was always fighting and everyone said I was always wrong.

Au   Do you have any idea of why you went to the clinical teaching program?

S   I never really did understand it until—well, nobody has really sat down and explained it to me as far as that goes. But, I mean, in my own ideas was that of a hypertensive child, I guess. That is the way I've broke it down. But nobody has really ever sat down and explained it to me.

Au   Well, that is too bad that nobody did. It makes me feel sorry that we didn't sit down and talk with you, although I'm not trying to justify that now. There were many times when we did try to analyze with you why you behaved as you did behave, but that was a long while ago and you were a young kid, and perhaps you have forgotten those attempts. And often times they took place when you were really upset and crying and kicking and fighting. I suspect that what you are telling me is that with kids like yourself with whom we are working now, we need to sit down with them frequently, and really try to give them more information as to where they are coming from.

S   I wish I knew more about what I was as a kid. I might understand myself better if I knew where I'd been as a kid. I often wonder why I am or who I am. I know my name, but I really think a lot about why I had all those problems and *why me,* I guess. Why me instead of someone else?

Au   What are some of the things you remember about the experience you had at the university program?

S   I remember Mrs. S.—I'll always remember her; she was really something else. I really liked Mrs. S. a lot 'cause she got physical when she had to get physical, and she talked to me when it took—you know—things like that. And ah, I remember Miss G., too. I didn't like her too much; I remember that. But, I remember her and I remember—I can't remember her name, but she used to type up all of our worksheets. And I remember a lot of students coming in—they had a two-way glass there—students coming in and talking to us.

Au   Do you ever remember spending much time with me in my office when you were a little guy?

S   I remember two conferences that we had.

Au   I can remember about 400 of them! In fact, I have recollections that you spent most of the first part of your first year with us sitting on my lap, which is about the only place that we could contain you. You were so hyperactive and disorganized. You were a very fine guy, and you had a good mind. Obviously you have put it to use. And, we were betting very strongly on you. As a young boy, though, you had many problems, so very many problems.

Tuesday, October 6, 1962: *During the two-and-a-half years Scott was enrolled in the clinical teaching program, behavioral samples were recorded approximately every fifteen minutes. Observer comments on* *two days in the early months of Scott's participation in the program indicate the nature of his behavioral problems.*

10:00: *Scott finished paper he was doing, put it in the cabinet without it being checked—took another. Miss B. went over, took it out and walked behind Scott to show him she was checking paper held above him. Scott put down new paper, and curled up in a ball under the desk.*

10:20: *Miss C. went in to check all papers put away without being checked. Scott reading with Miss G. Scott back in booth. Scott reading book putting page numbers on paper with sentences on it. Scott threw paper on floor—went to sit on desk top in next booth. No one paid any attention to him—picked up paper and continued work.*

Lightning and thunder begin. Keith—who had been reading with Miss G.—shouts "it's lightning; it hit me!" All children become very much disturbed, and run to see if they can see out the window. Steve climbs on top of booths. Keith turns around poking everyone. Scott shouts.

10:45: *Juice time—Scott drinks his in booth and because of concern about weather, Mrs. S. has a quiet walk with Scott, but Scott is hyperactive.*

11:10: *Scott acting up, by climbing on tops of chair, desk, then underneath; Miss G. had to come over and quiet him two or three times.*

11:40: *Scott jumps up and out of chair and throws himself on the floor. Miss G. had to come over and quiet him again.*

11:45: *Scott climbs under desk again with head toward back and feet up on chair seat. Miss G.—very firmly—says, "Get up." He does—sits awhile; when she leaves he goes back under the desk.*

12:10: *Ms. H. comes in to read a story. Because of hyperactivity of children, they turn their chairs around and listen from their booths. Scott obviously very distracted.*

Thursday, October 8, 1962. 9:00: *Scott is sitting quietly working in booth. Scott called Miss C. She is busy with Steve. Miss B. comes over; Scott says, "Get out of here!" He won't let her look at his paper but he finally does. After Miss B. checked it, Scott put it away. Scott at reading table reading out of workbook. Miss C. is working along with him. Keith is taunting Steve. Dictionary work—Miss C. asks Steve to hold on and ignore him—she had to leave Scott.*

9:30: *Scott goes back to cubicle to put his workbook down; he does so quietly, comes back to table with Miss C. to read. Scott reads very haltingly. He is still using the card to block out other stimuli.*

9:40: *Scott is back in his booth working on reading by himself. Miss C. stops by in rounds of checking each one. When John calls, Miss*

C. goes over there. Scott turns and looks, then calls Miss C. also to "Please explain this to me." Miss C. comes over and tells Scott, "I have others to help; you wait quietly when I'm helping them." Scott is quiet today. He is in control. Tremendous variability is his behavior from day-to-day.

Au   You were with us about two-and-a-half years. Where did you go after that?

S   I went to Perry Elementary School.

Au   Into about the fifth grade?

S   Exactly.

Au   How did you get along there?

S   Well, the first year was good, and then after the second year I was kind of shaky, because like uh, I was older than most of the kids in my class —it was the big setback, I thought. It is one of the reasons now that I kind of regretted going to the special education program, because I think it put me behind. I needed it, but I lost actual time. I really was further behind than I should have been. But I don't know, I can't really put the blame on anybody I guess but probably myself, but I was really—it was a big setback for me 'cause it made me know I failed again. A kid can take only so much failing. You know how it is.

Scott's appraisal of his difficulties at this time are accurate. He forgets, however, that in addition to his age and perception of the problem, his adoptive parents were struggling to maintain a home which ultimately housed Scott and six brothers and sisters. Parental efforts failed, ending in divorce. These issues and the tensions surrounding them were mounting at this time, factors which Scott cannot assess in their dynamic role.

Au   Once you begin to lose time you really lose it, don't you? You were a little bit behind also when you came to us, so that there was a period then in your life, beginning around kindergarten and up until about ten or eleven years of age, when you were losing ground until about the year and a half before you left us. Then you began picking up steam so that by the time you left us you were functioning just about the way a fifth grader ought to function. That is why we had you leave us at that point. But, you are quite right. You probably were a little older than the other kids.

When Scott returned to the regular grades he was admitted to the fifth grade. Some notations at this time are significant:

Educational comment *(California Achievement Test data): Reading: 1.5 grade (fall 1963); 3.5 (spring 1964); 4.3 (fall 1964); 5.4 (spring*

1965). Arithmetic total scores: 1.1 grade (fall 1963); 3.6 (spring 1964); 5.0 (fall 1964); 5.9 (spring 1965).

Psychological comment: *The present drawings show continued gains in control of impulsive behavior. The boy's reproductions of the Bender designs reveal adequate perception and copying of the configurations. The errors which were observed consisted of primitive loops, distortion of proportions, and difficulty in copying angles. The placement of the drawings and approach to the task indicate that Scott sets high standards for himself and is critical of his performance. Both the Bender and the H-T-P drawings reveal that Scott tends to decrease his anxiety by repeating familiar patterns of behavior and meticulousness concerning details. His drawings and stories suggest that Scott has many unmet emotional needs still, but that he has acquired the inner resources to tolerate frustration and to seek positive relationships with his peers and adults outside the family.*

Pediatric comment: *Scott has shown excellent growth patterns in the past year. He is now in good physical condition and there are no medical recommendations at this time.*

Neurological summary comment *(EEG): Mild abnormality in posterior head region; greatest on the right.*

The unanimous recommendation of the staff was to proceed to return Scott to his neighborhood school.

Au   Then after Perry Elementary School, where did you go?

S   To Clawson.

Au   Junior High School. How did you get along there?

S   I got along pretty good. I knew a lot of people 'cause I was from the south side, you know. I really didn't have any problems in Clawson. In fact, I made, well, the first year I did have a problem at Clawson. I was so depressed from Perry that I decided, you know, what's the use, and when I got to Clawson I met the principal. His name was Mr. Trask. I met him a few times and, uh, we kind of—we talked and everything, and I gave him my background, you know. And he was really understandable, and I mean *really* understandable. And we talked and we talked, and he decided to give me a break one day. If I passed 7th grade with a certain percentage—if I passed it clean, you know—he would put me up an extra grade. But, if I didn't, then, I'd have to just keep on going, you know. And, I blew it 'cause, I don't know—about then I was really anti-school, you know, for some reason. [The home situation was deteriorating very rapidly at this time. Extreme use of alcohol by the parents and resulting disintegration in the home was evident to all, including Scott.] And, so he, Mr. Trask, kept his patience with me through the three years, and him and the student counselors—they helped me out the most

—and a few of the teachers. It was rough—school, how I felt about myself, and things at home were getting worse and worse—my Mother drinking and my Dad, too. I've seen enough gin go down to float a boat. Mr. Trask used to let me talk to him about it.

Au Mr. Trask was a good principal.

S   Did you know Mr. Trask?

Au Sure. He had a good reputation.

S   He was a good man.

Au I didn't know him well, but I knew his reputation. I'd met him, of course. After Clawson you went where?

S   To Tinsdale High School.

Au Ah, yes, and how long were you at Tinsdale High School?

S   About a year. Let's see. I went through the tenth grade, and then I quit.

Au Why did you quit?

S   There was a number of reasons, like I had a big hang-up like after I got out of junior high. Home was hell. I started to get into drugs quite a bit, and uh, instead of going through school I kind of just slacked up. I didn't want to do anything for a time. So, I quit school, and I was about sixteen at the time, and I was out of school for a full year, forever really, so I decided, well, then I decided I was going to do something, you know, so then I went into the service. That was about a year-and-a-half after I quit school. Sweet sixteen. That was when everything started to fall apart. I was down and going to hell in a basket. I couldn't see any reason to keep going. The drug scene hit me then.

Au How did you get started on drugs?

S   Friends, I guess.

Au How far into it were you?

S   I was pretty bad at one time. I was in pretty bad shape. I was really hooked for about four months or so.

Au Hooked on what?

S   Heroin. I was shooting it regularly.

Au Where did you get the heroin? I don't mean the person, but where were you able to get it?

S   Right here in this city.

Au Was there a pusher around the school?

S   No, this was—I didn't get it anywhere that was school connected. It was outside school. You can get it pretty easy, if you have the cash.

Au Were the guys or the girls—was the crowd that you were going with also on heroin?

S   Well, yeah, quite a few of them were.

Au   When you say you were hooked and you were in a bad way, just how bad a way were you?

S   Well, later they had me on a methadone program for about four months.

Au   How did you get into that? How did you decide to get onto the methadone?

S   I just wasn't, you know; it wasn't, at first it was really nice, the drugs, I mean. I thought it was pretty cool, and then I decided it wasn't the way to go, you know. So, I just said to myself, I gotta get off.

Au   You made that decision yourself? Did you get busted?

S   No. In fact, I got a clean record.

Au   Did your parents know you were on drugs?

S   No, well, my parents weren't living together by then, and I was on my own. No one cared about good old Scott.

Au   You weren't living at home?

S   See, I got away from home when I was about sixteen or seventeen. You keep asking about home, but you don't know that I left home and got away.

Au   Why did you leave home?

S   Well, my parents broke up when I was fourteen.

Au   Well, tell me, Scott, where did you live when you left home?

S   I lived with about three or four friends. We, uh—

Au   Guys?

S   Yeah, well one was—I was living with this—OK, let me get this straight; it's been a while. I ran away from home, and I got caught. OK, they put me on a probation program. I was on probation for two years, and uh, Mr. Williams was my probation officer, and he, uh—this was just before my parents broke up, and after my parents broke up we had a real hard time at home. My father had six kids to take care of, and really it was too much responsibility for him. Oh, god. It was rough [tears]. I had to get out. I had to make the decision.

Au   I know this is hard to tell to me. Don't be ashamed to cry if you need to. I probably would too. Your mother left?

S   Yeah, and we had a big problem, and so I decided I was going to leave home, so I left, and I talked it over with my probation officer, and he put me in a place called St. Martin's, which was right up here on Howard Street. And Father Curtis was in charge; there was four of us in the house there, Tommy, me and another guy, and another—a guy named Kevin. I lived there for quite a while, and then my probation time was coming up, and I was about seventeen, that's right. And so, I moved out—I just decided to move out because my probation period—they were going to extend it so I could live there and I decided, naw, I didn't want to do it any more. I didn't need to live there any more. So then I lived with this girl—like, her husband had left her, and she had two kids and she was on welfare, and I said, what the hell, I'll just stay with her, for like she invited me, and we had an affair for about six to eight months and then I decided—that is when I was really starting to get hooked—I was really getting down on myself then, and then I just decided I wanted a change of pace, so I went in the service.

Au   Does Wendy know about the girl you lived with?

S   No, not then. She knows now. Like, Wendy and I were only going together on and off, you know.

Au   I'm asking that because I don't want to involve Wendy in anything. We aren't going to discuss this, but I don't ever want inadvertently to speak to her of this and hurt your relationship. You have leveled with Wendy?

S   Yeah, she knows everything.

Au   That's great; she knows you were on drugs?

S   Yeah.

Au   Was it difficult for you to get off of drugs?

S   I think the *decision* was the biggest difficulty, you know. 'Cause I had—it was a long time, and I wasn't sure how to go about it, you know, without losing face about it or anything. At first I thought, what the hell—what have I got to live for anyways, you know. I was enjoying myself, and I was free and I was by myself, and then I decided, where is it going to get me later? Most of it was the decision; that was the toughest.

Au   Making that decision was the tough deal, eh? Losing face in front of yourself or losing face with your friends?

S   A combination of both.

Au   How did you know where to go to get help?

S   Well, they had a program called Eleven Twenty-Seven, a street number. And, there was a doctor and, uh, I went up and it's all—you know, no police or nothing. You just go on in and talk to the people and everything. And I just started showing my face around there every once in a while, and, you know, just talking to people. And, I got a hold of this doctor—right now I can't even remember his name. But he is the one who started me on the Methadone program, and he says—he just told me the rest of it was up to me.

Au   So you just took the bull by the horns and said, Scott is going to do this, eh? And you were only on Methadone for four weeks?

S   Four to six weeks. I was pretty good, I thought. I really followed through. I really was proud of myself. I had to stay away from my friends and I had to try to find new ones. Anything to stay away from the needle.

Au   Did you have trouble during that time?

S   Not really; not much; I did a little, but not much—at least now I don't remember much trouble.

Au   You know, I'm very proud of you, Scott. I really am. You have really gotten a hold on yourself. Tell me about the army bit.

S   The army crap I really didn't like at all; the travel I loved. I had such a fantastic time. I was in Kentucky for two months; I was in Georgia for two months. I had orders for Vietnam. I went all the way to Oakland; turned in all my equipment, and everything and, uh, the orders were changed, so I came from Oakland and went back to New Jersey, and they sent me over to Germany.

Au   What kind of specialty number, MOS number, did you have in the army?

S   I was what they call a "63 Charlie," which is—I was a diesel mechanic.

Au   So in Germany you did what, primarily? Did you work on diesel engines?

S   Well, yeah, I had a really interesting job, I was a tow truck operator plus work service too. Like, if I couldn't fix it, I'd tow-it-in sort of thing. They wanted to put a mechanic on the truck, and I thought I was the most qualified, so I just grabbed it, you know.

Au   Scott, you told me over the phone that first night when we made contact after all these years that you were working on transmissions. I turned to my wife after I had hung up the phone, and said, "You know, I'm not quite sure, knowing what I know about Scott, that I'd ever let him work on my transmission." Because I can remember when you were a little guy you couldn't even put a puzzle or peg board together. You were having all kinds of eye-hand coordination problems, and here you are working in a very, very skilled mechanical situation with real fine-motor skills being required.

S   Yeah, well nowadays they require those skills. But do you remember all the stuff we used to do in the program: physical exercise, puzzles, walking boards, and stuff? That probably helped some. I was a clumsy little bastard.

    The program which Scott experienced is fully described in W. M. Cruickshank, Learning Disabilities in Home, School and Community (Syracuse: Syracuse University Press, 1977). Scott's memory of extensive training in gross-motor and fine-motor activities is correct, although no claim is made to support a one-to-one relationship between these activities and Scott's present type of employment.

Au   What did you do in Germany in addition, I mean outside, the army routine? Did you travel around a bit?

S   Oh, I've been through the whole Benelux countries; I've been to Austria,

Italy; and went to Greece for about three weeks. I did some traveling when I was over there; definitely had a good time.

Au   You made the most of it.

S   Yes.

Au   Did you go with guys, or did you go by yourself?

S   Mostly with other guys. Me and another guy went to Switzerland, and we went on a tour, and there were some girls from Canada. They were from Ottawa, and they were over there visiting their brother, and they just decided to go on the tour, and we were with them the whole time. We were gone for about two and a half weeks. We had a fantastic time— that had to have been about the best tour I was in.

Au   That's great. And when you went to Italy, you went to Rome?

S   No. Well, we went down to Italy in a Volkswagen. We went right just to the tip; we didn't go into Italy very far.

Au   In Austria where were you?

S   In Salzburg and all around Salzburg—like we went up to the Salzburg castle and along the Salzburg wall and up in the mountains.

Au   Besides drinking beer all over Germany, what are the kinds of things that you enjoyed seeing and doing when you were out on these trips?

S   The scenery was great, and looking up women! That was the big GI thing, though.

Au   And were you successful?

S   I've never had a problem with that. I'm not bragging, but I really never had a problem with finding women. I needed them and I found them everywhere and willing.

Au   What did you do for recreation?

S   We had organized recreation and everything.

Au   I meant when you were out on trips.

S   No, well we, yeah, we did a lot of that, but we—

Au   You did go into art museums?

S   Oh yeah, quite a few.

Au   Really, you enjoy art?

S   Well, sure, I enjoy the culture. Like they had going into Switzerland, into Berne. They got a wooden bridge, and that goes across one of the river there. And then on top of it, it has A-frames and every A-frame has a picture on it which is a step that Switzerland took toward her freedom.

Au   I've seen it; I've been there, too. In Lucerne, wasn't it?

S   Yeah, I really liked that, and then on the other side there was a museum, and then they had a restaurant-museum type of thing. We went into it, and that was the first time I had fondue. Man, it was great.

Au   The Swiss fondue, you were right in the middle of fondue country, weren't you? And you were in Holland and the Netherlands?

S   I went to Holland, and Amsterdam was the biggest place we went to. I got pictures at home of the two of us at the tulip fest. And we went to that place where they have a miniature village. Did you see that? That was really great. I loved it.

Au   Well, we'll have to compare notes on your travels, because we have obviously been in a lot of the same places. You seem to have made the most of your opportunities when you were overseas. Scott, you said in Europe you found women easy to find. How old were you the first time you had sexual relationships with a girl?

S   I'd have to say I was about sixteen, seventeen.

Au   Where did you learn about sexual intercourse—and having relations with girls?

S   I never really thought of that. It just happened, I think. I mean, I've never really read about it. I was kind of frigid, as a matter of fact, and I thought about it, you know, but I never really. It just happened one day.

Au   Did you worry?

S   Oh, yeah. That first time, oh, wow! My heart went thump, thump, thump.

Au   You are talking about worrying about that first experience?

S   Yeah, right.

Au   I didn't make myself clear. Did you worry about the fact that there might have been someone that you could talk this over with other than the guys on the corner? Did you have anybody that you could fall back on? Was there any sort of security that you had? Or, did you have to kind of feel your way through?

S   God, no, I didn't have anyone I could talk with! I was on my own except for the gutter stuff. I remember that you or somebody talked with us about it quite often in the program when we were messing around, but we were little kids then. I knew about sex, but I was little. It was later that I really needed someone to talk with. That's what fathers should be for, but not mine.

Au   You grew up by yourself.

S   I sure did. In seven children you have to grow up alone a lot, particularly if you don't have parents who care. But it was good too on sex. There was no hanky-panky with us, but we all knew how we were built. You know you and Mrs. S. were my best teachers on this, but I needed more —something that was always there. A kid's problems change as he grows up.

Au   What are you going to do with Todd? [Scott's three-month-old son.]

S   Well, I'm not going to leave him in the dark as far as—I'm going to let him know what is going on, you know, so he doesn't get himself in trouble, first of all. And you know, explain it to him. Like it hadn't been explained to me, you know. Let him know what's going on.

Au You had a pretty rough childhood, didn't you?

S It was tough.

Au You had a rough childhood up until you hit the army.

S Until *I* could do something about my life.

Au Yes, until *you* could do something about it is right. What are the things that gave you a feeling of responsibility, a sense of responsibility? How did you learn this, how did you fall in love with Wendy, and how did you begin to feel so good about Wendy?

S How does anyone learn responsibility? In my case there were a lot of stone walls ahead—real blockades. When I reached one of these—drugs, drunk mother, lousy father—when I couldn't get by, you just have to go around the thing. When you make enough of these decisions, you learn to be responsible for yourself. Do you know I was eleven, or maybe twelve, when I left the program and went to Clawson School. I remember that you often said to me, "Scott, you have a good mind. You will have to make many decisions about growing up." I remember those talks we had and they gave me confidence, I guess.

How did I fall for Wendy? That just sort of grew. I always felt good about her, but I had to convince myself that I was good enough for her. I wasn't when we first met. Drugs, the other woman I was sleeping with, no future. But Wendy is good; she's good for me. Wendy gives me, like, a sense of security, you know. Like she is a good woman. She takes care of Todd good. She takes care of me good.

Au You love her?

S Yes, very much, very much. She is easy to talk to and, uh, that's mainly how we really got it together 'cause we sat down and talked. We could understand each other. She gives me security. She's what it was all about when I made the decision to get unhooked or not to go farther. She didn't know it, but it made it easier for me to decide what road I'd take.

Au Did you have an affair with Wendy before you were married? Did you have sexual relations with her?

S Yeah, we did. It was a long time when we wouldn't, you know, in between times. It is just, I guess respect for each other, you know. But there was a while that we didn't.

Au Did having sex affairs with her have any effect upon how you felt about her after you were married?

S Not really, not really.

Au You really love her?

S Yes, I do.

Au   That's wonderful. How do you feel about Todd?

S   He is what everything else is for now. He's—I'm pretty proud.

Au   What is the biggest thing you can give Todd?

S   Love, I guess, and understanding.

Au   What do you and Wendy enjoy doing outside the house, or inside the house? I don't mean having a physical relationship at this point, but what are your social interests? Do you have groups of friends?

S   Yeah, we have quite a few friends. Of course, she works late. We are working at different hours.

Au   I know that interferes with social life, but what do you do weekends?

S   Well, we like to take in a movie every once in a while. We like the foster parents where my brothers and sisters are living, and we go out there and play cards with them on a Saturday night or something 'cause they are nice to be with. They are fun.

Au   Would you be willing to tell me about where your brothers and sisters are now?

S   Yeah, I got one that is in the army, my brother Tom. He's the next oldest to me. He will be nineteen next month, I think. Then, I got the rest of my brothers and sisters . . . there's seven of us all. They are all living together now, except for Tom in the army and me.

Au   One foster family has taken all of the other children?

S   Right. I helped work that.

Au   So that they can live together?

S   Right. Plus, they had one of their own. They were all separated in different places. We were all sad. It's a long story, but we finally got them all together.

Au   That is pretty good.

S   That is really good. I think that's what really made it for me and us all, 'cause they are happy now, you know. I mean they got a sense of security.

Au   And you see them? Obviously you do, you said that you go out to their home. Are they happy about being aunts and uncles now to Todd?

S   Oh, yeah. Every time we take Todd out they are all over him.

Au   That's wonderful. And uh, you were telling me you were adopted?

Scott was born in 1954. Little is known of the first three years of his life, but all evidence points to severe maternal deprivation and neglect," states the social worker. "His natural mother would leave him tied to his crib or to a chair when she went out, and would leave him for several days at a time with an elderly gentleman. There was evidence of physical neglect and abuse. Scott's natural mother is a niece of his adoptive father.

S   Yeah. I was adopted when I was three. It was like hell before, I guess, and even now every once in a while my real mother calls me. You're not supposed to remember much from that young, but I do. I can remember a feeling that now I can call "aweful lonesomeness." I was alone.

Au   Your natural mother still calls you on the phone?

S   Yeah. She usually calls me around eleven thirty, twelve o'clock at night, you know, after she has had a few drinks, and tells me how much she loves me and that she didn't want to do what she had to do, but she did it, you know. It's a twenty-year "I'm sorry," I guess.

Au   Does she live in this city also?

S   Yeah, she lives over on the north side.

Au   Do you see her, or does she just phone you from time-to-time?

S   I think I seen her in the last year. I've seen her about three times.

Au   Has she seen Todd?

S   Yeah.

Au   Well, you can understand too. She may indeed have some guilt feelings about the whole unfortunate experience.

S   Well, she does. Like, I don't really tune her off. I listen to her over the phone. But . . . god, I don't owe her nothing. I won't hurt her, I'll listen to her, but that's it. I've got a life to live—so do Wendy and Todd. That's where life really is now.

Au   Scott, you really have reason to be proud of yourself. You have just done a remarkable piece of work in getting a hold of yourself, going through that drug scene, for example. You could have gone down hill in a very dramatic way at that age, what with the kinds of things that you were going through then. It took a lot of guts for you to get a hold of yourself. I'm proud of you, if that means anything. How do you think all that happened?

S   How I got a hold of myself?

Au   Yes.

S   I just kicked myself in the head and said, "do it," you know, I guess. I'm glad that you are proud of me, and I'm glad you all came along when you did.

Au   Well, why didn't you become like some of the other guys? Or, why didn't you get into a situation where you couldn't keep a family together any better than your dad or mother could keep them together?

S   Well, I had a dream.

Au   A dream? What was your dream?

S   I've got certain things, and I got it broken down like a phased-type thing where I want to get so much accomplished in so much time, you know. And like, my first phase was, I wanted to get my stereo equipment. That was the biggest thing in my life at one time. And now I got really fine stereo equipment I picked up while I was in Europe, you know. And there was Wendy, ah, part of that phase; and then I just move on to another phase. Where I'd say, OK, now I want to do this and I'd work on it till it was done. And I got a new car now. I'm moving on to another phase where now I want to get a house. Wendy and I'd like to own a house.

Au   "Wendy and I"; not just you.

S   Yeah, right. Wendy is in everything.

Au   And when do you think you might get that dream house?

S   Well, we are not the ones to really rush into it. Wendy, we are kinda contemplating now whether we'd like to get an old house and remodel it, or just have one built. And, uh, . . . we've been looking around now for about two years. We really haven't found what we want.

Au   Keep looking.

S   You will know it when we find it!

Au   Do you think you will stay on working at the dealership? You enjoy working there, you enjoy the guys that you are with?

S   Oh, yeah. I will; it's a good time. I mean, it's not where you go in and punch a clock, go do your job and then punch out, you know. There is something different every day. That is the biggest thing I like about it. And the people you get along with, really great guys there. Except for the foreman. Sometimes you have to get time—I mean to get the good jobs which pay—you have to fight with him a little bit, you know. But, usually he is OK, too.

Au   Listen, exclusive of the clinical teaching program time—although you can include that, I guess, if you want to, but I'm not asking for compliments at this point—what is the most important thing that ever happened to you in your life up to this point? And also exclusive of marrying Wendy.

S   I'd have to say the military.

Au   What about the military?

S   Well, it helped me get myself on a schedule. I don't mean a schedule as a schedule, but it helped me get myself get used to a job. It gave me training to where I could do something I enjoyed doing, you know. Like, I went into the service knowing I was going to be a mechanic and knowing what I was going to do when I got out, you know. And, uh, I think that's the only thing that I can get to my level of . . . I'd have to probably say the Service, really, 'cause it gave me—

Au   A certain amount of structure. Is that the word you are seeking?

S   Yeah, right. And I got to really understand people, work with people to where I really wasn't used to doing it before, you know. Plus I had a chance to travel, too, which got a lot of things out of my system.

Au   Are you sometimes bitter over your childhood, are you sometimes angry with what happened to you as a kid?

S   A lot of times I really don't like thinking about it, you know. 'Cause sometimes it really makes me really upset because a lot of bad things happened, you know. But somebody else had it worse you know.

Au   Then you can turn it off, pretty much, begin to look to the future. You've got a beautiful future.

S   I like to think so.

Au   Well, you sure do. You have when you think of all of the wonderful things that you have made happen to yourself. Nobody's done it for you, that's for sure. When you think of the job you have, the skills that you have, the fact that you have Wendy. She is a perfectly charming person, and that little boy is something like you don't see very often. He is a charmer. You've got the future in the palm of your hand as much as any of us do. It is very exciting for me to talk with you. It is worth the trip just to come here and to get reacquainted with you.

S   Thank you.

Au   In very, very many ways, I hope that we won't have to let ten years go before I see you again. I'd like to keep my eye on you and on Todd. So, I guess maybe we will stop this now, and visit for a while with Wendy and Todd.

S   Thank you for coming to see me.

Au   The thanks are on my part.

   At this point Scott's wife and infant son entered and joined in the conversation. Todd, three months old was obviously the center of attention.

Au   Oh, how lucky you guys are!

S   Yeah, really, you know it.

Au   How does Todd sleep at night?

W   He has been sleeping through the night since he was six weeks old. And even before then he was sleeping, you know, four or five hours at a time.

Au   This is wonderful. I never thought I'd get to meet your family, Scott. This is a generous surprise you have provided me. When did you, where did you two meet?

S   We met, well—

W   About six years ago.

Au   Really?

S   It has been quite a while.

Au   Was this during your high school years?

S   No. We were at different high schools. We just kind of met—

W   No. I met him at my girl friend's house. He was going out with another girl, and I had a crush on him.

Au   That's great, and you won?

W   Yeah, I guess so.

Au   Six years ago. You are twenty-two, Scott?

S   I'm twenty.

Au   So, you were out of school? You weren't going to school?

S   When I met her?

Au   Yes.

S   No, I was in school.

Au   And how long did you go together before you got married?

W   We got married last year, so, five years.

S   Four or five years.

W   He was in the Service, and then all the way through the Service, and then after he got out he gave me an engagement ring for Christmas, and then we got married.

Au   That's wonderful! And did you write each other all the time you were in the service?

S   Oh, yeah. We were just talking about that tonight.

Au   How often did you get a letter from him, Wendy?

W   Oh, usually—a good letter—about once a week, and a mushy one about every two weeks, you know. I'd get good letters every week, but there would be a few mushy ones in between, too.

Au   That's all right.

W   They're all in my hope chest; I just stuck them all away.

Au   Did you? You saved them.

W   I've kept them a few years, and can look back and see how funny they are.

Au   Well, you'll enjoy them someday, that's for sure, and so will Todd! And the baby was born about three months ago, you said?

W   In June.

Au   You told me the date, but I've forgotten.

W   Twenty-second.

S   I went into the delivery room with them too! Boy!

Au   Did you? And how did you feel about that, Scott, being in the delivery room?

S   I didn't know how it was going to feel at first, you know, 'cause I'd— well, we'd gone to these classes to prepare us for it, you know, to let us know what was going on and everything. We went to about six weeks of classes on it.

Au   Did you?

S   And then after it all started happening, you know, this just seemed natural.

Au   Were you scared, Scott?

S   At first I was, but I wasn't, not too much, later—say about after the first hour I started getting tired, 'cause she started getting into the labor around midnight—she didn't have the kid until seven in the morning, and I had worked a long shift the day before with no sleep.

W   No, six. Don't push it any farther.

Au   Six. So about six hours of labor, Wendy, and you stayed at the hospital all that time, Scott?

S   Yeah, I was with her all that time.

Au   And had you seen movies about having babies? Did the six weeks of lessons and classes you went to really prepare you both for what was going to take place?

W   Yeah, pretty much; there were doctors would come, they would show you everything—how the baby was going to be born; what you were going to go through; what you were going to feel during labor and everything. That was pretty good, really. Because when it actually happened, I knew what was going on and all that. It was easy, you know, to handle, when you knew what was going on.

S   They showed you some of the Lamaze techniques to use before—you know, like breathing techniques. Most of it is just keep your mind off of it, you know, and they say breathing is just part of it, or you could recite poems and things like that.

Au   And did you recite a few poems?

S   No, I just sweated! She handled it real well, though.

Au   Did he handle it pretty well, Wendy?

W   Yes, except for when I started telling him to get a nurse or a doctor, then he started going back and forth and back and forth—it was terrible; he was more nervous than I was.

Au   Well, I suspect maybe that is normal, because there is not much he could do at that point except get a nurse or doctor. How long were you in the hospital?

W   Three days. They make you stay three days. I didn't want to stay three hours. The beds are uncomfortable, the food is terrible, and you can't have any visitors. And, I'm terrible if there is nobody to talk to me; I get terrible.

Au   Tell me, had you expected this baby? Did it come as a surprise to you that you were pregnant? Had you planned, or did you hope it might be sometime in the future?

W   I expected it. It was a surprise on his part, not on mine.

Au   Had the two of you talked about having a child about this time, or had you thought that it might come later?

W & S Later.

Au   You knew about it probably before he did because, after all, you were carrying the baby, so that you had a general idea that there might be something going on here.

W   No, he wanted to have it later, though, mostly; I wanted to have it then.

Au   I see. Did you trick him into having the baby?

W   No, he wanted the baby so I figured, you know, now or later—what did it matter? [laugh]

Au   Had you been using the pill before that time?

W   Well, I was kind of mixed up, you know, I was on several different things —none of them seemed to work too much. I was on and off on what I was using, so, in a way, it was, you know, easy. I didn't have much trouble getting pregnant.

Au   What were your feelings, Scott, when you realized you were going to be a father?

S   I was pretty happy. Well, at first it was a shock, you know—I didn't know how to handle it.

Au   When did Wendy tell you?

S   When she was—

W   Six, seven weeks—about two months it was. I told him, and all he did was walk around the house going, "Six weeks!" "Six weeks!" That is all he did; he didn't say "hello" to me; he didn't say anything; he just sat there and said, "six weeks"; ate his lunch, and walked out saying "six weeks." That is all he said to me; he didn't say one word to me—he just keep repeating, "six weeks."

Au   How did you feel about that, Wendy?

W   Oh, me? I was laughing. I thought it was funny.

Au   You saw the humor in it.

W   Yeah.

Au   What did the six weeks refer to, Scott?

S   That is when she told me; she told me she was six weeks pregnant.

Au   Why do you think you reacted that way?

S   I wasn't ready for it, I don't think.

Au   Were you unhappy, aggravated that she had waited six weeks to tell you?

S   No, I just wasn't sure.

Au   You weren't sure she was really pregnant?

S   I wasn't sure of how I felt, you know. I was kind of up and down, you know. I wasn't sure if I was happy, or why it took this long for her to tell me—I'm not really sure. I just wasn't sure at the time. Now I figure, well, maybe it was for the best.

Au   Of course, it is for the best when you see this young man. You know it is for the best now, I guess.

S   Right! Boy, are you right!

Au   Can you remember back to August 22, when the baby was actually born, how you felt, Scott?

S   I had a tear in my eye.

Au   Did you?

S   He was—like I watched him come out, and they took him over, and like he had a problem with respiration, and they had to take him downstairs, and I was right behind him the whole time. And, uh—

Au   Both Wendy and Todd were taken together downstairs?

S   No.

W   Just the baby.

S   Just the baby. Like he came out; he had the umbilical cord wrapped around his neck, and he had a problem with respiration. I went downstairs, and they had it all under control, and his heart tone had just come and everything, and it was great. I went upstairs and cried a few minutes and I was really happy.

Au   That's good; it was good for you to have cried. It's all right for men to cry sometimes. Tell me, did the physician know that you were following him downstairs?

S   Yeah, and really, I didn't bother to ask him; I just went. It was my baby.

Au   You just went.

S   Yeah, right, naturally.

Au   And what did the physician do?

S   He just—well, after he knew that I was coming, you know, he just told me to keep coming.

Au   What did he do with the baby?

S   He cleaned a lot of the stuff out of him; he had a lot of phlegm and buildup, and he had tubes going down and cleaning him out, and after they got him cleaned out he was all right.

Au   How much does he weigh now?

W   Well, about fourteen pounds, I think. It is not fat; he is just so long; he is getting so big.

Au   Scott, did you ever think that you were going to be a father?

S   I'd thought about it a few times.

Au   Are you planning to have more children?

S   Yeah, I'd like to have maybe one or two more; I'd like to have a girl next.

Au   Really?

S   Yeah.

W   If we can't have a girl next time, try again.

Au   You want some more children too, do you, Wendy?

W   Yeah.

Au   Where do you work?

W   Ah, Banking Operations Center—it is a computer center for the bank.

Au   How long have you worked there?

W   Three years.

Au   How long were you away from work when Todd was born?

W   Three and a half months.

Au   Three and a half months? And you went back? Who takes care of him during the day?

W   I do, and he (Scott) takes care of him at night. I work at night. See, the bank's work doesn't come in until night time, after the banks close and we have to have it ready for the next day. I work from 6:30 P.M. to 2:30 A.M. or to whenever the work is done. Scott is the best father of all of our friends. I am so glad.

Au   And Scott, you work then from—

S   Eight to five.

Au   So you see each other about three hours a day; is that right?

S   Yeah.

Au   When you come home at night—

W   Or at lunch and then we have—spend weekends together. But I miss being at home. But I look at it this way—I want a house, too. I want a house for Todd and any of the other kids we may have. So the only way I am going to get that nowadays is to work.

Au   That's probably true. How do you feel about it, Scott?

S   Well, I feel about the same way, you know. Like, I'd like to get a house and everything; there will be a time—later, for us. I'm just wanting to plan for the future now. This is the phase thing I told you about. Wendy knows.

Au   I think that's great, and good planning usually succeeds. Well, I have a feeling maybe we ought not to continue this part of the conversation too much more because, uh, I have a feeling that either Todd is going to fall asleep or else—

S   Besides, we are having too much fun. I like talking with you, and I am sure Wendy does too. You know this evening sort of makes things complete for me. It brings everything around. We've got to keep in touch.

Not much more needs to be said about Scott and his little family. Less than a year after this interview took place, Scott and Wendy were able to purchase a home and assume a reasonable mortgage. Todd grows as frequent pictures attest. Scott is pleased, for his dream has come true.

We think most of the credit for his mature achievement must go to Scott himself. Wendy, a later arrival in his life, saw sparks of worth and quietly waited until her influence and help could be effective. Scott has once again met Mrs. S., his teacher and over and over again refers to the significance she had for him. The early basis of success in the clinical teaching program undoubtedly played a role, however small, in assisting Scott to achieve maturity with a legally "clean" record as he so proudly states.

One day the total life history of a child and youth with a learning disability will be written. Interests in adolescence will be extended into adulthood and maturity. Such, however, is not the purpose of this book, yet some post-adolescent characteristics can be suggested which need thought and attention. Scott has indeed made a remarkable adjustment. He often exemplifies maturity beyond his years. In an earlier chapter it was stated that for some adolescents with learning disabilities their problems become alleviated only as they blend into adult society where personal variance is accepted more generally. Scott exemplifies this. He has some remaining needs, however, as do the others. The young adult who has or did have learning disabilities often now has a need to know why. "Where did I come from?" "How did I survive?" "What caused all of this?" Over and over Scott asks and echoes these questions.

One of the authors has promised Scott to share and to read through with him his boyhood clinical records, to explain the data included there, and to talk about the information sufficiently for him to obtain a full understanding. It is Scott's record. There is no reason to deny this information to him now. He needs to know. His childhood in large measure constitutes a void, and this accentuates his insecurities. He described himself as sometimes feeling without "root." We hope that in reading and understanding his childhood records, a perspective may be provided which he does not now possess. We feel that this may be a normal procedure with most learning disabled adolescents and young adults. The data can serve as concrete evidence of the perceptions of others regarding them, their achievements, their social relationships and their difficulties.

Early clinical relationships with Scott have developed into wholesome friendships among adults—Scott, his wife, one of the authors, and the latter's wife. While having dinner together at a restaurant,

Scott needed to talk, as he often does. For nearly an hour he monopolized the conversation in a personal catharsis, unloading feelings and attitudes which were private and controlling. From this we deduce the necessity of very long-term counseling as a requisite for many young people with learning disabilities as they move into adulthood. The schools may not be permitted to dissolve their responsibility for youth at eighteen years of age. Better still is the development of a close relationship between the Scott-like people and one who can listen, understand, and place developments into a reasonable focus.

Scott and Wendy need a different kind of counseling and advice as well. At three years of age their son Todd represents classical symptoms of hyperactivity, perceptual processing deficits, and an attention span which is almost negligible.

Part III

THE SECONDARY SCHOOL

10

The Learning Disabilities Faceoff

Lᴇᴛ ᴜꜱ ᴛʀʏ ᴛᴏ ᴠɪᴇᴡ the secondary school as an incoming learning disabled student might experience that entry. The student has moved from an elementary program where he attended a self-contained learning disabilities program in the morning and a regular sixth grade class in the afternoon. He had three teachers: a learning disabilities teacher, the sixth-grade teacher, and a physical education teacher. He enters the junior high to be confronted by the presence of a thousand bodies, banging lockers, halls, halls, and more halls. The schedule is handed to the student; he cannot read it. He discovers through the help of others that he has seven periods per day and nine different courses. Two classes meet on alternate days: two on "M" days and two on "T" days. This is simple the first week because the "M" day is Monday and the "T" days are Tuesday and Thursday. Not so the second week. "One must remember which classes you had Friday to know to attend the alternating classes Monday." Of course, of course. So many teachers with so many styles and voices and paces . . . only five minutes between classes . . . where is the locker? . . . what is the combination? . . . which is right or left? These are the wrong stairs. Late. Need a pass. The office? Which office? Left the book on the bus. Everyone else has friends . . . look at them laugh. Can't understand what the assignment was. The girls are pretty, the boys are big. They don't know I can't read. Why not, why not? Tomorrow will be better. The bell is ringing—no pencil . . . hurry it up . . . don't crawl . . . sit still . . . listen . . . pretend . . . so much talking . . . Neanderthal man . . . sets . . . regrouping . . . not . . . not soccer, oh, . . . please, not soccer.

So it begins. Someone will help; the panic will be relieved, but too often adolescence will crush in to compete with the helpers. Each of the youths included in Part II of this book indicates in his own way the confusion he experienced as he left the shelter of the elementary school;

Scott through his "conference" with the junior high school principal;
Andy in the accentuation of his paranoia and avoidance of "fights."
Others express this in still other forms.

WHAT DOES THE LEARNING DISABLED ADOLESCENT LOOK LIKE IN THE SCHOOL?

What do the teachers see? How does this learning disabled person appear
to other students? To the teachers trained in selected subject matter, with
a six-period daily class load, this student on first glance looks much like
all the new seventh-graders. A bit more shy, or self-conscious and blun-
dering, perhaps a little more clumsy and a bit more restless. But soon he
stands out as frequently late, often without materials or assignments, unable to listen or to follow oral directions. When twenty-eight of his classmates are able to write the assignment down and independently pursue
their classwork, why can't he? He can barely read. What can a teacher of
History of Western Civilization do with a boy who cannot read? He never
leaves his seat, but he is in perpetual wriggling motion. He seems tense
and nervous, and yet he yawns and yawns and yawns. Can he hear well?
Perhaps he needs his eyes examined. He says all of the wrong things at the
wrong times, and the others tease and laugh at him unmercifully. He is
growing up and he is physically self-conscious, but he seems so young
and unready for this experience. Whose responsibility is this child? Why
didn't they teach him to read in elementary school? His handwriting is
atrocious, and his erasures make holes in his paper. One would think he is
a perfectionist until his paper is turned in—a mass of smudges with most
of the illegible, misspelled words strung together in a stream-of-
consciousness arangement—the content of which bears little relation to
the assignment and looks for all the world as if it rode to school under the
wheels of the bus rather than in a binder.

To his peers he is strange—a little too loud and never quite on
target with his comments in class. Even out of class, his jokes seem to
have no beginning or end, rather just one extended middle. Sometimes he
has a chip on his shoulder but other times you have to feel sorry for him
because he can't seem to do anything right. Nobody likes him. They think
he's retarded—sometimes he even drools. You should see his locker!
There's a girl who can't read in social studies, but that's her only problem.

Not this guy. He forgets everything, even when it's time to go to the special education teacher's room. He seems to have so much trouble paying attention and doing things right and yet he can be so mean to other kids who don't do as poorly as he does. It's too hard to understand.

HOW CAN THE SCHOOLS SERVE YOUNG PEOPLE WITH LEARNING DISABILITIES?

In discussing programs and models of delivering service at the secondary levels we must remember the newness of learning disabilities as a category. Although there were a few elementary school classes scattered across the country before 1963, they were labeled NH, BI, MBD, BD or some such descriptor. Since 1963, there has been a steady development in programs for children with learning disabilities. Most of these programs fall into one of the following organizational models: resource room, self-contained learning disabilities class, partial day self-contained, or regular class with teacher consultant services to the teacher(s).

For the most part these services have been on the elementary level. Although some school districts have been providing services to secondary learning disabled students for several years, the majority of programs have been established since 1972, and in many cases there is not a choice of program models. This is especially true at the high school level, where self-contained classes are rare and available services usually consist of a resource room and/or teacher-consultant.

There are a number of reasons for the lack of continuity of services, as well as for the absence of certain types of programs altogether.

1. The literature is sparse in material focusing on the secondary learning disabled pupil. There is little in the body of reported research or even clinical studies to clarify our picture of the learning disabled adolescent.

2. There are few educational assessment instruments with norms for adolescent students. The fact that we have been unable to clarify the quantity or severity of the assumed discrepancy between performance and potential has been used as a reason for the small number of identified and served students at the secondary level.

3. Very few university teacher preparation programs have pro-

vided specific curricula or practica concentrating on adolescents with learning disabilities for their trainees; thus, there is an extremely limited supply of well-trained personnel.

4. There are very few methods or materials for remediation with demonstrated efficacy for this population.

One further problem which has probably influenced not only the quantity and timing of services to youth with learning disabilities, but also the particular emphases of the programs, is a notion which has arisen in large part from the propagation of a phrase found in most popular definitions of learning disabilities, that children with learning disabilities *are those with average or above-average intelligence* with disabilities in one or more of the following areas: reading, writing, mathematical computation, or reasoning (see Figures 1 and 2). The emphasis is always placed on the near normality of these children. We are assured that their handicap is "hidden" or "invisible," and that were it not for a small but important flaw, they would be like the "best of the normal."

This constant reminder and caution regarding the all-but-normal state of the learning disabled has set up expectations on the part of both teachers and parents of attainment of near normal function, and even of *cure* or recovery. It is not unusual for parents, anxious about under-achievement, to be told, "Don't worry, he'll be just fine," or "Just get her to buckle down and apply herself."

One of the characteristics of children with learning disabilities is hyperactivity. Professionals have observed a marked decrease in hyper-active behavior as boys and girls enter adolescence, and reports of improvement in *that* condition have been, at times, overextended and generalized to other learning disabilities. This has given support to the notion that learning disabilities, unlike deafness or mental retardation, diminish or disappear at adolescence. The confusion is increased by the fact that improvement and compensation *does* occur. We would be the last to suggest that change and positive development are impossible with the learning disabled child; on the contrary, we believe that early and careful intervention often yields outstanding progress. The gains made by the young men who attended the clinical teaching program described in Part II represent positive indication of what can occur. Referring to those same men, however, one can see that some of them still demonstrate attributes and residuals of disordered learning not now manifested in poor reading or mathematics.

We have seen young students whose difficulties were discreet enough that when the proper technique was applied, the student's spelling, handwriting, or reading problem was overcome; the student actually appeared to be *cured*. Many more students make just enough gains and adjustments to look more *lazy* than *disabled*. They continue to struggle against overwhelming odds when dealing with the multifaceted demands of the secondary curriculum and routine. It is almost as if a new set of disabilities or differences within the child are provoked into being by the new setting and its requirements.

It is, then, this *new* learning disabled student, the adolescent in the secondary school, who confronts us and our inadequate definition which states that he is *not* physically handicapped, sensorially impaired, or mentally retarded, and has average or above-average intelligence. We are left with an intriguing definition of exclusion: we know more about what the student is *not* than what he *is*. Secondary educators who have had little or no orientation to the problem of learning disabilities or individualization of instruction accept this definition as gospel, and place the responsibility for lack of progress wholly on the adolescent youth.

It is ironic that avoidance of identification with the mentally retarded may have inadvertently deterred appropriate programming for learning disabled students, particularly in the area of adaptive skills and career or vocational education. This is not to say that all is well in services to the mentally retarded. Certainly some critics with data have sound arguments against, for instance, the self-contained special classes; however, we have for many years offered secondary students identified as "mildly or educably mentally retarded" alternative classes, adjusted curricula, and special vocational preparation. Whether this has been the correct route will not be determined here; but, in fact, those individuals designated as "EMR" do graduate, do find employment, do marry, and do function independently in the community.

With few exceptions we apply small educational band-aids to the learning disabled adolescent. We make some attempt (often the same for years) at remediation of academic skills; have them sit through regular college preparation classes; offer little or no vocational counseling or training; and then wonder why such a disproportionate number of adjudicated youth with "normal" intelligence are reported to have learning disabilities. The fact is that many are equipped for nothing: they cannot read and cannot fill out a job application; most cannot gain entrance to or compete in college; some cannot manage their lives or even organize themselves to seek assistance. They do not understand their own differences and they have no applicable vocational skills.

None of the young men in Part II of this volume had access during secondary school years to special services for the learning disabled.

After their participation in the elementary clinical teaching program, and in spite of academic gains and certain vocational successes, each boy except perhaps Scott, demonstrated little understanding of the relationship between his own skills and the world of work. This is especially true of Andy, who continues to be confused and naive as he speaks (almost in one breath) of being a CPA, managing a truck stop, and working as a custodian.

We must decide not only what organizational model we will use to deliver services, but what the content and focus of the programs will be. For the junior high students, the focus will probably continue to be mainly academic with a strong skill remediation component. By the time the student has reached high school, priorities will need to de determined. As Irvine *et al.*(1978) remind us, "while in high school learning disabled pupils may also be capable of learning much academically, their academic time clocks are running out"(p. 267). In deciding whether the emphasis will be learning skills of a vocation, development of basic literacy, or academic instruction with a bypass of reading, each student's case must be scrutinized separately. Programmatic options will be required, along with individualized planning, to develop priorities and make decisions for individuals within a population we have already described as having great diversity of personal attributes.

WHAT PROGRAM OPTIONS ARE ESSENTIAL?

We suggest a model (see Figure 3) which provides the following as a minimum in contrast to Deno's concept (1970):

1. *Self-contained classes* should be available with provisions for those few students who need a full day of intensive small group situations. The five youths discussed earlier each received a solid educational start in this form of the school program. The personnel of these self-contained classes have a peculiar challenge. They must be able to offer reading and writing instruction to students who are so deficient in those skills that they are rendered helpless in regular classes where the time spent would in fact just contribute to the distance between the student's potential and his performance level. Because the student will be in the class all or almost all of the time, however, the teacher will need to offer instruction in several subject areas, while providing opportunities for social development to avoid the possible escalation of "specialness" that can occur from isolating and perhaps stigmatizing adolescents. A third and essential

SELF-CONTAINED CLASSES	RESOURCE ROOMS	LD SPECIAL'STS	JUNIOR HIGH OCCUPATIONAL OR CAREER ED	HIGH SCHOOL VOC TRAINING	WORK STUDY PROGRAMS	COUNSELING SERVICES

FIGURE 3 A continuum of service options

part of the challenge is the need to interpret the whole matter to the adolescent, who hates to be different.

2. *Resource rooms* would provide selected periods of remedial instruction and supportive tutoring for those who need them but can benefit from attending regular classes in some subjects. Although there are several different types of programs described as resource programs or resource room programs, most provide one to three hours of direct instruction in basic skills, by a trained teacher of learning disabilities, as well as some support in completing subject area assignments. In addition, most of these students will need consultation to the teachers of the regular classes they attend.

3. *Learning disability specialists* with skills in consultation can provide help for those students who can maintain their position in regular classes, as long as the general education teachers receive some assistance in making necessary instructional accommodations. In other words, these specialists must be competent not only in specific techniques for learning disabled adolescents, but familiar as well with course content and the requirements of various subjects. Above all, these specialists must be able to offer, in an acceptable manner, suggestions for materials and means which will allow subject area teachers to make adjustments in their manner and mode of presentation—as well as alternatives for the student's written responses.

4. *Occupation or career education* should begin during junior high school years, to permit pupils to explore systematically vocational opportunities and to expose the learning disabled student to the realities of various occupations. This preview of occupations and their requirements and requisite skills should include information about college education. Although higher education is not thought of as a "job"—certainly for a learning disabled individual who wishes to pursue education beyond high school—it is as essential to have a clear understanding of what that will entail as it would for another student to be aware of the typical requirements of a vocation, such as sheet-metal working or building maintenance.

5. *Vocational training* in the high school should be designed specifically for the learning disabled adolescent, or it should have the capacity of individualizing programming to accommodate a student with specific skill deficits. Many school districts now offer vocational training units called Skill Centers. Unfortunately, most of these units require an eleventh-grade status for entry and little support for those with deficient reading or writing skills. We would advocate, as a minimum, early entry as well as tutorial support for learning disabled students.

6. *Work-study programs* could offer the student opportunities to try out skills "on the job" with school faculty supervision, while also providing opportunities for continued academic and vocational study on a part-day basis. The most impressive work-study programs are those which employ a full-time coordinator-supervisor, one who matches student needs with community employment opportunities and then offers both students and employers necessary support. This type of program is particularly important for those learning disabled students who have difficulty generalizing their learning to a variety of situations.

7. *Counseling services* should be available for the learning disabled adolescent. These may be group and/or individual in focus. The counselor might be the special education teacher, the school guidance counselor, school psychologist, or another professional sensitive to the most common pitfalls for the adolescent with learning disabilities—as well as the peculiar difficulties some learning disabled young people have with understanding and responding to the abstract concepts and long streams of language so characteristic of counseling sessions. Some learning disabled students have poor perception of social situations as well as problems of impulsivity, short attention span, and specific language disabilities. For these students, *group* sessions may be especially useful. The group offers a small, controlled environment for trial interactions with feedback and interpretation available. Although the groups may be psycho-social in their focus, they can also serve as opportunities to actually *teach* certain social/behavioral skills which most students develop in the normal course of school attendance, but which escape "absorption" by the learning disabled adolescent. Some of the best work in this area has been implemented in the Child Service Demonstration Center for Urban Secondary Students with Learning Disabilities in Pittsburgh. Naomi Zigmond and her associates outline that work in their (undated) replication materials, entitled, *Guide to Implementation.* Their content for the group sessions emphasizes school survival skills ranging from study skills to "teacher-pleasing" behaviors.

Essentially, then adequate programming for the learning disabled adolescent student requires that a continuum of services be available. For several years, special education administrators have found it helpful to use a model of program development described by Deno as a cascade model, in which a variety of programs are available and students are placed according to severity of handicap, with those considered to be mildly handicapped enrolled in the least restrictive program and the most severely handicapped enrolled in special facilities. Another way of describing this model would be in terms of intensity of service, with those in need of intensive service being placed in special hospitals or schools; those needing slightly less intensive service in special self-contained classes; and so on through program options, but usually considering a one-to-one correspondence between severity of disability and nature of service.

The nature of learning disabilities in adolescents dictates a set of even more flexible program options. A student may need intensive remediation in one or more skill areas, but be able to cope successfully with a full slate of regular classes; another student may need less intensive work on basic skills, but be unable to function adequately in regular classes because of attentional difficulties or an inability to organize material adequately. Yet another student will need almost one-to-one instruction in reading and writing, but still be ready for vocational training and actual work experience. We could continue to describe variations and combinations of individual student needs, which are at times so disparate that they seem incongruous, and certainly do not lend themselves to simple solutions in planning.

It would seem, then, that instead of the vertical or cascading system of program types wherein a student is assigned according to severity of handicap, we must think of the continuum of services in a more horizontal manner (Figure 3), allowing choices and permutations in programming which will meet the diverse individual needs of this group of students. Figure 4 utilizes a bar graph to show how one particular student's program was developed from components available on the continuum.

WHAT CAN PUBLIC SCHOOLS LEARN FROM ALTERNATIVE AND PRIVATE PROGRAMS?

Of the learning disabled teenagers we know who have attended private residential schools for students with learning disabilities, each has made impressive progress. This has caused joy for parents of those students and for lamenting on the part of less affluent parents who are unable to offer their children such treatment. Certainly the situation will remain where very few learning disabled students will be able to attend the necessarily expensive private schools. But what can we learn from them? What do they do which is so different, and how much, if any, of it could be incorporated into public school programs?

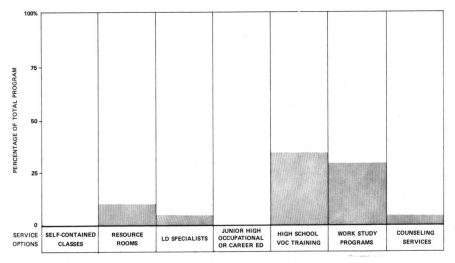

A sample intervention program for Andrea B., grade 11, Deauveaux High School:

STUDENT OVERVIEW:	Primary difficulties:	severe reading disability, socially awkward, shy
	Strengths:	intelligence, artistic talent, well organized
PROGRAM DEVELOPED:	Regular classes, 25%:	Civics, Driver's Education
	Resource Room, 10%:	Fernald lessons, 40 min./day
	LD Specialist, 5%*:	Consults with regular class teachers and Voc. Center Staff
	Voc. Training, 35%:	Print Shop and Graphics
	Work Study Program, 30%:	Walco Wallpaper Co., design transfer apprentice, 12 hr/wk, $2.35/hr
	Counseling Service, 5%:	½ hr/wk individual session with guidance counselor 1 hr/wk L.D. group meeting with guidance counselor

*Indirect service; specialist consults with instructors

FIGURE 4 An individualized intervention program developed from
the continuum of services

Private schools are able to immerse the learning disabled student in an entire program tailored to his or her needs. Rather than one or two periods per day of remedial instruction or tutoring slipped into a day of classes with non-handicapped learners, the private school offers its pupils classes in social studies, English, mathematics, arts, physical education, and languages. Moreover, offering a student a total program of "special" classes does not present the problems encountered in placing the student in a self-contained learning disabilities classroom housed in a public school whose majority is non-learning disabled. There are, of course, dangers in some private schools of creating or sustaining a learned dependency, but these are probably offset by the risks students are willing to take in such a totally supportive environment.

We know of a few large school districts which have chosen to develop alternative programs for the learning disabled that duplicate in part the private school model. These programs offer what might be described as a "departmentalized self-contained" program. Those particular programs, located in some public school systems in the states of Michigan and Virginia, are so young that they, like other secondary learning disabilities programs, have yet to report evaluation data with which we might assess efficacy.

Most school districts of small or moderate populations will feel hard-pressed to meet even the minimum program options described earlier, let alone provide the whole cadre of teachers (trained both in selected subject areas as well as in learning disabilities) needed to provide an alternative full-day departmentalized program for learning disabled secondary students.

What then can we take from the models and successes of the best private schools? In scrutinizing the curricula and methods of teaching reading in a few of these programs, we had hoped to find that these schools had discovered *the* select reading approaches which *definitely* work with learning disabled students. Alas, such magic was not to be. Is there a critical variable which accounts for so much more success by these programs than is reported by public schools? One factor that stands out in contrast is *consistency*. The review of a reading disabled, public high school student's cumulative file often reveals something akin to a catalog of commercial alternatives to reading instruction, with a different program being used each year—or one (apparently inappropriate) primer being used over and over again in spite of negligible gains made. Private schools, on the other hand, seem to make a decision regarding appropriate instruction and stick to it day after day unless periodic assessment reveals no gains.

The best of these schools are aware of expected accountability to students and parents, and therefore provide rather *frequent evaluation of student progress*. What happens is actually a shift in responsibility; whereas public school personnel assume the resistance to improvement to have its bases in the inherent deficiencies within the student, the personnel of private school programs have acted as if *they* had the responsibility both to find an appropriate method and to match it to the child's learning differences to effect achievement.

The other element of the special school program which may deserve attention and review is a particular type of *reinforcement.* In reviewing curricula and typical schedules of private schools, we found a certain set of demands made upon the student more often than in the public school programs of learning disabled students. This set included especially a relatively large production of written language. It appeared also that while a great many accommodations were made for non-reading students, including alternatives to printed materials, students were required and expected to read any material which could be acquired and was within their grasp. Our experience supports the notion that exercise in written expression reinforces reading achievement and that reading itself (practice) is one of the most productive facets of remediation.

It has not been our intent, in this brief examination of these alternative programs, to discourage public educators or to suggest that the only way learning disabled students will be helped is by enrolling in $12,000-per-year private programs. These schools have some clear advantages. Our real purpose was to consider which components of these programs might be incorporated in the public school curricula. There is no apparent limit to the ideas school administrators might gain by first-hand examination of those programs that have demonstrated a high rate of success with learning disabled students. In conclusion, we would endorse as a minimum those three aspects of private school programming cited in this section: (1) consistency of programming; (2) systematic monitoring and evaluation; and (3) complementary task reinforcement.

When Scott, Tom, Andy, and Ron were of junior and senior high school age, there were no options for the learning disabled in high school. Some progress has been made; a small number of model programs has been federally funded and other services have been developed with local district funding. We have moved beyond the point of merely acknowledging that students who have suffered from extreme differences in learning ability and style do not as a rule outgrow those problems during the summer following grade six, seven, or eight. If we are to serve these students' best interests, we will need to continue examining alternative models and researching selected programs.

11

Assessment and Planning

ASSESSMENT OF LEARNING PROBLEMS
IN SECONDARY SCHOOL STUDENTS

Many of the junior and senior high school students labeled learning disabled are identified as such early in their school careers, or at least while in upper elementary school. Whether this is true, or an initial referral is made at the secondary level, a specific assessment of the current status of learning problems is always warranted.

In the previous chapter we stressed the importance of monitoring and assessment. Appropriate programs of testing are included within this phase of the programming we endorsed. There are two major reasons for testing children: one is to provide information necessary for administrative decision-making program eligibility and/or placement. The other reason, the one which will receive greatest attention in these pages, is to collect data for planning, and for the adjustment of a student's program of coursework and remedial instruction.

As the reader is probably painfully aware, there are few tests of learning process or performance which are designed for students of secondary school age, either norm or criterion referenced. Because of this fact, as well as an appreciation of the diversity within the population of children called learning disabled, we find it more helpful to speak of a *set of procedures* rather than a standard *battery* of tests.

The model of assessment which forms the basis of our thinking begins a chain of procedures which should, with careful management, provide a continuous loop of monitoring and readjustment of goals and objectives so essential for adequate service to these complex students (Figure 5). Four of the related stages in the assessment and planning chain are

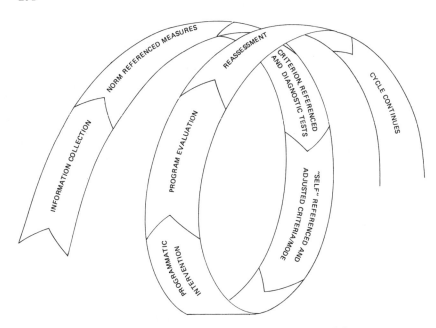

FIGURE 5 A model of continuous services for the adolescent
with learning disabilities

represented in Figure 6, and a description of those stages follows. Figure 7
is a suggested worksheet to assist an evaluator in planning throughout the
first four stages.

Stage I: Information Collection

The first stage of this process includes collection of information
necessary for the development of an assessment plan. This stage should
clarify the objectives of testing and place the process in historical perspective. The objectives often evolve from questions which are prompted by a
review of the student's school history and reports of current concerns:

Question: Is there one specific aspect of the reading process with
             which the student has the most difficulty?

Objective: To measure the student's success with word attack prob-
             lems using real and nonsense words.

I. Information Collection	II. Norm-Referenced Measures	III. Criterion-Referenced and Diagnostic Tests	IV. Self-Referenced and Adjusted Criteria/Mode

Clarification of referral concern
 	
History
 	
Observation
 	
Records Review
 	
Interviews with student and significant others (family, teachers, physician, tutor, etc.)
	Achievement
	
	Cognitive
	
	Language
	  receptive
	  expressive
	
	Personality
	
	Neurological
	
	Medical
	
	Vocational
		Math
		
		Reading
		
		Spelling
		
		Handwriting
		  form
		  speed
		
		Abstract reasoning
		
		Written language performance
		
		Visual perceptual processing
		
		Locus of control
		
		Self-concept
		
		Motor speed and accuracy
		
		Allergies, diet
		
		Manual performance
			Test similar educational behaviors as in criterion-referenced tests, but *adjust* conditions, e.g.:
			
			Break tasks into smaller units
			
			Give specific aide such as abacus or number line
			
			Give color-cued paper and encourage to use cursive back-hand slant in handwriting
			
			Try reading comprehension measure with student sub-vocalizing as he reads—have him use a guide to read

FIGURE 6 Four stages of assessment model

Question: Would a reading method which includes more simultaneous modes of input and practice be more effective than the largely visual, basal approach tried for so long?

Objective: To measure student's success with a trial of two multisensory approaches to reading [Fernald and Gillingham-Stillman].

Stage II: Norm-Referenced Tests

Once objectives are established, the purposes of the assessment should be more apparent. In the cases of secondary students often there will be current norm-referenced data from intelligence tests and standard achievement tests. If this is not the case, it may be helpful to begin the assessment with standardized norm-referenced tests in order to (1) give a global picture of the student's performance in relation to that of a representative sample of peers; (2) eliminate areas that need no further probing; and (3) pinpoint levels at which criterion-referenced or diagnostic testing should begin.

When a student is having very little success in reading and writ-

Assessment Planning Worksheet

REFERRAL CONCERNS (Note concerned party if appropriate)	EDUCATIONAL EVALUATION QUESTIONS OR OBJECTIVES	PROPOSED TESTS (In order of presentation or numbered)	RESULTS AND/OR SPECIAL COMMENTS

REFERRAL CONCERNS (Note concerned party if appropriate)

1._____

2._____

3._____

PERTINENT COMMENTS FROM RECORDS (Note source)

_____
_____
_____
_____

PRE-ASSESSMENT DATA AVAILABLE
School History
   Regular Education Programs

_____
_____

   Special Services

_____
_____

PREVIOUS EVALUATION
Test
Date
Results

Test
Date
Results

Test
Date
Results

CURRENT SCHOOL PLACEMENT
Regular Classes

_____

Special Services

_____
_____

OBSERVATION(S):

When_____

Where_____

By Whom_____

EDUCATIONAL EVALUATION QUESTIONS OR OBJECTIVES

1._____

2._____

3._____

4._____

5._____

PROPOSED TESTS (In order of presentation or numbered)
CODE:
NR = norm referenced
CR = criterion referenced
I = informal or adjusted
     measure--usually examiner constructed

RESULTS AND/OR SPECIAL COMMENTS

Student_____ b.d._____

Evaluator_____ Date_____

PROPOSED TRIAL TEACHING OR ATTEMPTS AT TESTING COMPETENCIES WITH ADJUST-ED CONDITIONS	RESPONSES	QUESTIONS, CONCERNS, PRELIMINARY RECOMMENDATIONS

FIGURE 7 Assessment planning worksheet

ten language tasks, but is able to work somewhat independently in math, it is not unusual to receive a referral report which states: "This student is a virtual non-reader, although he seems to enjoy some easy books. Math is his best subject and he does well in art." Although one might assume that this seventh grader is reading on kindergarten level while doing seventh grade math, the administration of a standardized achievement test indicates the following performance:

Word Recognition . . . . Grade Equivalent 3.2

Reading Comprehension . . . . Grade Equivalent 2.4

Mathematical Computation . . . . Grade Equivalent 3.8

Mathematical Concepts . . . . Grade Equivalent 4.8

Review of these scores provides ready understanding of the *impressions* given in the report; however, the actual grade level equivalent scores give more realistic and concrete information for further testing. Had we acted on our assumptions from the report, we might have wasted a good deal of time in diagnostic testing of reading at too low a level, and on the other hand, might have greatly frustrated the student with math problems well beyond his skills.

Stage III: Criterion-Referenced and Diagnostic Tests

In the third stage of the assessment, criterion-referenced and diagnostic instruments are used to clarify the extent and nature of the difference that was established in the first two stages of the process.

In Stage II of the evaluation, a student's scores on individual tests were compared to standard or group scores, giving us information on the areas and degrees of difference. Because criterion-referenced tests measure a student's performance in terms of specific curriculum objectives, we are able to gain a clearer picture of the strengths and weaknesses in a given area.

Let us suppose that we discovered in Stage II (norm-referenced testing) that a tenth grade student had arithmetic computation skills on a fifth grade, sixth month level when compared to the norms of a reliable standardized achievement test. This score gives us very little specific information for actual teaching. We would then, in Stage III, test the student on items within the math curriculum, using either a standardized criterion-referenced test such as the *Key Math Diagnostic Arithmetic Test* or items selected from local mathematics curriculum material. We might discover that the student has adequate skills up through eighth grade material in numeration, geometry, and measurement, but fails to meet acceptable criterion (say 80 percent) on items representing skills in computation utilizing subtraction, division, or multiplication above third grade level. The student is unable to compute the addition of two-digit numbers if the process requires carrying over. The same student is unable to add even a chain of three single digits mentally (without visuals or pencil and paper).

It seems obvious that this type of testing offers much more specific information for developing educational objectives for the student. A student might have acquired skills in such an uneven pattern for a number of reasons (irregular attendance, poor instruction, emotional disturbance) and it may suffice now to set about intensive instruction of a standard format in the selected areas of deficit. If, however, the irregular and deficient development of arithmetic (or reading or other) skills is due to specific learning disability, then we may need still more information. It would be helpful to know which methods have been attempted and what the responses were. Whether or not we are able to clarify the history of instruction with the student, we have identified some specific weaknesses, and now it is essential that we determine *why* these deficits exist. We are referring not to etiology here, but to more specific learner characteristics which may have rendered the student unable to assimilate concepts and skills, and those ways in which the student *does* learn.

Stage IV: Self-Referenced and Adjusted-Condition Testing

During stage III of the process we clarified and made more specific *what the student could not do.* Now as the fourth stage we must find out under what conditions (if any) the student is able to *accomplish or learn those tasks.* We often refer to this stage of the assessment as "trial teaching," and we consider it especially crucial in the assessment of students who have been involved in special education or remedial programs for any length of time. It is appalling to review the educational histories of some learning handicapped adolescents and be confronted with the months and years we have been (with all good will and concern) trying to teach them certain skills. From the point of view of the student it is more than appalling! It is essential in these cases that we take the opportunity to look at the student not in relation to national or even local norms, or even with a curriculum reference, but *using the student himself as the reference*. We must try to ascertain his or her individual qualities or styles of learning, and then attempt to match instruction to those needs.

An example of adjusting conditions on performance items in the case of the student who was unable to perform on addition problems requiring regrouping, would be to set up a problem requiring regrouping but using objects, such as beads or match sticks, so that the student can physically regroup. If the student masters the task under this condition, an attempt should be made to move the student to a less concrete level by setting up a problem on paper with slash marks or using coins and currency to teach the concept. There are, of course, endless examples of adjustments which might be made. They might involve adjusting not only materials, but mode, sequence, and even criterion. Trial teaching involves a keen understanding of both task and learner analysis, and makes heavy demands on the teaching experience and methodological repertoire of the evaluator. For this reason, a teacher experienced in teaching students with learning disabilities is usually the most appropriate evaluator.

There will be a limited time or number of times a student may be seen by the evaluator. This often amounts to a total of two or three hours, which will necessarily restrict the trials and adjustments that may be attempted as well as limit the depth or extent of those adjustments. An evaluator with extensive experience in direct instruction with learning disabled pupils will have the most appropriate selection of methods and materials to make these trial teaching sessions efficient. This will usually be an experienced teacher.

It may be possible to extend the trial teaching and "adjusted condition sequence" over a longer period of time, by placing the student with a skilled teacher or in a diagnostic classroom on a temporary basis. If properly monitored, this approach should offer more reliable information for decision making in developing individual educational plans.

HAS THE PROCESS GIVEN ADEQUATE INFORMATION FOR PROGRAM PLANNING?

We began our discussion of assessment with the objective of offering a set of procedures which would provide a natural progression from historical review through testing and trial teaching to rational decision-making in regard to specific plans for the learning disabled teenager. But even after all data from the actual assessment have been analyzed and the results organized as a foundation for planning the program, a weakness in the system should be noted. Good, individual performance data have been gathered; every attempt has been made to ascertain the instructional conditions which are optimal for the student; however, most of this has been done in an artificial setting. Adjusting conditions in a quiet, distraction-free office or small classroom bears important, but limited relevance to the pressures of the real world of secondary programs in which these students must "make it."

Adjustments and numerous compromises will need to be made if the plans are to be accepted and acted upon by general education personnel. Before these adjustments are made a thorough assessment of the *ecology* must be undertaken. This will include examination of those non-learner conditions which nevertheless impinge on the youth's performance.

WHAT WOULD AN ECOLOGICAL ASSESSMENT INCLUDE?

We have described an assessment of the learner, and we have noted that learners do not exist in isolation, nor do they carry with them out into the halls or classrooms a set of "test conditions" within which they may operate. Any adequate program development will require examination of not only learning styles but also teaching styles and environmental conditions.

Teachers, like students, have individual differences and styles. Most secondary students will encounter one or two teachers each semester whose styles or personality they do not like. For a learning disabled student such encounters represent a mismatch which may lead to educational and interpersonal crisis.

How can we make decisions about the "right" kind of teaching for the learning disabled student? Is there a best method for *all* learning disabled pupils? We think not, but there are probably *best teachers* for individual students, and the choices may be crucial in attempting to insure successful functioning.

Before we describe teaching qualities, let us develop a reference by examining an outline of qualities of learning disabled secondary students which we have observed and those reported to us by teachers as important to students' school performance.

SOME SPECIFIC PROBLEMS OF LEARNING DISABLED ADOLESCENTS

I. Attending or attention problems

   A. Auditory

      1. cannot listen or concentrate on teacher's comments

      2. cannot concentrate when there is a discussion

      3. cannot concentrate when there are extraneous sounds such as whispering, wind blowing, doors closing, students talking in the halls, etc.

      4. cannot listen when there is visual interference such as many children between student and speaker, lights, tree movement, things on walls, etc.

      5. cannot attend to verbal input only, when there is no visual reinforcement such as writing on the board, pointing, or pictures

      6. critically affected by such variables as speed and pitch of speech

   B. Visual

      1. cannot find or keep their place in written materials, whether in books or on the blackboard

      2. cannot watch a film or slides or other visuals and later revisualize that material or even comment on it

      3. cannot attend to written material unless it is presented in "small doses," and those only when highly structured—two or three math problems at a time rather than 20 or even 10; large, well-spaced type, with few pictures, small pages, large margins

      4. cannot work without guide cards or their fingers, pointers or other aids to follow written work and move along a line of print

      5. cannot pick out important detail from complex visuals, especially maps and graphs and charts

   C. Physical (Physical activity problems may be a *reaction* to the abovementioned difficulties in attention)

      1. extremely restless

      2. squirm endlessly

      3. yawn frequently, and with little correspondence to amount of sleep

    4. must be tapping or touching something all the time with fingers, hands, feet, tongue

    5. have dreadful posture; both sitting and standing

II. Major problems executing work in regular classrooms

  A. Following directions given either orally or written

  B. Copying assignments from chalkboard

  C. Copying actual work material from board

  D. Organizing a response to assignment, i.e., What comes first? What do I need? Where do I get it? When am I through?

  E. Formulating questions and approaching teacher for clarification

  F. Lacking skills specific to the task, e.g., reading, writing, spelling, dictionary use, map reading, etc.

  G. Estimating time

  H. No confidence

  I. Self-consciousness, embarrassment

  J. Difficulty in sequencing at all levels

One often hears secondary school teachers and administrators state that, if these pupils have all of these problems, they do not belong in high school. "We're educators, not psychiatrists," one high school principal told us recently. This man does not remember the definition of his own discipline, for a major aspect of education at all levels is to *provide practice, severe and systematic training, in the acquisition of skills.* This is exactly what the learning disabled adolescent requires. Secondary educators too often have taken the easy way out and have retreated to content, serving the needs of only a fraction of their clientele.

WHAT DOES THE ENVIRONMENT
OF THE SECONDARY CLASSROOM LOOK LIKE?

There is more to the secondary school environment than classrooms. We mentioned the confrontation and confusion of halls and lockers, stairs and offices. For this example of an ecological assessment, however, we will concentrate on the classroom, its structure, and the related teaching styles.

Classes have been called structured, teacher centered, open, traditional, multimedia, individualized, formal, informal, and various other terms. Definitions of these terms and types of classrooms vary, and connotations are the rule. It should be more helpful, therefore, to concentrate on behavioral descriptors of the elements of classroom structure and style in this step of the assessment. There would be little productive, for instance, in stating in a report that, "Janice will function best in a traditional classroom." We will need to be guided in our examination both by the list of traits of the pupil under consideration and a set of questions. Our major concerns are: (1) What will the impact of participation in a certain class be on a particular student, and how disruptive will the presence of the learning disabled student be to the class? (2) What about the class will or or will not be facilitative of the student's optimal performance?

WHAT ABOUT STRUCTURE?

A word which has become almost synonymous with learning disabilities is *structure* (Cruickshank 1977). We firmly believe that many learning disabled students need a superstructure of external organization to support them—especially in early adolescence. But the word *structure* has had at least as many interpretations as "open education." There are all kinds of structure, and just as it will not suffice to state that Janice needs a traditional classroom, it will not be satisfactory to state that "Stephen needs a structured setting," unless you are sure that you and your listeners share a common understanding of the term. Let us examine a classroom in which a learning disabled child is thought to be disruptive.

Some classes are harder to disrupt than others. The tighter or more constant the routine and order in a class, the greater its vulnerability to disruption by a learning disabled pupil. Let's take a "tapper" or a "squirmer," for instance.

Picture any class seated in six columns of straight rows, with the teacher seated in center front. The teacher has reviewed some material via lecture, and has directed the class to quietly write a two-paragraph summary. Our tapper prepares for the work by getting paper and pencil, but just as the students begin to write, he begins to tap his pencil. His pencil tapping becomes louder and more rapid. The teacher notices it is distracting some of the students and asks the tapper to stop. He stops tapping the pencil and begins to write. But now his foot begins to tap and then his teeth. We sometimes call this behavior an enactment of the *balloon prin-*

ciple; if you "squeeze" or inhibit one behavior, a substitute behavior will pop out elsewhere.

What if he were, as well as a "tapper," a student with severe deficits in the skills required for written language? Any deviance, either of a behavioral or academic performance type, will be noticeable and disturbing in a class whose rigid structure demands homogeneity.

In contrast, in a class where students naturally shift positions, chairs, tables, and other equipment when asked to complete a project, "tapping" would not be as disconcerting. If options are offered for assignments, differing skill levels might be less noticeable and less of a hindrance in the students' execution of a relevant product.

Have we demonstrated in our example that learning disabled students will do better in open, flexible classrooms which allow freedom of movement and conversation? Certainly in some cases, but not necessarily. In fact this type of class could portend doom for many learning disabled students. The crucial thing to keep in mind is that an ecological assessment is not an examination of the relationship of the *class* of all learning disabled or the *class* of all secondary school classrooms. It is, rather, the exploration of the interaction between *one student* and one or more elements of the environment under certain conditions.

TWO DIFFERENT TEACHING STYLES

One of the most important aspects of the teaching style to assess is the dominant mode of presentation of material.

Think again of the "tapper/squirmer." What would happen to him in a classroom where each student is expected to enter, assess one's own current level of achievement by scanning the chart in an individual work folder, identify the day's work accordingly, check out a given set of materials, proceed with an experiment, write an analysis, and finally determine the homework assignment from a large chart with specific assignments corresponding to levels of achievement, but dependent on the self-checked accuracy of the day's experiment?

If the "tapper/squirmer" has the characteristic difficulty organizing himself and sequentially proceeding through such a series of steps, he will require a more direct and repetitive imposition of structure. Once again, we may be faced with a dilemma. The class just described offers opportunity for this restless student to move legitimately; it also has work individualized to such a degree that the student's performance weakness would not be as obvious and he could work at his own pace. But, is there too much independence required? Can he manage to progress with any consistency within a system of such delayed feedback and evaluation? Does he need an auditory supplement to the visual directions? These are some of the questions which must be addressed.

An additional example of the relationship of mode of presentation and specific learning disabilities is derived from an actual experience of one of the authors while supervising student trainees.

A student teacher working under direct supervision of a special education teacher-consultant spoke of her concern for a ninth grade student whom she felt was being misunderstood by a particular teacher who called him "impudent, lazy, obstinate, negative, and hostile." The teacher (we will name her Ms. French) agreed to an observation of the boy (Paul) in her class (social studies), and in fact insisted that she welcomed the opportunity to have some verification of his offensive behavior.

There were approximately twenty-five students in the class, seated in orderly rows of individual desks. Paul was seated four rows back, but directly in line with the teacher's desk. As soon as the bell rang, Ms. French called the class to order by saying, "All right, students, the bell has rung, and we need to get busy with the assignment. You will notice there is a worksheet on your desk. On page one, do a, b, c, and 1 through 4 under d. Now you'll need to work quickly, because we are due in the auditorium at 10:55. You should finish by 10:45. When you finish, put your papers by the planter on the table and wait quietly in your seat."

Most of the students started to work immediately. Paul had slouched slightly in his seat; he picked up the worksheet pages and glanced at the first page with a frown on his face. He flipped through the pages, shaking his head. He glanced in the direction of his classmate on the right, and then on the left, and then sat up straight and looked at the papers again; his mouth formed a grimace of disgust, and he tossed the papers forward on the desk and slumped down in his chair.

At this point, Ms. French crooked her finger at Paul and said, "Paul, come up here—and bring your worksheet." It was clear from the tone of her voice that she was annoyed. When Paul had reached her desk, Ms. French took the paper from him, and slapping it down on her desk, began to repeat the directions in a rather forceful and exaggerated manner. As she spoke she pointed to each item with emphasis (and apparent anger). When she had finished, she pointed to the clock on the wall and said, "It is now 10:15. You must finish by 10:45." Loudly, and with obvious sarcasm, she added, "That will be when the short hand is on the 11, and the long hand is on the 9!" Rather than seem embarrassed by this, Paul followed her pointing with eagerness. Ms. French then poked Paul's arm and said, "And Paul, this is the planter [touching it]; when you finish, bring your worksheet and put it here." At this point, Paul returned to his seat and began to work.

Ms. French walked over to the table where the observer, presuming that Ms. French might be uncomfortable about the scene having been observed, was discreetly taking notes. In fact, it became evident that Ms. French felt somewhat relieved—and possibly vindicated—that there had been a witness to what was Paul's typical behavior. She leaned over, and in a much subdued voice said, "You see, if I really *give* it to him, he does it!"

It appeared to the observer that Paul was unable to process long streams of complex oral directions without directed visual clues. Further investigation indeed did disclose that his eventual understanding of the instructions was due not to the loud and rather cross manner in which they were repeated, but rather to Ms. French's speaking more slowly and with more emphasis, while pointing to each item. Paul could not tell time, and thus, Ms. French's graphic description of the position of the clock hands was a welcome clue.

Paul had a very different reputation and performance record in his Unified Studies (English and Social Science) class. The Unified Studies teacher gave assignment sheets out each week on a mini calendar with holes punched so that it could easily be placed in the students' ring binders. Each class lesson was taught with the aid of either film or filmstrip or with a demonstrated experiment. All procedures were reviewed and clarified before students were requested to work independently or in pairs. Tests were untimed and usually multiple choice or fill in the blank, and a tape cassette recording of the test was available for those with reading difficulties. Points were not subtracted for misspellings, but students were expected to locate correct spellings and demonstrate improvement after the graded tests were returned.

WHAT IS THE ROLE OF THE STUDENT IN THE ASSESSMENT?

We often neglect one of the richest resources available to a complete assessment—the student himself. We are so committed to being helpers that we sometimes fall into the trap of "doing unto," without adequate and sensitive consideration of the feelings and self-knowledge of our charge—the learning disabled teenager himself or herself.

In addition to a thorough explanation of the entire assessment and planning process to the student, we would suggest a structured interview regarding classroom learning style.

The following questions could form a questionnaire. These particular questions are directed to the teacher. When used with a student, the format should be changed so that the questions read, for instance,

1. Do you work best
    a. in quiet?
    b. with background noise?

It is very helpful to utilize all of the questions directly with the students. They feel that they are a part of the planning for their own lives, that the adult is interested in them as individuals, and that full explanations of some situations can be provided in the informal atmosphere of a conference-interview. Among other important questions that need consideration by the teacher and learning disabled student before planning a program are the following:

1. Does the student work best
    a. in quiet?
    b. with background noise?
2. If given the opportunity, how would the student choose to do independent work:
    a. in semi-seclusion?
    b. at desk in midst of group?
    c. on floor?
    d. other?
3. Does the student have problems with instructions:
    a. oral only?
    b. visual (printed on paper or chalkboard) only?
    c. oral with visual input?
    d. only with multi sentence instructions, either oral or written?
4. Does the student need material restructured to facilitate completion:
    a. shorten?
    b. isolate items on page?
    c. highlight with color or different typefaces?

    d. small segments of items given over a limited time?
    e. intermittent checkpoints?
    f. multisensory?
    g. other?

5. Does it help the student to be given multi-media aids:
    a. material on audio tape?
        (1) with headset
        (2) in conjunction with printed material
    b. individual slide or flimstrip viewers?
    c. dictaphone?
    d. Talking Book material?
    e. teaching machines, e.g., Tutorphone, System 80, etc.?
    f. calculator?
    g. other?

6. Is the student able to ask for assistance?

7. Does the student have age-appropriate material with which to work?

8. Does the student have inconspicuous and socially appropriate methods for dealing with memory problems:
    a. meaningful doodles?
    b. notes?
    c. reminder codes?
    d. finger multiplication?
    e. wallet-size spelling demon cards?
    f. wallet-size multiplication, division, decimal charts?
    g. calculator?
    h. calendar?
    i. other?

9. Do you have adequate skill level information for planning:
    a. achievement levels in math, reading, general information?
    b. writing skills?
        (1) handwriting
        (2) typing
        (3) spelling
        (4) mechanics (punctuation, capitalization)
        (5) sequencing
        (6) phrasing
        (7) paragraphs

    With the four steps of the assessment process plus the examination of the ecology, the professionals responsible for the assessment, in consultation with the student, parents, and other essential team members, should be able at this point to choose from the elements of the continuum of services (Figure 3) to form the student's program. Then the challenge begins to peak. Plans are laid. Will the program be adequate? Have the correct interventions been chosen? Are the best settings available? Are all parties resilient enough to weather the inevitable unexpected variables? Continuation around the loop will be necessary to answer such questions. Interventions must be monitored and carefully evaluated.

A careful and thorough process has been described. We have the procedures to suggest the best program; now we will move to some specific examples and suggestions for remediation and compensatory instruction.

12

A Course of Action

TEACHERS AT THE SECONDARY LEVEL often recognize that their preparation has not equipped them to work with youth with learning disabilities. "What do I do?" is the often-heard refrain from thoughtful teachers who wish to do the right thing for their students. It would be unusual for a teacher not to be confused in the presence of a student who on the one hand appears sophisticated and who has good handwriting skills, but whose written work, on the other hand, reveals reversals, gross phonetic spelling, faulty punctuation, and sentiments of antagonism to the task (Figure 8). However, in the single "sentence" illustrated in Figure 8 there are to be observed the elements of learning disability which can guide a total program of intervention. Since most intervention techniques are emphasized only with elementary educators, it is to be expected that secondary school personnel may be confused when facing students who have some of the most complicated of all learning difficulties.

Although we might have joined the handwringers in saying, "We can't do anything because no one knows what to do," we found ourselves faced with a different dilemma: how to reduce the scope of these last chapters to realistic limits. Rather than indulging in a smorgasboard approach or treading into unknown territory, we have chosen our areas of concentration by examining the list of most common and confronting school problems of the learning disabled adolescent and culling out those items which match our expertise—and our biases. These decisions will necessitate the further search by educators into other important areas which are only briefly touched here: career exploration, vocational training, handwriting, social skills, effective oral communication, and college survival skills. Our focus here and in Chapter 13 will be on problems of reading, organization, study skills, and written language.

We include this discussion as an example of the manner in which

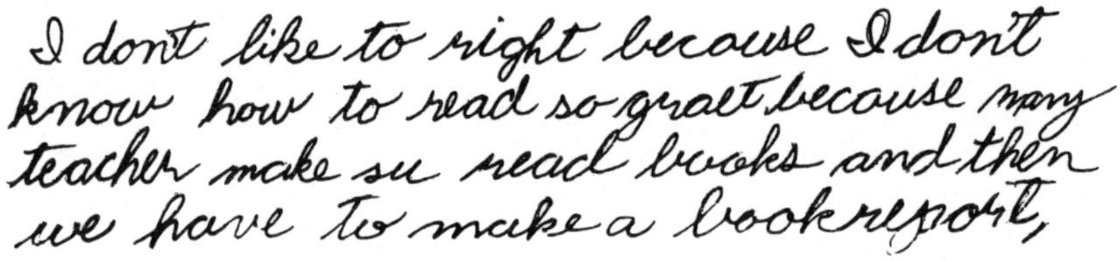

I don't like to right because I don't know how to read so great because many teacher make su read books and then we have to make a book report,

FIGURE 8 A three-time eighth grade repeater and her writing

secondary educators must muster their efforts to meet the needs of learning disabled students. We stress that this is a single example of the care with which all teaching and learning must be approached. While we shall focus here on reading, similar specific steps must be taken with mathematics, social science, and all else which the learning disabled student attempts in the junior and senior high school years. Even those who recognize the need for precise organization of school skill training often neglect the need for similar care in social skills and vocational planning.

TWO ESSENTIAL COMPONENTS

We have found two underlying principles to be of great value in developing remediation for learning disabled students.

1. *Task breakdown.* We are not speaking here of task analysis, which usually describes the requirements of a task, although analyzing the task may be an important step. While this ordering or reordering of tasks must be done initially by the teacher, the goal should be the assumption of this skill and responsibility by the student. The student eventually should be able to say, "Now, let's see. The first thing I do is—, and then I will—" and so on to task completion in a stepwise progression.

2. *Multisensory input.* Although a few adolescent learning disabled students seem overwhelmed by stimuli, and may need to receive information, not only in small units, but with as little stimulation as possible, *most* learning disabled students by the time they are in secondary school are at a disadvantage when instruction is of a single modality input, i.e., auditory only (lecture) or visual only (silently read direction or a captioned silent filmstrip). It seems essential for these students to have at

least a paired-modality input with themselves assuming as active a role as possible, e.g., following the print while listening to a taped or oral reading of the material, being allowed to vocalize (whisper, mumble or speak) one's own reading of print, or having the instructor point to pictures or diagrams while verbally describing the activities or experiments being studied.

It should be helpful to keep these two important components in mind for the most effective utilization of the suggestions which follow.

READING OR NON-READING:
A SOMEWHAT DIFFERENT PROBLEM AT THE SECONDARY LEVEL

Students who enter the junior high school, and those who move on to high school with minimal reading skills, need to have this problem examined within a new context. When students have failed to learn to read by grade three, we do not deliberate over whether their problems should or should not be remedied. We are not always successful; nevertheless, we automatically *attempt* to teach the young student to read.

It is our bias that we should *continue* to try to teach any young person who wishes to learn to read (see Chapter 13); however, priorities must be re-examined for teenagers and young adults, and questions must be asked.

How well does the person read now?

How old is the student?

How much school time is left?

Does the young person have the strong desire and emotional resource left to struggle with the problem?

What differences will it make?

What are the student's vocational or further study goals?

What does the person *need* to be able to read?

Is there a promising approach significantly different from those previously tried?

It is a sobering experience to confront ourselves and the student entering grade nine possessing a grade two reading level, with the information that, if he or she continues to gain reading skills at the past rate, a grade three level will be achieved by graduation; if the rate of skill acquisition is *quadrupled,* he or she will leave school with a grade six reading level after grade twelve. This highlights the fact that perfunctory practice can easily replace serious efforts with the expectancy of actually learning. Whatever is done must take into account the motivational state, the available energy of the youth to keep working on a problem, in short the hope. In the following pages, there is the weaving together of method and motivational conditions.

The Method of Choice

If after a thorough examination of the issues and questions, after the student and teacher decide to pursue reading remediation, it will be necessary to choose a method of instruction. At this point the assessment information discussed in Chapter 11 will prove valuable. A review of the information collected in Stage I (see Figure 6) will reveal which programs and techniques have been tried in the past. *Efforts should be made to avoid trials of methods and materials known to have been ineffective.* Performance on reading tests and probes in Stages II through III (Figure 6) should give clues to the *nature* of the student's reading disability.

Although not infallible, we have found samples of written spelling, either from original writing or dictation, to be reliable guides to methods of choice in reading instruction, and we typically include collection of these samples during our assessment of adolescents with reading problems.

THREE ERROR PATTERNS

Sometimes the clinical problem per se indicates the method which may prove beneficial to the learner. Boder (1971), for example, identifies three groups of poor readers by analysis of spelling patterns. Her *dysphonetic* group corresponds to the category called auditory dyslexics by Johnson and Myklebust (1967). Students in this group tends to demonstrate bizarre spellings except for those words in their sight vocabulary (Figure 9). These students seem to have primary deficits in auditory processing and (in spite of those who believe that Johnny can't read) do not respond to

strong	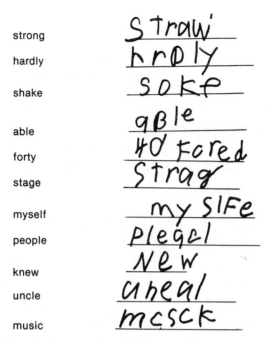
hardly	
shake	
able	
forty	
stage	
myself	
people	
knew	
uncle	
music	

FIGURE 9 Spelling of a dysphonetic youth (auditory dyslexia)

phonics training as a primary teaching mode. They need a whole-word approach until they have a well-established reading vocabulary.

The second group Boder cites is the *dyseidetic* group. The readers of this group differ from the auditory dyslexics in that they spell correctly *only* those words which are phonetically consistent (Figure 10), and many of their spelled words are easily identified even though the spellings are incorrect. Johnson and Myklebust identify this group as visual dyslexics, and they recommend reading instruction which emphasizes phonetic training. We would agree that the members of this group, if taught very systematically through a highly structured phonetic approach, can make impressive progress.

Boder mentions a third group which reflects characteristics of both the former two groups. These readers (far more often non-readers) with *mixed dyslexia* tend to have difficulties resistant to most typical remedial techniques, and often remain non-readers throughout adult life. Boder would recommend multisensory approaches for this group.

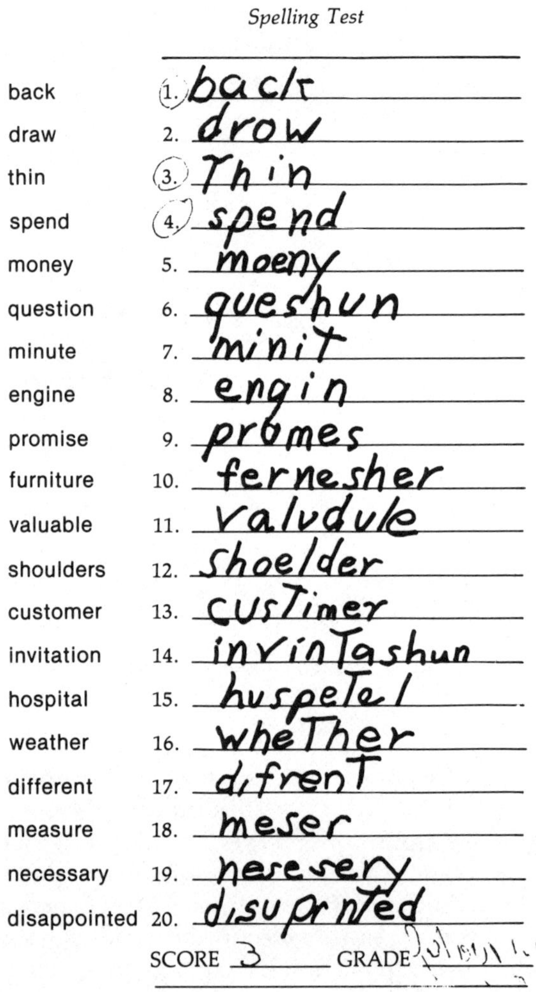

Spelling Test

back	1. *back*
draw	2. *drow*
thin	3. *Thin*
spend	4. *spend*
money	5. *moeny*
question	6. *queshun*
minute	7. *minit*
engine	8. *engin*
promise	9. *promes*
furniture	10. *fernesher*
valuable	11. *valvdule*
shoulders	12. *shoelder*
customer	13. *cusTimer*
invitation	14. *invinTashun*
hospital	15. *huspeTel*
weather	16. *wheTher*
different	17. *difrenT*
measure	18. *meser*
necessary	19. *nesesery*
disappointed	20. *disuprnTed*

SCORE 3 _____ GRADE _____

FIGURE 10 Spelling from dictation of a dyseidetic boy aged 16-6

AN IMPORTANT VARIABLE DICTATING OUR METHOD OF CHOICE

We would encourage the use of the above categories to aid in the selection of the most appropriate method of instruction. We have been particularly impressed by the success of users with the alphabetic-phonetic approach of Gillingham and Stillman with the dyseidetic group members. However, considering some of the questions we recommended asking when we began this discussion, what about the students who are simply fed up with remediation and are so discouraged that nothing short of a miracle will work? We think that these students may be in the majority of the severely reading disabled group found in the secondary schools.

Do we have a miracle? Almost. It is our firm conviction that the work of Grace Fernald in the 1920s through the 1940s has not been improved upon as a method of choice for discouraged disabled readers. One of the most important qualities of this method is that the teenager gets instant success. The method begins with the use of finger-tracing a word volunteered by the student himself and written by the instructor. After tracing the word as many times as necessary and saying the word as a whole while tracing, the model is removed and the student writes the word from memory. Getting the older student to try this may be difficult, because the tracing seems so childish. Our experience indicates the technique is so powerful that if one can get the young person over his initial embarrassment, he or she will be so impressed by the success that a major battle will be won. The actual method proceeds with a language experience approach, requiring much verbal exchange and demanding much individual assistance from the instructor. We feel the successes dictate that it is a worthwhile expenditure of professional time.

One of the authors was demonstrating this method to a group of teachers and was using a small group of secondary level students as volunteers in the demonstration. One student was a very big 13 year-old boy. He was sad looking and very obese. There was little in his appearance about which one could make positive comments. When asked if there was a word any of the students wished they could spell, he immediately raised his hand. "OK, what's the word?" said the teacher/demonstrator. An absolutely unintelligible response was given which, after two or three attempts, finally caused the demonstrating teacher to ask for help. The boy's regular teacher in the audience stated that the pupil was asking to learn his own last name! "What is it?" "SCHENKLENBERGER," responded the teacher. The moment of truth was at hand!

The youth began finger tracing over the word written on the blackboard: verbal support accompanied tracing; more tracing; more verbalization, etc.,—then erasure. The model was removed and the youth was asked to spell his name on the blackboard. A deathly silence pervaded the room as the teachers watched fifteen letters accurately appear in front of the boy.

As the boy was congratulated for a genuinely successful performance, some tears trickled down his face. "It's the first time he's ever done that," said his teacher who came up to congratulate the youth. "But not the last," said the young man. What indeed is the self-concept of a 13-year-old boy who, because of the length of his name, cannot spell the one thing which gives him identity? The instructional effort may have to be replicated before complete recall is automatic, but motivation to learn reduces the repetitive nature of instruction when success experiences are present.

The reader is encouraged to refer to Fernald's original work, *Remedial Techniques in Basic School Subjects* (1943), for a complete understanding of the method, as well as inspirational case studies. For easy reference, we include here a discussion and outline of the method which has proven to be a useful guide for the many instructors who swear by this approach. First, we believe that teachers can use a method which has proven to be a successful guide for many others. Second, the Fernald method highlights the task breakdown approach which must accompany all instruction for the learning disabled pupil—the challenge to secondary educators.

LEARNING DISABILITIES AND THE FERNALD METHOD OF READING INSTRUCTION

We have emphasized a multisensory approach to teaching pupils with learning disabilities. In selecting reading as our first example of how the secondary school can respond to this group of students, we have emphasized that the Fernald Method is our method of choice for those who are discouraged learners. Such is not to say that other methods have little value. If a method of teaching can be shown to match the specific learning disabilities of the pupil, it should be tried. This is the essence of the *psychoeducational match* described elsewhere (Cruickshank 1977).

There are six quite distinct steps to all reading instruction in the Fernald Method.

1. Trial or Initial Step (Step 1)

The first step in the complicated art of teaching reading, the initial sessions with the pupil, is in itself composed of three distinct parts.

First, tell the student we have a "new" way of learning words which we want him or her to try. As we explain the new approach, we often indicate that the method was actually developed more than forty years ago by a psychologist at UCLA who worked with children and youth who were intelligent, but had very serious reading problems.

Second, explain that we are not quite sure why the method works, but that it has been very successfully used with junior high and high school students as well as with young adults with severe reading disabilities. This explanation often wards off the repulsion to the *tracing*, which may seem babyish to many teenagers. It also indicates to the student that the teacher does not consider himself or herself to be omnipotent, but is entering the learning-teaching situation as a participant and guide.

Third, let the student select any word he or she wants to learn, regardless of length, and teach it to the student by the multisensory method suggested above. It is often good to teach three or four words in this initial session. The student will probably be surprised at retention of these words in subsequent sessions. Confidence, motivation, and the feeling of joint enterprise between the learner and the teacher are the keystone concepts and objectives of this initial session or set of sessions.

2. The Story (Step 2)

As soon as possible isolated words should be integrated into stories or other forms of reading words in a logical and consecutive order. Reading is more than learning to write individual words as in Step 1. It is important that soon the learner achieve concepts of sequence among words, progression of ideas, and logical outcomes to what is being read. We start with those things which are known to the young person and which have a high interest for the student even though they may not have the same values to the teacher: cars, girls, jobs, sports, for some boys; boys, clothes, sports, marriage, for some girls we have known and with whom we have worked.

The student ultimately should be encouraged to write from his or her own experiences. Before this can be done, however, the instructor may need to discuss many points with the student, and try to locate specific interests and activities about which the student would enjoy writing or conditions where being able to write, even at a minimal level, will make life easier. As soon as these have been located, the story should be developed making a one-point outline (list) first and later blocking in the story. Some students will be able to write their own stories as words are provided. For others, the story should be taken down by the teacher and then read back to the student for corrections and additions as the student feels they need to be added. When this is done, the story is dictated to the student and the words needed to be learned are taught by using the appropriate aspects of the method, that is, Steps 1, 2, or 3. These two preliminary steps successfully completed will provide the teacher with the information needed to determine in what depth Steps 3, 4, 5, and 6 will need to be pursued.

3. Words into Stories (Step 3)

As the student moves into Step 3, while the teacher's role is still dominant, the pupil begins to assume some minor self-direction. Table 1 includes sixteen sub-steps which at most must be followed in detail; at the least, they contain very important check points of which the teacher must be constantly aware. Table 1 can serve as a good guide to the teacher who seeks to follow the Fernald Method.

Items A through D of Table 1 are very basic. Here the student asks for a word and the teacher ascertains that the student understands the meaning of the word and that syllabification and pronounciation are correct.

Following this the teacher writes the word on a large piece of paper (Item E Table 1). Here again, a specific set of steps are to be followed by the teacher:

1. The teacher says the word syllable by syllable while writing it.

2. The teacher is careful not to distort the sound of the word.

3. The teacher determines that the student carefully watches the writing as it is done.

4. The teacher holds the paper so that the student can see it easily.

5. The teacher underlines each syllable after finishing it.

Item E is a teacher activity. The student is more than a passive observer, however, and maintains the role of carefully watching what the teacher does.

At this point (Item F) the student pronounces the word, and then

TABLE 1
Step 3: Teacher Responsibility Predominant

Item	Activity
A	The student needs a word and asks for it.
B	The teacher checks to see if the student knows the meaning of the word and if it is in his or her vocabulary.
C	The teacher consults the dictionary for correct pronunciation and syllabification, if necessary.
D	The teacher pronounces the word for the child and confirms that the student has the correct pronunciation.
E	The teacher writes the word for the student with crayola or marker on a large (3″ x 10″) paper.
F	The student pronounces the word, then starts to trace.
G	The stimulus is removed and the student writes the word on scrap paper saying it syllable by syllable as he or she writes it.
H	The student now writes the word in his or her story, saying it while writing.
I	When the story is completed the student reads it to the teacher.
J	The story is typed within 24 hours for the student.
K	The following day the student is given the typed copy of the story.
L	The words learned are reviewed in isolation; any missing are re-taught.
M	The student then files the words learned in file box.
N	The student is motivated to write another experience.
O	The student asks for a word.
P	The student checks his or her word file to see if the word is there.

Those familiar with the Fernald Method will observe that our *Steps* 3–6, inclusive, are comparable to Fernald's *Stages* 1–4, inclusive. We have chosen the term "Step" (a) to prevent confusion with an earlier chapter in this book, and (b) to unify two preliminary phases (*The Trial* and *The Story*) into a total six-step sequence.

begins to trace and pronounce the word repetitively as is necessary. Again a carefully developed procedure is to be followed:

1. Student starts to say the words syllable by syllable as he or she starts to trace.

2. The student traces with either or both the index and second finger.

3. The student's syllable pronunciation and tracing are kept together.

4. The student does not distort the sound of the word.

5. The teacher checks to see that the student carefully follows the contour of each letter.

6. The student pronounces the word in full after it has been traced.

7. The student continues to trace until he or she feels sure that he or she has learned the word.

It is perfectly obvious to the reader by now that this is an adult-dominated procedure. It is such, because no longer can one afford to permit the learner to make mistakes or to proceed too rapidly into areas of learning for which the learner is unprepared. Permissiveness has no role with the learning disabled pupil until accurate learning has taken place. Permissiveness requires choice. Individuals who have experienced a lifetime of failure operate from a trial and error base, and this is likely to produce more failures. As controlled teaching and learning takes place, and as success experiences accrue, choice becomes possible and more and more permissive self-direction can be handled by the student.

With Item G (Table 1) the stimulus is removed and the student should be ready to write what he has traced. If he cannot, a repeat of earlier steps is required. Now the teacher (1) watches carefully for errors; (2) stops the student at the first sign of an error; (3) returns him to tracing again if necessary; and (4) then when successful compares the student's word with the teacher's written word. A success experience has taken place, and it is time for positive reinforcement and encouragement by the adult.

The student now writes the word, saying it while writing (Table 1:H), and then when the story is finally completed he reads it back to the teacher (Table 1:I). At this point the teacher (1) checks on all of the learned words, (2) notes any words which are missed which were not called for in the writing, and (3) teaches these and any additional words which were spelled incorrectly. Insofar as spelling is concerned, a correct product is finalized. The story is now typed (Table 1:J) for the student. All punctuation mistakes are corrected, by the teacher or aide, and the learned words are underlined. Syntax is corrected by the teacher, because at this point the emphasis is on reading and spelling, not on grammar.

As is indicated in Table 1:K, the typed copy is returned to the student the next day, and the following substeps are observed:

1. The student reads the story silently.

2. The student is asked to note any mistakes that he may have missed.

3. The student reads the story to the teacher.

4. The teacher checks on all mistakes.

5. If there are mistakes on words previously learned, the teacher teaches them.

6. If words are missed that were not missed the previous day, these are taught.

If all has gone well to this point and if motivation and encouragement has taken place as a consequence of actual accomplishment rather than the typical "try-and-you-can-do-it" approach, the student will usually be addressing the task in a wholesome and positive manner. Sufficient success experiences will have come his way to make him feel that the activities of tracing, responding, and tracing are indeed important activities. We should like to point out that in these early stages, the teacher needs to recognize the mental health of the adolescent. It is best to begin the developmental process in a room where privacy can be insured, and where the learning disabled adolescent will not become the brunt of teasing by his peers if they observe the elementary nature of the activities in which their friend is involved.

Items L through P in Table 1 are self-explanatory. It should be emphasized with Item P that if, after the student asks for a word (Item O) it is found in his file, he relearns it, for obviously it has not yet become thoroughly integrated into his usable set of reading tools. If the word is not there, the teacher teaches using the steps outlined in this section, starting at the beginning.

4. Transition from Teacher to Student (Step 4)

Table 2 contains a list of the major considerations which the teacher must keep in mind as the developmental program continues into the next phase, the beginning of repetitive student successes. Step 4 is almost identical to Step 3, except that tracing is no longer a necessity. When the student moves from Step 3 to Step 4 there is a period of transition, forward and sometimes backward. There is a period of uncertainty. Conditioning has not been completed as yet. The student will usually know when it is still necessary to use the tracing. Dale, age 17 years and severely handicapped in the reading skills, laughingly once said to one of us, "I've

TABLE 2
Step 4: Transition from Teacher to Student

Item	Activity
A	Student asks for a word.
B	Teacher checks the dictionary for correct pronunciation and syllabification if necessary.
C	The teacher checks to be sure that the student knows the meaning of the word and that it is in the student's vocabulary.
D	The teacher pronounces the word for the student.
E	The teacher writes the word for the student.
F	The student looks at the word and says it to himself, but does not spell it.
G	The student studies the word until he or she is sure that he or she knows it.
H	The stimulus is removed and the student writes the word.
I–P	These activities are the same as noted in Table 1.

got callouses on my fingers from that damned tracing, but I guess we'll keep it up for a while longer. It works." The motivated student usually knows when the crutch is still needed, and in his own way acknowledges that need. It cannot be said that there is any particular place where Step 3 stops and Step 4 begins. It is a process of gradual change and development.

If the reader examines Table 2, using it as before as a guide, it will be observed that Items A, B, and C are identical to those found in Step 3. With respect to Item D, the teacher pronounces the word for the student. At this point the student pronounces the word after the teacher while the teacher carefully checks the pronunciation. The aural reinforcement by both teacher and student is essential. Items E through G again are similar to those in Step 3, and they serve as important reinforcers to the learning which is taking place.

With Item H, the role of the student becomes more aggressive in the learning process. The stimulus is removed, and as previously the student writes the word. Now important roles are changed between teacher and student:

1. The *student* says the word as he or she writes it syllable by syllable.

2. The teacher carefully watches for error.

3. If the *student* starts to make an error, the student is stopped at once.

4. If the *student* makes an error, the student again is shown the stimulus, the teacher pronounces the word again for the student, and the student repeats it.

5. The *student* studies the word as before till the student feels secure.

6. The *student* again writes the word as before.

7. When the word is written correctly it is compared by the *student* to the stimulus.

8. The *student* writes the word a second time without the stimulus.

9. The *student* writes the word in his or her story.

On one occasion a learning disabled student, Terry, was working alone writing his words into his story (Step 4, Item H). The room was quiet, and the teacher had left him momentarily to assist another youth on the far side of the room. All of a sudden it became apparent to Terry what he was doing and could do independently. Spontaneously and without thought or awareness of where he was, he blurted out, "My god! I'm writing and reading!" When the other students got over their shock of the outcry, they with their teacher applauded quite genuinely. What better motivation can one ask for?

5-6. Reaching for Independence (Steps 5-6)

Steps 5 and 6 are essentially contained in Tables 3 and 4 to which the teacher is now directed. In Step 5 the student is able to learn from the printed word; the teacher no longer writes the words. Tracing and verbalization to support tracing are no longer a part of the routing, except in unusual circumstances.

The basis of the Fernald Method, and one recognized by the authors as significant to all learning, is the concept of conditioning. If the reader will carefully consider the steps and the items contained within each, it will easily be seen that the method is based on a stimulus, verbal repetition, response (writing word), and a positive reinforcement coming from the ego satisfaction of actually learning. Success is essential or there can be no positive reinforcement. Total repetition of the process when it

TABLE 3
Step 5: Student Reads the Printed Word

Item	Activity
A	The student meets the unknown word in a reading situation.
B	The teacher tells the student the word.
C	The student repeats the pronunciation after the teacher.
D	The teacher makes note of the word in her record.
E	At the end of the reading the teacher teaches the word missed.
F	The student looks at the word in print.
G	The teacher pronounces the word for the student after checking the dictionary for correct syllabification.
H	The student repeats the pronunciation.
I	The student studies the word till the student feels he or she knows it.
J	The student writes the word on 3 x 5 card.
K	The teacher checks for error and stops student at once if error is made.
L	The written word is compared to the printed word.
M	The word is written correctly twice.
N	The words are reviewed at the end of the lesson.
O	The words are reviewed again in 24 hours.
P	The student files the word in file box.

is not successfully accomplished is absolutely necessary. Learning which with the normal child appears almost incidental to growth is for the child or youth with learning disabilities a step-by-step process of conditioning. It is the same process that the normal child goes through, but with the latter, conditioning and thus learning is not disturbed by perceptual processing deficits, neurophysiological dysfunction, or by the various sensorimotor problems. It is thus a process without major trauma in contradistinction to the often observed struggles of the child with learning disabilities.

Table 3 contains a list of steps which, if followed carefully by the teacher and learner, provide a matrix through which the student progresses from "the unknown word" (Item A) to high-level comparison of the written and printed word (Item L).

Table 4 continues this process, moving from words to words in

TABLE 4
Step 6: Student Moves toward Independence

Item	Activity
A	The student glances through a paragraph; notes all the words he or she does not know, sounds these out, and reads the paragraph.
B	The student asks for any word he or she does not know to get the meaning of what he or she is reading.
C	The student is told the word, repeats it, and goes on.
D	The teacher records the word for later reference if it is comon to the student's everyday language.
E	The student is never made to sound the word when he or she is reading, nor is it sounded out for the student by the teacher.
F	At this stage it is important the student be given sufficient help to make the reading fast enough and easy enough so that the mechanics involved in the process of word comprehension shall not distract the student's attention from the content of what he or she is reading.
G	At the end of the lesson the teacher teaches missed words; using VAK (visual, auditory, kinesthetic) or VAKT (visual, auditory, kinesthetic, tactile), if necessary.
H	All words are reviewed at the end of the teaching period.
I	All words are reviewed 24 hours later and on further delayed recall.
J	The student reads as much as he or she wants to about anything that is of interest to him or her.
K	Material should be such that the student will continue to read to find out what he or she wants to know.
L	The amount of training depends upon the educational age the student must reach.
M	The student should have sufficient reading to make it possible for him or her to recognize new words.
N	The student should have established an adequate reading vocabulary.
O	The student's concept development allows him or her to read and perceive word groups as such.

sentences and paragraphs (Item A), to relatively independent reading (Item J) and ultimately to a relatively sophisticated stage of reading fluency (Item O).

We wrote earlier that the Fernald Method was powerful. Experience has demonstrated its functional worth. We are not suggesting that all learning disabled students will develop into outstanding readers. Some will; others will be able to deal with college and high school reading requirements with reasonable speed and comfort. Still others will achieve lesser levels of competence commensurate with their inate mental ability, motivation, and freedom from serious emotional or other physical disabilities.

There is at least one way in which a learning disabled adolescent can be assisted to participate more fully in the academic life of his school. Reading and writing probably are the most important skills for any person to possess. As such instruction in these areas constitutes a major responsibility, not only of the clinical teaching specialists and teachers of English, but for teachers of social science, driver education, vocational arts, and all other subject areas of the secondary school.

13

A Secondary School Dilemma

In AN EARLIER SECTION OF THIS BOOK the question was posed: "Is there life after high school?" Any volume on adolescents who have learning disabilities must concern itself with the post-school years and into young adulthood. These youths do not cease to live or to struggle as they approach eighteen years of age. We have already seen that Scott has made a successful adult adjustment, and that three of the four other young men in Part II of this book have made their ways with varying degrees of success. No one of these individuals, however, had sufficient intellectual capacity to attend college or to move into the professions. This is a different problem. There are youths with learning disabilities who are capable of attending college, and this places an added burden on the high school (and on the college or university when such an applicant appears). One must look carefully at the high school curriculum as well as at the needs of the post-school demands on those with learning disabilities in order to ascertain the modifications or adaptations which the schools must make for these college-bound young people.

Without question, reading and writing are the most primary skills required of anyone, whether in elementary or secondary school, in higher education, or in after-school years. Reading and writing are also most often of greatest difficulty for learning disabled adolescents. In this chapter we shall examine this issue in the light of two young men who first made our acquaintance when they were in their early twenties—still struggling to reach a satisfactory adulthood.

Students who cannot read obviously do not engage in writing activities—other than copying. Often, so much concentration is invested in reading instruction for disabled readers that writing is all but ignored. It is not surprising that even those reading-disabled students who eventually develop some facility in reading often achieve only primary levels of written expression.

Since the 1950s, elementary school curricula have been so dominated by ditto sheets and fill-in-the-blank workbooks that deficits in writing skills have not been especially noticeable or disturbing. In recent years the universities' cries of indignation over the poverty of written expression demonstrated by incoming students have sparked some response from the secondary schools (whose personnel, of course, demand that the blame for their graduates' failure in writing be shared with their elementary school colleagues who passed the student on without the "basics"). At any rate, with keen awareness that there is widespread mediocrity (at least) of written performance, elementary and secondary school educators do seem to be raising their expectations and increasing demands for original written work. While this is an important and positive revision, it makes exposure of especially serious writing deficiencies of learning disabled students a certainty. Whereas the typical student will probably develop reasonable skill in expressive writing by the move back to more frequent demand and systematic group instruction, we suspect that there will be learning disabled students whose writing will be noticeably discrepant even after exposure and treatment.

SPELLING DIFFICULTIES

We are faced then, with a problem which has confounded special educators, and has, for lack of any obvious solution, been for the most part ignored. Disturbances of written language are complex and resistant to treatment. Probably the least complicated of the difficulties, although not easy to remediate, is an isolated spelling disability. Poor spelling may, in fact, be the least common denominator of learning disabilities. It seems that even in cases where all other symptoms or disturbances in learning disappear, extremely poor spelling often remains. It is not uncommon to find adults with dreadful spelling who will admit that they had other learning difficulties in early school years. We have observed students whose reading skills are adequate, but whose spelling is so poor that they are almost paralyzed by a written assignment.

Good, and especially "natural" spellers (those who *never* make an error and seem to know the spelling of almost any word familiar or unfamiliar) are often baffled and even annoyed by poor spellers; we know good spellers who seem to equate spelling skill with IQ. These skillful spellers who rarely need to consult a dictionary are quick to query, "Why don't you look it up?" And how surprised they seem when the poor speller responds, "How can I look it up when I don't know how to spell it?" or "I didn't look it up because I didn't know I had misspelled it!"

The spelling from dictation of a 13-year-old boy with a history of learning disabilities (Figure 11) provided some explanation for poor per-

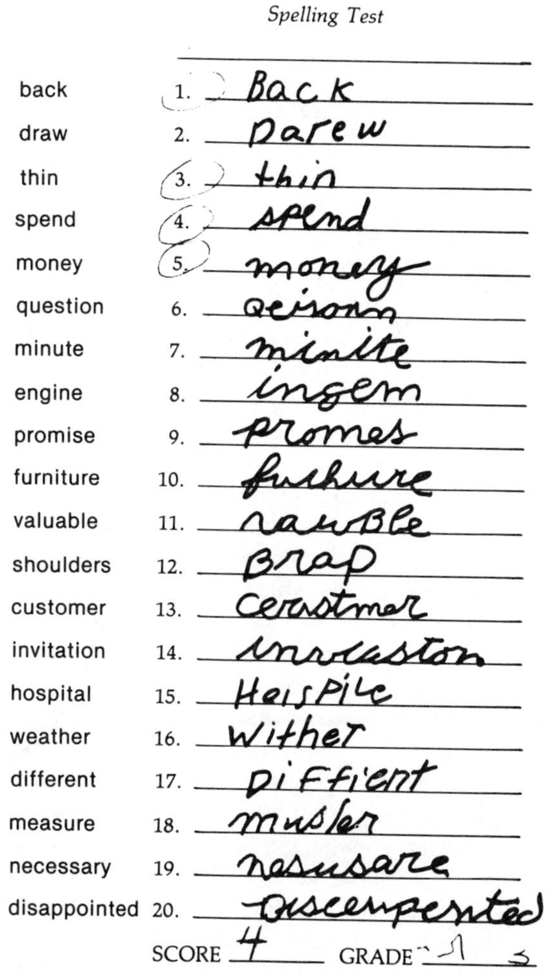

Spelling Test

back	1.	*Back*
draw	2.	*Darew*
thin	3.	*thin*
spend	4.	*spend*
money	5.	*money*
question	6.	*aeironn*
minute	7.	*minite*
engine	8.	*ingem*
promise	9.	*promes*
furniture	10.	*furhure*
valuable	11.	*nawBle*
shoulders	12.	*Brap*
customer	13.	*Cerastmer*
invitation	14.	*inrlaston*
hospital	15.	*HeisPile*
weather	16.	*Wither*
different	17.	*Diffient*
measure	18.	*musler*
necessary	19.	*nasusare*
disappointed	20.	*asceuperted*

SCORE __4__   GRADE __1__

FIGURE 11 Spelling from dictation of a 13-year-old seventh grade boy

formance in school. This student was thought to have been almost "cured" of his learning problems. A nonreader until fifth grade, he was by seventh grade reading on a high fifth grade level and was expected to function in regular classes with minimal support from the teacher-consultant. This young man, however, was failing every subject except mathematics. The most obvious aspect of his school behavior was his lack of production. He rarely handed in daily assignments and had never produced a major assignment. When asked directly what he thought was the matter, he responded consistently, "I don't know." When he was asked if he *could* complete reports, he answered, "probably, if I put my mind to it." This answer seemed parrotted, and so some probing was attempted. Even though his spelling subtest score on the *California Achievement Test* was a grade equivalent of 7.7 which correlated exactly with his grade placement, a *dictated test* of spelling was given. An examination of his performance in Figure 12 should leave us without surprise that he does not write! The fact that this student could perform well on a multiple-choice spelling test such as found in the *California Achievement Test* indicates that he was able to *recognize* correctly spelled words but not to *recall* the visual image necessary for spontaneous written language.

Students who spell in a similar fashion often say, "I spell phonetically." They do indeed put down sets of letters which *might* represent the sounds, e.g., invita*shun*, min*it*, *codet* for *couldn't*. These students usually do not have difficulty with phonetically consistent words, such as *thin, men, fat*. They are confounded by diphthongs, diagraphs, and the host of irregularities in English spelling. By middle school years the spelling vocabularies of the typical student are full of words containing these irregularities. But it is not only words such as *ghosts, corps, biscuit,* and *siege* that cannot be retrieved by the student with poor revisualization; his better auditory perception and memory leave him baffled by endings of *middle, nickel, approval, grateful,* and *until*—words which flow automatically from the pens of most high school students.

Spelling demands more of the person than revisualization. One must also have the ability to discriminate, recall, and sequence sounds, and finally to transfer these sounds to their appropriate symbol representatives through a motor output (writing or typing) without losing the proper order. There are a few students who are able to spell orally, but are unable to write those same words without error. Unfortunately, oral spelling is as useless a skill as "multiple choice spelling" (such as found in those who do well *only* on achievement test).

Learning disabled students who have poor auditory skills, but

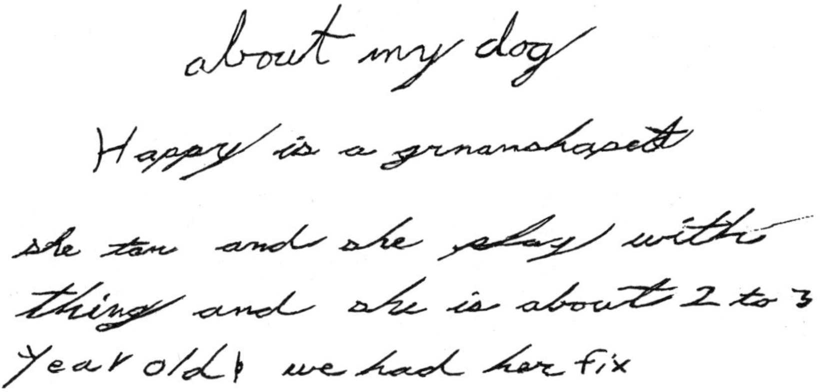

FIGURE 12 Written language of 14-year-old boy with verbal IQ 102
and performance IQ 126

some visual memory and visual organization ability, tend to leave off
endings, omit vowels or whole syllables, and produce bizarre spellings of
unfamiliar words. An example of this type of difficulty is to be seen in the
writing of a 14-year-old student with severe auditory processing disability (Figure 12). This intelligent boy was unable to recall more than three
digits in correct sequence and could not verbally reconstruct words as familiar as *examination* or *hospital* when they were spoken to him syllable
by syllable as in *ex-am-in-a-tion.* He was able to spell correctly many of
the base words in his reading vocabulary, but his spelling of seldom-seen
words was so peculiar that his "translations" left most readers as surprised
as the reader may be to know that "Happy" is a *German Shepherd* (Figure
12) dog.

SO WHAT? WHO CARES?

Should we worry about the spelling of adolescents with learning disabilities? Is it really an important area for investment of time and effort of
either secondary school teachers or the students?

Like all other questions regarding the remediation of learning
problems in adolescents, these questions must be answered by considering the particulars of an individual student's situation: the age of the stu-

dent, the academic goals, other disabilities and strengths, probable career choices. For Jim, who is discussed later in this chapter, spelling and reading assumed extreme significance only as he became an adult and was employed.

Most people care, even though we occasionally hear such statements as "As long as you can read it, it doesn't matter about the spelling." The father of a learning disabled girl with whom we worked astonished his daughter and her tutor by pulling a very worn, folded piece of paper from his wallet and explaining that he never returned to his job of seven years after he overheard his fellow workers howling about a note he had left his partner, "Ur dtr called she cant pick up the car in garje."

What Should Be Done?

1. *Spelling should be taught in the most natural manner, that is, through the vocabulary of the student, not by arbitrary lists.* This will require individual instruction so that the student may have words provided as he or she needs them. The Fernald Method, which utilizes language experience stories, provides an excellent format for this type of spelling instruction (see Chapter 12). Another procedure is to generate the spelling words through assigned writing activities from the student's content area courses; thus, a book report or an essay assigned to a student could serve as the vehicle for spelling instruction.

2. *Instruction should be geared to the particular type of spelling disability observed.* Students whose words are recognizable because they use gross phonics (Figure 11) will usually respond to a highly structured phonetic or alphabetic phonetic remedial approach such as the Gillingham-Stillman method (1965). Students with poor auditory skills will be frustrated by such an approach, but they are likely to be responsive to a whole-word multisensory approach like the Fernald technique. Clinical diagnosis and assessment of need must characterize the secondary school instructional program, and clinical teaching which complements the observed need is always in order.

3. *There is a two-dollar "commercial" guide available.* After years of attempting to structure high-quality individual programs of spelling intervention, we were amazed to discover that inside the covers of a book which had lain on our bookshelf for the same number of years was all that we had done and more! If we could make only one suggestion which might be suitable for *all* persons who suffer from miserable spelling

problems, we would recommend the revised version (1976) of Harry Shefter's book, *Six Minutes a Day to Perfect Spelling.*

Other Problems of Written Language

Learning disabled students often sit through years of typical instruction and even learn to read well without assuming the basic rudiments of punctuation and such organization aspects of writing as sentences and paragraphs.

Just as younger learning disabled children must be carefully instructed in buttoning, handwriting, cutting, and other skills which children usually pick up by exposure and infrequent demonstration, older learning disabled students with symbolic disorders will need to be taught aspects of writing such as insertion of commas, periods, quotation marks, and parentheses in a similar highly structured manner.

We have already committed ourselves to *not* reinventing the wheel, and our appraisal of available texts and articles supports our bias that the work of Myklebust (1965) and Johnson and Myklebust (1967) represents the best guides to theories and educational procedures for disorders of written language.

AN EXAMPLE OF A DISORDER OF WRITTEN LANGUAGE

One of the most baffling of learning disabilities and most perplexing to secondary school educators is the disorder of syntax and formulation. The writing of students with disorders of syntax and formulation often contains errors of tense and punctuation and word omission. Because the disorder usually occurs in students who are fluent in spoken language and reading, the alarm for assistance is often sounded late, if ever. This is a very typical problem and is found in many highly intelligent youths with learning disabilities. Two of the present authors have had the opportunity to admit a young man for graduate study who aims toward completing the doctorate degree. He cannot read or write. He is seriously learning disabled. He is a recent graduate of a highly respected eastern college, and has performed in an exemplary manner. At times, he has had as many as fifteen readers working for him as he struggled to maintain his daily assignments. He is not atypical, and if he joins the university student body to which he has sought admission, he will be one of several who in varying degrees represent the same type of problem as he demonstrates.

For those of us whose writing bears the usual correspondence with our spoken language, it seems unfathomable that a person who would state, "Yesterday I saw the mailman avoid our box because the snow wasn't shoveled," could actually write, "Yesterday I see the mailmen avoid a box it wasn't shovel." For a student interested in academic pursuits beyond high school, this handicap is difficult to keep hidden.

Such was the case of a 23-year-old man (whom we shall call Raymond) who referred himself to a university affiliated clinic for evaluation and assistance. His high school years were personally torturous. We include his story here at length because it so clearly highlights the dilemma experienced by content-oriented secondary school personnel and students with disorders of written communication. Raymond's graduation from college was blocked by his inability to pass an "exit examination" in written composition. Because his experiences are different from those of the young men in Part II, and also because we feel his statements regarding his disability and educational experiences have implication for other learning disabled youth and their educators, we share a portion of a verbatim transcription of the assessment interview with Raymond. At 23 years of age, Raymond has completed his fourth year in two liberal arts colleges, having failed two years during elementary school. As one reads this dialogue, it is important to ask the question, "where does the fault lie?" Is Raymond's problem that of the college, or does the social promotion policy of the secondary school have to assume a major portion of the blame for Raymond's plight? Is there any evidence of clinical teaching provided in either the secondary or the elementary schools which Raymond attended? The reader must be reminded that Raymond is a self-referral to a clinic, in contradistinction to the young men whose interviews are carried in Part II.

The clinician states, "Raymond, in terms of this writing problem you say you have had for so long, what about the identification of it—or intervention and remediation of it. Did you have any assistance?"

"When I was younger I went for, to the Red Cross for speech pattern lessons (articulation therapy), and I don't recall very much about it, but that's about all."

"That's all?" asks the clinician. "What happened when you had this problem all through school? Was nothing ever done about it?"

"No, nothing was ever done about it other than I failed two grades, grade two and grade six, and it came out in spelling mostly in my first grade school years, and then it just continued in writing and got worse."

"But you were able to get by and you were able to take your SATs and do all right. It seems as long as it was just multiple choice questions you could respond. It is when you have actually to write a composition that you have trouble. The problem now, nearing graduation, is that you can't graduate without achieving writing competence, is that correct?"

"That's right, a test of writing competence is required to graduate."

"What is the test like?" asks the clinician.

"It is fairly simple. You go into a room and you have two hours to write, I'd say seven paragraphs. And so it is not so very hard to pick a topic or to think of something, but it is the writing that kills me. The grammar just comes apart with the spelling and, you know, other things."

"Raymond," said the clinician, "please tell me a little about your background, just enough so that I understand where you have come from and how you got to the place you are today."

"Well, I spent two years at St. Barnard's College in Bakersville, and then I left the school for academic reasons—like I didn't feel it was of high academic quality—so I transferred to Martin College, and I notified them in writing that I had a writing problem, and there was no problem with admission. I went into the courses. I'm a history major and poli sci, so there is quite a bit of written work required and the grades were lower than what I could have gotten. With term papers I had help with from someone. Martin College went through a phase where they were loosening up their writing requirements, and within the last half year or so decided to tighten them again. They are very much involved in it, and so it came down to the writing competency test and I wrote it five times—four or five times—and also I had a poli sci paper, my senior paper, I'd written at the other school and it was acceptable and everything but the Department of Political Science at Martin wants me to write a new one. It was about fifty pages, and I refused to get involved after writing one already to do another one."

"What do you plan to do if you get your degree there in poli sci and history? What happens?"

"Well, I will get the history degree, but not the poli sci. Since I wouldn't write another thesis, I won't complete that one even though I have completed three 400 levels. I'd like to go on to graduate school, but first of all I'd like to take care of this problem. If not, I would like it identified first and my approach organized, because I don't think I could apply to any graduate school with any chance. Like I wrote the LSAT Test for law school, and it really hurt me because that deals with grammar and things like that."

There is sufficient detail here to provide the reader with the dilemma Raymond faces, and which the secondary school people undoubtedly struggled with as well. The latter failed; Raymond persevered to his present level, and he is aggressive regarding his desire to continue his education. However, the problems Raymond faces in reading, writing, and spelling are severe, and they will continue to present him with serious hurdles unless he obtains much outside assistance. The capacity is present; the skills are not. A few examples of his academic characteristics will suffice to illustrate the type of problem he has and, more important, the demands which these youths make upon secondary education which this level of schooling must meet.

For example, the clinician asked Raymond to write a short paragraph describing the room in which he was sitting. Figure 13 shows the result of his effort.

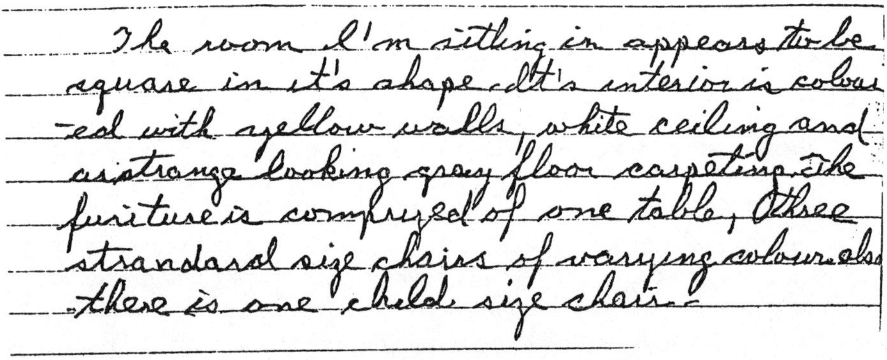
The room I'm sitting in appears to be
square in it's shape It's interior is colour
-ed with yellow walls, white ceiling and
a strange looking gray floor carpeting the
furniture is comprized of one table, three
standard size chairs of varying colour. also
there is one child size chair.

The room I'm sitting in appears to be square in it's shape. It's interior is coloured with yellow walls, white ceiling, and a strange looking gray floor carpeting. The furniture is comprized of one table, three strandard size chairs of varying colour. also there is one child size chair.

FIGURE 13 Raymond's writing when task was clearly delimited and concrete in nature

We later obtained the actual examination paper Raymond wrote for his college "exit examination." Figure 14 is illustrative of the total examination. Figure 15 is a typescript of the production he submitted. It is obvious that as a college senior this young man has writing and spelling problems which are severe. These problems, if analyzed carefully, are seen to be not those of a careless pupil. They are not typical of those who have experienced environmental deprivation or who have grown up in a home where little value was placed on education. There is a distinct pattern to the errors which are made, each of which involves some or all of the visual, auditory, or kinesthetic modalities.

Raymond states, "I go in there with something like that, and I get this flack from the academic chairman who says, 'You have to have this or there is no way you are going to graduate.' And I felt like jumping on top of the table, you know . . . after four years, you are crazy."

"I don't blame you a bit," said the clinician. "I think we can send a supportive statement without any difficulty, and I think we will ask for some exception in terms of the format in which you take the test. But it would seem to me that you still should be committed to trying to correct the writing deficiency, because whatever you want to do, you are likely to choose a very academic area. Even if you went into a business ed/ history combination, it is still going to require an expression of thought on paper. And, probably any program is going to have some kind of master's paper or thesis, so although you could look forward to having a secretary respond to dictation in later years, in the meantime, if you are going to have any peace with yourself, you are probably going to need to be able to write.

"To give me a further understanding of your problem and what we may be able to do about it, I'd like to record something on tape and then ask you to listen to it and transcribe it in writing." Figure 15 illustrates Raymond's attempt to deal with written material presented in this manner.

Raymond's performance on the transcription task indicates that this is *not* a profitable approach for him. Instead, it was recommended that the educational procedures set forth by Johnson and Myklebust (1967) for disorders of formulation and syntax (pp. 230–39) be followed. It is interesting to note that Raymond himself stated several times his need for the most basic of the Johnson-Myklebust plan: (1) the need to move gradually from concrete to abstract writing; (2) the need to improve his awareness of errors; and (3) the need to develop specific skills in proofreading for grammatical and spelling errors.

Readers may be interested to know that the administration of Raymond's college did decide to waive the exit examination requirement for Raymond after receiving a report explaining his difficulty. We must

The events that led to the Ambassador's resignation as it appeared in the press followed a certian pattern which could be best described as having two stages. Stage one involds the raise of the relatively unknown common American in the act of defending his country against against the thankless herd of smaller countries in the United Nations. In this stage we find the devolpment of a hero that the country desperatly desires in the wake of it's post-Watergate slump. The second stage is one in which the public is feed a tickle of information that our new hero may not be getting the support of that un-elected administation in Washington. As time goes on the tickle of information turns into a flood that shows Moynihan fighting off hostile enemies only to continue in the U.N. for his country's sake. From here we move into the final part which is the actual resignation itself.

The events that led to the Ambassador's resignation as it appeared in the press followed a certian pattern which could be best described as having two stages. Stage one involds the raise of the relativly unknown common American in the act of defending his country against the thank less hord of smaller countries in the United Nations. In this stage we find the development of a hero that the country so desperatly desire in the wake of it's post-Watergate slump. The second stage is one in which the public is feed a tickle of information that our new hero may not be getting the support of that un-elected administation in Washington. As time gose on the tickle of information turns into a flood that shows Moyihan fighting of hostile enemy only too continue in the U.N. for his country's sake. Form here we move into the final part which is the resignation itself.

FIGURE 14 Copy of original bluebook exam from required competency exam in composition; underlinings and corrections were made by a college faculty member; verbatim transcript from bluebook original; Raymond age 23

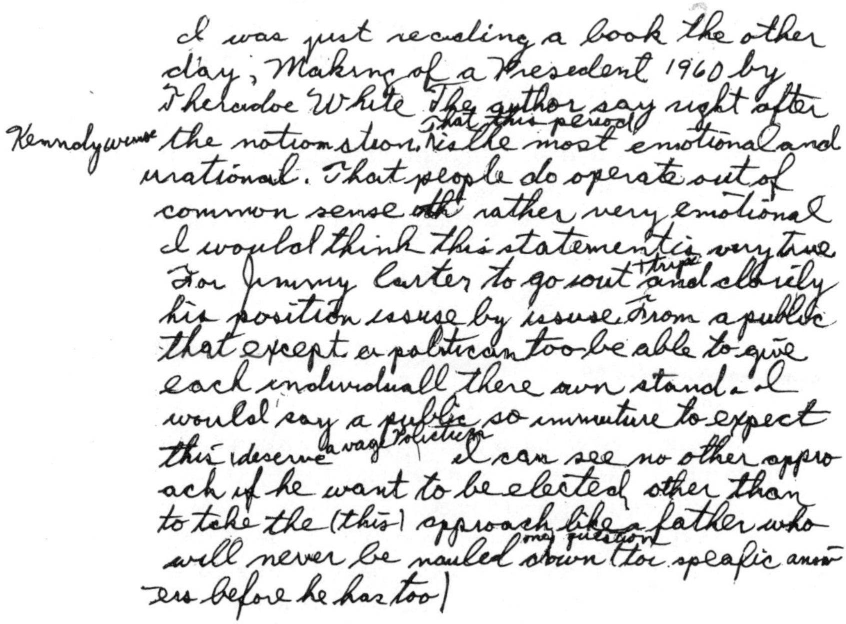
I was just recaling a book the other
day, Making of a President 1960 by
Theradoe White The author say right after
Kennedy were the notiomsteon. is the most emotional and
irrational. That people do operate out of
common sense oth rather very emotional
I would think this statement is very true
For Jimmy Carter to go sout and clorily
his position issuse by issuse. From a public
that except a poltican too be able to give
each indiviuall there own stand. I
would say a public so immature to expect
this deserve I can see no other appro
ach if he want to be elected other than
to take the (this) approach like a father who
will never be nauled down (to speafic answ
ers before he has too)

FIGURE 15 Raymond's writing from his own taped dictation

also say that Raymond's qualities of perseverance and reasonable self-appraisal are not characteristics commonly found in learning disabled young adults who have suffered similar frustrations. It will be essential for educators to reach students with similar problems much earlier in their school careers.

JIM: A VERY LATE BLOOMER

Jim dropped out of school as a truant when he was fourteen. His family was apathetic toward his problem and his behavior. He floated until he was 16 years of age when the work laws of his state permitted him full-time working papers and employment. He then obtained a job as a sweeper in a large satellite plant of a major industry in a metropolitan area.

Jim was a handsome adolescent, and even though he could not write or read, his pleasant personality and sense of humor endeared him as a young adult to the men with whom he worked. He was gradually given more and more responsibility, and he remained in this employment because it provided the security he needed, an income, the recognition that he was not a complete failure, and a life structure in terms of working hours and environment which was satisfying.

At 20 he met Nancy, fell in love, and married. At the time he referred himself, they had an 18-month-old child in whom they both invested tremendous interest.

Recognition at work continued to come to Jim, and at 22 years of age he was made a foreman with responsibility for approximately 50 other employees. Only his boss knew about his reading and writing problems. Nancy was supportive and encouraged him. He was unhappy as he clearly stated when, finally, through a chain of mutual friends, he learned of and referred himself to a clinic for assistance.

"What's your problem, Jim?" asked the clinician.

"I have a basket full of them," he replied, "and I'm tired as hell of the whole mess. I can't read; I can't write; I—"

"Surely you can read some—?"

"No, I can't, and I'm not giving you a line. Did you ever have someone have to confirm the X on the payroll being yours? Well, I do every week. I can't drive because I can't pass the written test. I can't keep our checkbook, because I can't figure. I can't, I can't, I can't."

"How do you get along in your job?"

"The boss," said Jim, "is great. He knows about me. He lets Nancy come to work every day or so, and she reads everything I need to know or need to tell the men. She's quite a gal. You'll meet her one of these days, I suppose."

Further discussion led to an understanding that Jim was accurately reporting his deficiences. With learning disabled individuals, it is necessary to ascertain the lowest level at which a success experience can be obtained in reading, number concepts, or writing and then, at this point begin an appropriate education regimen. On a second visit, the clinician said to Jim:

"Today we are really going to see what you can do, not just talk about it."

"If you're talkin' about reading, it won't take long," laughed Jim nervously.

"We're not going to start directly with reading, for I believe what you tell me, that you can't read. Jim, here's a 'ball' made of pieces of yarn. Please find and pull out a piece of red yarn and give it to me." (This material, about the size of a softball, is composed of short, loose pieces of many colors of cotton yarn.)

"If you say there's a red one there," said Jim, "then it's probably there, but I'm not the one to pick out a little piece of red stuff from the rest. I can't do it."

The clinician placed some small pieces of colored construction paper on the table before Jim.

"Give me the papers which have some red tint in them," he directed.

"How much time do you have?" was Jim's reply. "Does this have something to do with the fact that I can't read?"

Getting some 8½" x 11" pieces of construction paper, the clinician pushed back the furniture and provided a large open space in the middle of the room. "Jim, take your jacket off and lie down on the floor on your stomach. I'll do the same."

Placing four pieces of colored paper near Jim's head, the clinician said, "Now, put your nose on the blue one." Immediately this was done successfully. "Good, now on the green one. Fine, now on the yellow. Great. Those were all done correctly."

Jim had demonstrated eye-head coordination, but he possessed terribly inefficient eye-hand skills. "Sit up and put your foot on the pink paper, Jim." Inaccurate targeting was demonstrated in response. This was repeated also in terms of eye-foot responses to other commands.

Apparently the lowest level at which eye-motor skills could be successfully established repetitively was in terms of eye-head coordination. At 23 years of age, would Jim be willing to perform and work at a preschool level? "Let's try it," said Jim, when the situation was fully explained.

"With no guarantees," said the clinician a bit defensively.

"Now look who's scared," smiled Jim.

Teaching materials of this nature are essentially non-existent. The clinician converted the Columbia Test of Mental Maturity from an intelligence test into a 100-item eye-head multiple choice learning experience while at the same time he had home-made teaching materials of the same nature constructed. Step by step, on a logical developmental progression, Jim moved in two one-hour sessions per week from eye-head learning to eye-foot, eye-knee, eye-hand, eye-elbow, and always, when possible, with supporting verbal behavior ("eye-mouth") coordination. Abstract materials ultimately were substituted for the concrete items utilized in the multiple-choice instruction. Varieties of content were employed in the teaching materials. Three years passed, and Jim was functioning slightly in excess of a grade three level in reading and arithmetic. He was signing his name on the payroll. He had a driver's license. (In his state, the reading test for a license was at about a third grade level.) He could keep score at the bowling alley. Nancy's visit to the plant dropped in frequency to about once a week on the average. The two were elated with Jim's progress. At this point, Jim chose "not to sweat it out any more," knowing that he could always return to the clinic if he wished to try to improve his skills further. He knew that a ceiling was probably relatively close at hand, although he also knew that he would be instrumental in determining what the level of that ceiling actually would be.

A FEW COMPARISONS

Raymond and Jim, both 23 years of age, both products of the public schools in their respective communities, demonstrate some similarities. Raymond is the product of an economically secure home; Jim came from a home in which socioeconomic opportunities were limited. Yet Jim had inner controls as did Raymond which helped him survive adolescence. The school personnel viewed Raymond as intellectually capable, but they made little effort to understand his severe problem. Although Jim was legally a truant at fourteen years of age, the school's leadership really did not want him, and they made no effort to get him back into a regular attendance pattern. His severe learning disabilities became a cross, and he carried it alone.

Both young men were learning disabled. Both had problems of written communication. Each had problems which were remissible, if proper educational regimens had been established in both elementary and secondary schools. This was not the case. Although home and community agencies may have to share in the wasted years which Jim experienced, responsibility rests directly on the personnel of the school systems. A further examination of this public educational responsibility will be the topic of the next and concluding chapter.

Solutions to the problems of these former secondary students are not going to be found in college preparatory curricula, in content-oriented teachers, or in standardized achievement tests and their results. The future of these and the five other youths included in Part II are not going to be secured by social promotion, by failing a grade as a therapeutic procedure, or by truancy unattended and uncorrected. Disorders of written communication, the disability highlighted in this chapter and so pronounced in the secondary school setting, require a clinical teaching regimen in the secondary schools which is based on the specific known needs of the students.

14

Can Secondary Education
Meet the Challenge?

THERE IS A LARGE GROUP of learning disabled youths in the junior and senior high schools of this nation whose needs are not being met. Just how large this group is is not known, for anything nearing an accurate census is unavailable in spite of so-called authoritative statements to the contrary. Federal, state, and local educational agencies publish incidence figures, but these are not based on accurately collected data or definition. The parent organizations are quick to indicate the size of the problem, but these are at best educated guesses, and are usually far from accurate. What the problem is in size at the secondary school levels is unknown, although within any good school system personnel are usually available so that local need could be determined. It is safe to say that in every grade level of the secondary schools of this nation pupils with learning disabilities will be found. In the aggregate every secondary school has enough students with learning disabilities to warrant a program to serve the needs of these young people. Numbers cannot be used as an excuse for no program.

It is also safe to say that the secondary schools rarely provide a program which will ensure a safe journey between early adolescence and the independence of the first job for those with learning disabilities. This is a period of personal disappointments, discouragements, failures, dropouts, sometimes tragedies for the young person and his or her family members.

If the learning disabled student does graduate from high school, a competency waiver graduation perhaps, new stresses are bound to be experienced as the young person seeks to move into the adult world. The worst may yet have to be experienced. But for the moment we speak of the secondary school per se.

On the other hand the attempt by many parents to obtain educational programs for learning disabled adolescents is filled with stories of disappointment and frustration. Recognizing that a few examples will not be accepted by some as characteristic of the whole issue, our experience with this problem over several decades in many school systems of this nation, leads us to believe that these few examples are more typical than atypical of the problems learning disabled youths face in the secondary schools. Expressing the essence of the problem, they illustrate the reason that more than 50,000 parents have banded together in the national Association for Children with Learning Disabilities to attempt to remedy the situation.

1. A distraught father called long distance to one of the authors to seek advice and help. His son had been told by the high school principal that he would probably be granted a diploma but that it would be stamped "dyslexia" across the face, a sadistic and illegal action to close out a long history by the youth in his attempt to complete the requirements for graduation.

2. "No kids who can't read will get into my driver class," stated a teacher. "How can you expect them to read the traffic signals? Learning disabled kids have no place here."

3. A mother reports that she has seven children. "I have spent more time in school with Joey [a learning disabled youth] than with all of the others combined, not to get him a proper program because that doesn't exist here, but to get them [the school teachers and administrators] to accept him as a person of some worth."

4. In a rural high school twelve students with severe reading problems are assigned simultaneously to a reading teacher and to an aide who must work in a room approximately 7 feet by 10 feet in size. Since this is an impossibility, half of the group must work outside the room on the floor in the middle of a major hallway. (No child of any community leader was included in this unfortunate situation.)

5. No individualization of instruction was provided in——— High School. Three learning disabled students with severe reading problems in grade ten were included in the English class where, at the time of a consultant visit, the reading included Shakespeare's *As You Like It*.

6. The principal of a very large high school was accompanying a consultant to a mathematics class in which a young man with learning disabilities was to be found. On arrival, in a loud whispered voice audible at least to all the pupils in the first five rows, the principal said, "That's him, the red head back there on the left. Looks normal, doesn't he? He could do it if he tried, but I think he's plain lazy. You should see him on

the school bus—a ladies' man if there ever was one. Doesn't do a damn thing worthwhile in school though. Might as well not be here." By this time the entire class was either smiling or expressing real hostility to an adult who publicly treated one of their group in this manner.

7. In a moment of frustration an English teacher, new to the school, posted both Sara's and Jerry's written papers, along with the other productions of her grade eleven class, on the bulletin board as part of an exhibit for a forthcoming parent visiting night. Sara begged that hers be removed from public display. The teacher refused stating, "It's high time the people understood your refusal to even try." Defeated, the girl returned to her desk. Jerry thumbed his nose at the back of the teacher's head to the amusement of the rest of the students. The teacher's comment to the consultant: "You see what I put up with every day." During the two-day visit, the consultant surreptitiously removed the offending papers from the bulletin board and slipped them in his brief case. Later when the consultant, the teacher, and the principal were together and when the climate was right, the teacher's frustrations were recognized, the papers were returned to her, with suggestions as to how the situation could be handled to her credit and in support of the two learning disabled students.

8. A mathematics teacher is almost totally unaware of adolescent development and psychology, and is completely unaware of the problems of Neil, a learning disabled pupil with severe memory problems. He cannot understand why Neil, sixteen years of age, handsome, and popular, cannot solve problems involving multiplication or division. When the consultant asked the teacher for the last test, and asked that it be redone again by Neil and at the same time gave the boy a pocket calculator, all problems except one were computed correctly.

A legion of other examples of educational ineptitude could be told, many more tragic or critical than the ones included here. Does this mean that secondary education administrative and teaching staffs are generally comprised of callous and unsympathetic educators, by thoughtless and sadistic leadership or by those hostile to the ones they are employed to teach? Evidence accumulated over the years would indicate that secondary education has its share of misfits in the public schools (Cruickshank, Paul, and Junkala 1969). However, total responsibility for failure to meet the challenge of the learning disabled adolescent is broader than the individual teacher or administrator who may taint the reputation of the total core, although the individual cannot abrogate his or her responsibility.

Teacher education programs for those wishing to enter the secondary schools are almost devoid of courses or experiences in the areas of psychology, individualization of instruction, or adolescent development. They are devoid of any emphasis on the education of exceptional children and those with learning disabilities. Teachers cannot be expected to respond to the unusual challenges of disabled learners when they have had absolutely no formal background or awareness of what these problems are. However, even when in-service programs dealing with learning disabilities are provided for secondary school personnel, they are often poorly attended or are attended by many with an avowed declaration not to agree.

So great is the adherence to the teaching content that the learner is lost. The long-standing hostility which exists—often with good reason —between university faculties in colleges of liberal arts and in the schools of education usually finds the former in total command when the curriculum for future secondary school educators is adopted or revised. A future junior high school teacher of mathematics, for example, who must complete a major in mathematics, a minor in chemistry, elective courses in physics, and who must begrudgingly meet programmatic requirements in English, a second language, and physical education, among other things, does not have much time to understand those he or she will be teaching. Simultaneously, the faculty of the school of education demands that this budding teacher experience courses in the methods of teaching mathematics, the history of the state educational system, the junior high school curriculum, two lengthy practice teaching assignments, and perhaps a course in adolescent psychology which stresses facts and statistics rather than human dynamics. Content is the primary emphasis. The new teacher— and many with experience—are mystified when in grades nine or eleven they encounter grade two or grade three readers, spellers, or writers.

Underlying the obvious aspects of learning disabilities is a long list of characteristics or determinants (see Figure 1). Visual-motor perception, auditory- and tactile-motor perception, memory, concept formation, figure-background discrimination, association, and dissociation—these among others are all essentials to the learning skills of any pupil. Yet an understanding of these significant factors, requisites to the learning of all children and youth, is rarely included as a part of teacher education programs. If teachers, to say nothing of administrators, possessed knowledge of the normative aspects of these essential learning characteristics, they would understand much more easily the child or youth who deviates and is learning disabled. Maldevelopment of the audio-motor functions results in disorders of spoken and written language. Maldevelopment of visual-motor functions produces ineffective writers. The inability to differentiate figure from ground produces poor readers. Faulty memory lies at the bottom of poor arithmetic performance. Inability to properly sequence, intersensory disorganization, inefficient visual targeting ability, tendencies to dissociate and perseverate, short attention span, and myriad other subtle psychological problems turn nice kids into failures, and these usually with an emotional overlay which clouds the true problems. If secondary level administrators and teachers do not understand these not-so-subtle issues, the needs of the students are not going to be met. Life-long psychological injuries may be imposed upon the youth. Learning disabilities is an area of child growth and development where the adults and environment which surrounds the child or youth must make the accommodations. The young person cannot.

LEARNING DISABLED ADOLESCENT NEEDS AND THE SCHOOL'S RESPONSE

Educators, particularly at the secondary level, have for years been caught in a dilemma. On the one hand they have heard the call for individualization of instruction and that their responsibility was to meet the needs of students. On the other hand college and university personnel, and indeed some segments of the community, have decried the concept of the high school for life and living, and have insisted that English, Latin, chemistry, mathematics, physics, and other subjects traditional to the secondary school be required of all students. Over and over again one hears traditionalists say that such and such a student "doesn't belong here," although never are appropriate alternatives suggested.

Secondary education in the United States must respond to the atypical student. We are a democracy, and as such young people should expect an educational program commensurate with their needs. The junior and senior high schools in the United States philosophically contain the necessary potential to support all students, but the adherence of their faculties to the single goal of traditional academic excellence defeats the attainment of the broader obligation and forces many exceptional youths to remain outside. Public Law 94-142 may force secondary schools to extend their services in more appropriate ways to learning disabled youths and to others, but it is unfortunate after decades of inadequate function that federal law must ultimately be created which requires program modifications. Are there not wise secondary school leaders who are capable of leading the program ahead of imposed legal restrictions? What is required to meet the needs of the learning disabled student in the secondary school?

Qualitative Assessment and Responsive Educational Program

Psycho-educational assessment is the cornerstone of the educational regimen whether at the elementary or secondary school level. Perhaps it is wiser to state that *continuous* assessment is the cornerstone, for in particular with learning disabled pupils and students, the status of the individual changes rapidly in accordance with the adequacy of the instructional program. In this field the educational program must fully reflect the findings of the assessment procedures.

Old concepts of assessment have no place here. The intelligence quotient and the mental age are only crude indicators of potential, and are not particularly helpful in planning a dynamic program. Qualitative assessment, using a variety of techniques, is required (see Chapter 11). A retooling of most of the skills of school psychologist is essential. The educational program will be dependent on an understanding of the student's ability in various areas. If the psychologist indicates there is a figure-ground pathology, for example, the educational response with respect to reading and mathematics must address this problem. The presence of dissociation will dictate the way in which handwriting and mathematics are taught. While we make no claim for a one-to-one relationship between gross- and fine-motor training and the acquisition of basic learning skills, we do feel that it is essential when these issues are demonstrated on psychological tests, that some time each day be set aside for such motor training.

Too often the educational aspect of assessment is completely overlooked in this process. But teachers have at their fingertips many somewhat traditional materials which, if examined qualitatively, can be of great value in individualizing instruction.

We are reminded of an encounter with a former student several years ago. The woman was a school psychologist who had taken an interesting position in Alaska. She was an itinerant psychologist/special educator for several tiny schools in remote areas, all of which were reached by a combination of small plane, snowmobile, or dogsled. She told how she had arrived at the schools with her psychological tools and an eagerness to be of assistance to teachers and children. It did not take long for her to realize that the teacher (usually one to educate eight children of various ages and language backgrounds) was not interested in waiting six weeks for the psychologist to return with a report stating that a student was functioning one and one-half standard deviations below the mean, placing the student in the borderline range of intelligence, etc., etc. There were no special schools for these children; they would get whatever learning they could in these tiny regional schools. This is not atypical to what most learning disabled children will receive wherever they are found in public school programs. The teachers wanted materials and methods with which to reach the students immediately, not labels or diagnoses. This too is not different today with teachers in almost every school system in the United States. And so the school pyschologist asked herself: "What five or six things, weighing less than 60 pounds and compact enough to fit in a snowmobile, could I carry as standard equipment to meet the incredible variety of special needs I find in these isolated schools?"

It has been several years since this question was asked, and we cannot yet claim to have a 60-pound solution to the special education needs of rural Alaska or elsewhere, but there may be some value in sharing a preferred list of items for the teacher of the learning disabled adolescent.

At the end of this chapter is such a list of items to aid in the support of learning disabled teenagers. It is offered without qualification or annotation, with an understanding that its contents will not solve the problems of all students and teachers, but may serve to spark ideas, and aid the teacher in a wise selection of materials from the ever-increasing offerings of commercial publishers and teacher-made tools which are specifically addressed to the needs of the learning disabled student.

We do not suggest that all secondary school teachers should become specialists in the area of learning disabilities. We do suggest that all teachers and other secondary school personnel be fully aware of the unique learning characteristics of the learning disabled student, so that wherever the student finds himself he will also find an understanding adult who can, with the pupil, utilize the specialist personnel to assist in the most appropriate manner and thus assist the student in profiting as fully as possible from any instructional program in which he or she may be registered.

Together with faculty and staff members who are oriented to the learning disabled adolescents and their problems, there must be available in every secondary school, mainstreaming notwithstanding, a specialist or team of specialists who, either in self-contained or resource rooms, can address the serious learning deviations which characterize every one of the youths included in this book, and which cannot be handled by the regular teaching staff members. Even Jim (cf. Chapter 13) could have profited by socialization and prevocation activities of a comprehensive high school, if specialist personnel had been available to do with him the things which were not started until he was 23 years old. Had there been good clinical teaching programs, Scott and Andy might have been held in school longer, John assisted in his serious reading and writing problems, and more realistic prevocational explorations provided to all of the youths than that which they experienced, if they experienced any at all.

The specifics of the clinical teaching program have been described fully elsewhere, and need not be re-stated here (see Cruickshank *et al.,* Chapter 5, 1961; Cruickshank 1966; Cruickshank 1977; Bailey 1975; Weis and Weis 1974). For a variety of reasons, it has been found frequently that a well-prepared teacher (or teachers) of learning disabled children, certified as elementary school educators, can be assigned effectively to the junior or senior high school programs to carry out the clinical teaching activities. The issue of elementary preparation is minimized, and these staff members are fully accepted as members of the secondary school teaching faculty. However, the methodology with which they are uniquely familiar is exactly what many secondary students need as educators and psychologists attempt to ascertain the lowest level at which success experience can be consistently performed. At that level the educators proceed to develop a total program geared to bring the youth to the maximum of his ability while at the same time keeping him as close as possible to the social, academic, and vocational activities of his peers. Clinical teaching specialists should be available to interpret the youth to the regular classroom teachers, who must see the role of clinic teaching specialists as significant in meeting the total needs of the learning disabled youth. The teachers cannot be expected to work alone, however. At the same time there is no place for the often-heard exasperation of the secondary academician who says "That kid has no place in my class." Such an attitude is totally defeatist.

At this point let us examine several aspects of the secondary school program and observe how regular staff members and clinical teaching specialists may work together in behalf of the learning disabled student.

Driver Education

Driving an automobile is just about as close to a recognized positive adult activity as a high school student can come. It is certainly a skill that is anticipated with pleasure by the youth, with fear and concern by many parents. For the learning disabled youth there is no less an attraction. Driving an automobile signifies to him and his friends that "he has made it."

Many driver education teachers are loathe to include learning disabled adolescents in this program. In earlier chapters, John, Jim, Ron, and Andy either avoided driver education classes or sought instruction where they would not be compared with others. There is no reason why these students should not be admitted to this program and receive its benefits. Details of instruction must complement the apparent learning disability. Repetitive experience must be provided. Final examinations may need to be administered orally if reading constitutes a problem. Beyond these factors, what of others?

Carl has sequencing problems. Consider what this means in starting or stopping a car. To start: (1) gear shift in park, (2) turn key, (3) release brake, (4) put gear shift in forward (or drive), (5) put foot on accelerator. This sequence may require seemingly excessive practice in comparison to other students, but it can be learned.

Mary has visual discrimination problems. Red, green, and amber of the traffic lights may require drill in discrimination not needed for other students.

Joey has problems of visual targeting. Bringing the car to a full stop at a given white line may involve much repetitive drill, for not only is visual-motor activity involved here, but judgment of distance, estimation of speed and distance, and motor sequencing involving brakes and gear shift are all inherent in the act of stopping the vehicle. Intersensory organization is manifest here.

Memory deficiencies and judgment are primary problems for Susan. Parking a car, backing into a space, and the backward-forward motion of the car which is frequently involved in parking constitute real problems for her—problems which she overcame with patient instruction and carefully planned drill.

Visual spatial orientation is Jerry's problem. Bringing the car to an appropriate halt in the garage required many attempts until the instructor helped him to find visual cues at his right and left side rather than judging distance from the wall while slowly moving forward, e.g., aligning the window mount on the car with a mark or object on the garage wall and stopping at the point where they intersected.

A willing driver education teacher together with assistance from the clinical teaching specialist can devise ways for overcoming the problems described here. In a rural high school the driver education teacher arranged for 17 learning disabled students between 16 and 18 years of age to have a special learning experience daily for twelve weeks during the summer. While didactic instruction proceeded with modified materials and techniques, the school play yards were used for actual driving experiences for a long time. Each learning disabled student was assigned to a volunteer non-learning disabled peer-driver for 45 minutes out of the daily 1½ hour class. In the presence of both, the learning disabled student's problem was carefully outlined, and each day segments of the total skill were practiced with both students working together. Each student had a car assigned to him which was provided either by the school, his family, or the local parent organization.

At the end of the summer the final examination was administered orally. All passed. As a group the students presented themselves at the license bureau where again the written portion of the test was administered orally. All passed. Fourteen out of the seventeen students passed the road test, and the unsuccessful three were successful two weeks later on a second try.

Socialization Experiences

Socialization appears to be the keystone of adolescent development. The school's responsibility in this phase of adolescent growth may be minimal or at best supplementary to that of the home and community. For the learning disabled student, this usually is not the case. For one who has had a young lifetime essentially characterized by failure experiences, social skills producing popularity with one's peers may be elusive if not completely lacking. Dancing is difficult to do when one is "all feet" and has a history of motor incoordination, clumsiness, and poor directional skills. It is interesting that with the exception of Ron, none of the youths included here ever mentioned parties—dances or others—in which social skills are learned. If the high school has no responsibility here, the home and community certainly do.

It appears to us, however, that the secondary schools, through a good program of social and physical education, have a significant role in teaching the skills which make it possible for the learning disabled youth as an adult to feel comfortable in social situations of all types. If dance, swimming instruction, gymnastics, and related instruction assists the learning disabled adolescent to feel more comfortable with his physical self, then indeed this needs to be a part of the secondary school curriculum.

Good body concept, directionality, motor coordination, and concepts of rhythm are often areas of deficiency for the learning disabled youth. Many times one hears learning disabled adolescents state "I can't" when urged to participate in a social activity. This attitude, related to a long-term failure history, can be replaced by positive self-concepts as fear-producing social activities are practiced and become success experiences. This, in contrast to the normal adolescent, must be a planned educational intervention.

Sex Education and Human Fulfillment

After the many years and the voluminous amount of writing on the topic, it hardly seems necessary to address the issue of human fulfillment education. We shall merely emphasize the necessity of providing basic and total information to learning disabled children. In this area of human development, these youths are no different than other adolescents in their need to know.

However, as one talks with learning disabled young people, it becomes obvious that in the urgent effort to meet and rectify the specific learning problems, the issue of sex education in its broadest definition has been ignored. When asked, hear John (Chapter 7) state that his knowledge probably came from "locker room garbage," although his father he recalls vaguely, talked with him once or twice when he was around the age of twelve. Ron's information (Chapter 5), such as it was, came from the reading materials of friends; Scott's (Chapter 9) from "the gutter." Andy and Tom apparently never had any consistent positive source of information (Chapters 6 and 8).

As we talk with learning disabled adolescents, we are impressed that almost universally they complain that this is an area of total ignorance. Sol Gordon's book, *You,* is a source of excellent psychological and social information for adolescents. Even this, however, contains reading material of a level higher than that held by many learning disabled youths. On one occasion one of the authors spent about a half hour a day reading this book to a 16-year-old learning disabled boy with a severe reading problem. As the reading proceeded into the area of physical maturation, boy-girl relations, and the issues of sexual intercourse, contraception, and pregnancy, it was punctuated by "Golly," "Not really," "I didn't know that," and a variety of other responses from the listener. The youth said that, although he came from a large family which prided itself on its integrity and respect of one another, sex as a topic was not discussed. The young man said, "I thought we avoided this because it was part of my screwy learning problems and not a problem for everyone else. Boy, was I wrong. I'm not different from other guys like I thought all the time." We do not believe this young man is atypical. To the contrary, we believe he is typical of the great majority of learning disabled boys and girls with whom we work.

We stress again that all children and youth require well-organized information in the area of physical and sexual maturation. The failure experiences of the learning disabled youths which cover their life-times, their perceptual processing deficits resulting in reading deficiencies of a major order, and concomitant misconceptions about their body, body parts, and functions, serve to impress on us the widespread need for appropriate secondary school educational planning and implementation in this area of human activity. To assume responsibility for the information area alone is insufficient for the learning disabled student. The information in the area of human fulfillment must be processed in a way in which learning disabled adolescents can understand and integrate it into their lives. This is not easy unless all information is transmitted to the young person verbally. Reading will be a significant hurdle for the majority. Most, if not all, of the considerations we give to the academic subjects in the next section will also be applicable in this important problem area, too.

Academics and the Technologies

Human fulfillment education, like English, social sciences, mathematics, science, and other secondary school classes, will probably be carried on in group instructional situations. The subjects which have been mentioned here each normally involve a great amount of reading by the student. The learning disabled student in these circumstances is now faced with almost insurmountable hurdles, and the best intended teacher or the best planned program of "mainstreaming" is thwarted.

Numerous parents, parent groups, and volunteers have mustered their energies to minimize this problem. Reading assignments are placed on tapes, so that the learning disabled youth can listen to the material which others read. It is the acquisition of knowledge which is important, not the method of acquisition of knowledge. Individuals with severe reading problems are now eligible for use of the Talking Book previously restricted to blind persons (see suggested list of materials at the end of this chapter). While there is often delay in obtaining orders, almost every-thing needed by the junior high school and senior high school students is included in the Talking Book catalogue, and if early planning between youth, parents and teachers is undertaken, the discs can be on hand at the time the student needs them.

In some communities small groups of volunteer readers at each grade level assume responsibility for taping textbooks and collateral reading. The tapes are kept for future use and for future years for other students. In this fashion the learning disabled student is able to keep abreast of his fellow students, and indeed many do exceedingly well under these circumstances. Examinations and quizzes are likewise read orally to the student.

The greatest hurdle to the success of the program is the traditional notion on the part of some teachers that the only way acquisition of knowledge can take place is through reading. Experience disproves this old wives' tale. If modern technology is available, it should be used *within the school* as well as outside the school.

An example of near tragedy for a learning disabled young man comes from the field of mathematics. The student was enrolled in a grade ten general mathematics class. The young man had severe reading and memory problems. He knew concepts. When it came to multiplication and division, however, he usually failed because he could not remember the necessary combinations. When it was suggested that the student, since he understood the processes, be permitted to use a pocket calculator in school, the teacher responded "Not here. None of them in this class. They have got to stand on their own."

The Superintendent of Schools intervened in this situation, particularly when he recalled having seen a calculator affixed to the inside of the mathematics teacher's checkbook! Shortly, any student who could demonstrate knowledge of process, was permitted to bring and to use a calculator. The superintendent went so far as to place several calculators and a supply of batteries in the mathematics department for those students who might not be able to afford to own a personal item.

The issue here is not the availability of technology; it is that of outmoded attitudes. Technology has not yet progressed far enough to solve all of the problems of the learning disabled youth, but some things are available to help and others such as home computers are on the horizon. When these aids are available they should be used, for they go far in bridging the gap between actual achievement levels of the learning disabled students and the expectancy level of the school. The learning disabled students can often compete if they have the appropriate tools to assist them. The learning disabled students should have every possible piece of technology available to them and they should be taught to use every crutch possible in dealing with basic arithmetic, reading, and spelling facts.

Self-Concept Enhancement

In many school systems in Michigan a gross-motor program has been instituted in the elementary schools. Using the Haptic Perceptual-Motor Development program (Wilson and Mann), 25 children spend 50 minutes a day with a teacher. The children are divided into groups of five each, and these circulate through five different motor tasks, spending about ten minutes with each one. An aide or teaching assistant is assigned to each motor task, and these aides often are recruited from the group of learning disabled high school students, some spending five mornings a week with the program, others less.

The significance of utilizing high school pupils in this manner who are themselves learning disabled lies in the changed attitudes of these students. "It's the first time I've even been asked to do anything in the school," states one learning disabled boy. "I know how hard these things are for some of those kids," says another. "I get a real satisfaction out of helping these little kids," says a grade ten learning disabled girl. "For the first time, I feel I am contributing something. People are always trying to help me, but I never had anything to offer before."

John (Chapter 7), almost in anger it will be recalled, said that he had thought about becoming a teacher and working with children such as he used to be. "I can understand how they feel." The school did not serve John's needs, but the young men and women serving as teaching aides are receiving an important type of learning themselves, namely, an understanding that they can make a contribution. Thoughtful planning on the part of school personnel can expand this example into many others, each serving to enhance the positive self-concept of students with learning disabilities as well as those with other types of handicaps. Taking tickets at the school dance door may not be a full substitute for participation, but it goes far in keeping the exceptional student in the normal course of adolescent activities.

WHAT HAPPENED TO PARENTS IN THIS PART OF THE BOOK?

We discussed parents and the importance of their relationship to their teenagers extensively in the first part of the book, and yet it seems we "went to school" without them. Do we feel that parents of learning disabled adolescents have no part to play in their youngsters' education?

Of course parents have a role. Their understanding and encouragement as the youth struggles with school encounters is often the crucial support needed for success. But in this section of the book we have been talking about formal teaching and school learning. We do not feel that parents need to be school teachers. Both parents and teachers have essential functions, and learning disabled teenagers, if they are to succeed in accommodating and relieving their difficulties, will need to play their roles to the fullest.

Some parents are fine teachers of mathematics or reading for their children, but more often than not parental teaching efforts abort into misunderstandings and frustrations. And why not? Most parents were not trained as teachers, and even parents who are teachers are emotionally bound to their children in a way school teachers are not. This important emotional attachment and investment clutters and complicates a formal teaching-learning process.

The adolescent with learning disabilities has managed to cope with confusion and frustration all day, and if, when he finally enters what he thinks is the haven of his home, he meets yet another academic challenge, he now feels safer and freer to vent his anger and exasperation on his parent. Parents, also, are liable to express emotions with their own child that they would not with others. And so in many instances there is no gain made in reading or mathematics or other subject areas, and actual damage may be done. A teenage boy or girl who has spent six or seven hours at school needs to be *someone other than a student at home.*

Parents can be of great help in the area of homework. Many learning disabled students find homework an insurmountable hurdle. In the case of the usual reinforcement-type homework, the problem is often not the content, but rather organizing the material, structuring the time so that each thing gets done, and then knowing when and how to ask for assistance. When confronted with the more open-ended type of assignments such as studying for exams or executing long-term assignments like a written essay or a major report, the problems are more difficult ones to tackle and the strategies suggested earlier for in-school instruction of study techniques may be helpful to parents.

Parents sensitive to the adolescent's need for independence and success will find ways to offer the necessary structure and to be available with assistance, but discreetly. This is probably easiest when there are other school-aged children in the family who also need to do homework. Frequently learning disabled students are "assisted" so much that they fall into a sort of learned helplessness. Making demands on them to solve a problem of a brother or sister or young friend may activate personal resources they are unaware of and inadvertently offer the necessary structure to pursue a solution to a problem of their own.

There are many steps parents can take to support academic growth of their learning disabled youngster, and the following suggestions are offered for their consideration.

1. *Support the best efforts of the school district in offering services to these students.* Many, many services to handicapped children exist because concerned parents joined forces with professionals to educate the public and pressure the system.

2. *Watch for opportunities for incidental learning.* Particularly responsive to home "study" and reinforcement are the notions of space and time; and these concepts are often weak or missing from the repertoire even of high school students. Remember that Ron at age twenty-three has difficulty with left-right orientation or knowing which hand to use (cf. Part II). Parents will find many suggestions in the literature recommended by such parent-professional organizations as the state or national Association for Children with Learning Disabilities. Consultation with the learning disabilities specialists who work with the young person in school should be helpful in pinpointing areas of deficiency which may yield to informal, "family style" beefing up. Because the temporal-spatial domain is such a common problem area, we would use it as an example, and suggest that parents might

    a. Make a practice of *verbalizing* directions and positions (north, south, right, left, between, beneath, beyond, contiguous etc.).

    b. Ask the teenager to catch the weather report on TV and make a game of predictions—but be careful, keep the *teaching* down and the parent *interest* up because it's more likely to be contagious.

    c. Keep a calendar of birthdays, and include your children in sending small but funny or intriguing cards, riddles, or gifts to relatives and acquaintances as surprises. This will keep the young adolescent in touch with the sequence of the months as well as other calendar characteristics (seasons, number of days in month, number of weeks in month and year).

    d. Comment on time often; estimate aloud how long it will take to fix the entire dinner, and what time you will need to begin preparation in order to get to the hockey game.

    e. Play games like "older" versions of "I'm Going to Take a Trip, and

I'm Going to Pack—" These are fun for teenagers when the trips are to Outer Space, The North Pole, Scandinavia, or Australia this month, or only to states south of the Mason-Dixon Line.

f. Play Twister or similar games, even if it is necessary at first to give the learning disabled person "cheat notes" or a tiny "L" on the left hand, and piece of tape on left foot. Be sure to try to "wean" these props as part of the fun.

g. Use the after-dinner table time for short discussions. This is a good time to make plans for trips—his, hers, or all or yours; to estimate costs of these trips and of wanted treasures. This is also a good time to air feelings or dilemmas of the parents' own. The learning disabled youth may be somewhat insensitive to the feelings, desires and problems of other family members, and probably has not known as much of what you've been thinking as you imagined.

3. *Have the youth do the measuring* for your household project of new curtains, screens, cupboards, etc. Be sure to have the youth tell you the dimensions and write them down. Again, do not contrive a *lesson,* but request the effort when it's really *needed.* There are so many times when we do things ourselves which would be valuable exercise for our children.

4. *Don't be guilty of belonging to the I-can-do-it-faster-myself club.* The time you "waste" having your youngster gather and mix the cake ingredients, measure and saw the porch step, weigh out the co-op food order, or count the family's collection of coins will be negligible compared to the potential gains your child will reap from frequent experiences such as these.

5. *Home learning need not occur under constant tutelage.* Your son or daughter may, in fact, resist any advances he perceives to be "school teaching," "too young," or "babyish." Look for opportunities to send the youth on errands, to have him or her do the babysitting or tutoring. Give the student an age-appropriate memo board, notebook, an address or phone book, or pocket calendar to encourage organization.

6. *Encourage the young person to engage in non-academic activities.* These may be sports, hobbies, work, travel—anything that bypasses the most trouble, i.e., some learning problems, and give the youth a "break" to consider him or herself as other than handicapped. "A kid can take only so much failing" (Scott, Chapter 9).

These young persons need committed, creative teachers who can bring enormous energy to the task of instructing, and creative parents who will engage their talents in helping these boys and girls find the young men or young women in themselves. Parents need to help the youth keep a perspective. Parents need to help these young people see that they are other than school failures.

Most of us disdain a batch of burned cookies, or our inability to fix a dripping faucet; we've never forgotten our grades in statistics; we are annoyed if we are merely average in golf or tennis; we are embarrassed by a fall in public or even one verbal blunder at a social gathering.

Failures more stinging than any of these are *hourly* occurrences for most learning disabled youth. Few of us could have tolerated even one day of the learning disabled student's encounter with failure let alone one hundred eighty days a year for 12 years! John (Chapter 7) says, "I've heard the words 'poor reader' a million times!" His experience is not unique. Think how we respond to a single mistake, and remember some of these students have experienced virtually *no* success.

Perhaps it is best summed up by an excerpt from a letter recently received from a young man now twenty-six, who at thirteen was almost non-functional in school, and creating perpetual disaster at home:

> I knew you would be surprised that I graduated from the University. It took me five years instead of four, and although I don't have the problem with speech anymore, and I really don't have a reading or writing problem—although you see my spelling is still terrible—I seem to have retained all kinds of difficulties that can't be seen. I still get very very tired when I write or read. I still can't follow written directions very well —and all of the organization I have when I work disappears when it comes to studies. And I still have to say every date out loud when I write it, or it comes out mixed up (grate from an archaelogiest, right?)
>
> Anyway, I decided not to go to graduate school, even though advanced degrees are necessary in this field. I decided I would rather just be an assistant all my life than to suffer the agony of being a student three or five more years! Do you know that I never saw a single movie or had a date the whole time I was in college? Actually I did date when I was home, but never once while I was at school. I couldn't even have many friends who were guys, because, hell, who wants to spend their time with some guy who has to study 6–10 hours every day?
>
> I know I sound sorry for myself and bitter, and that's not what I meant. I know I am luckier than most dyslexics. I had a lot of help and most of my problems are just like you told me they would be—invisible —but now I feel like running out on the sand and shouting "God, I don't want to be a student anymore, I just want to be a *person*!"

IS THERE LIFE AFTER HIGH SCHOOL?

Since 1973, Michigan law has required that public school authorities provide necessary services to handicapped children and youth, including those with learning disabilities until the chronological age of 26. While this law is in no way being fully administered yet, it places a new dimension and responsibility on the public schools, for a designated obligation now exists to serve these young people into the years of early adulthood. Other states, while not extending services as long as Michigan does, nevertheless have also determined that services are needed beyond the chronological ages of 16 or 18 years. It is obvious that the trend is set, and undoubtedly it will be extended even longer in the future. This thrust to provide services to the handicapped and to young people with learning disabilities brings the school more and more into pre-vocational and vocational placement activities. The new laws also overlap with the lower age level of the federal Vocational Rehabilitation Services administration (16 years) and the state counterparts. Certainly the potential for assisting learning disability students into the world of adult work and careers exists as it has never before. However, great problems exist between anticipated goals and present reality. It is well to examine some of the factors which can both impede and assist in the full flowering of a strong program.

Counseling

Just as with general educators, so psychologists, and administrators, guidance and vocational counselors who may work closely with students with learning disabilities must become fully aware of the nature of the perceptual and learning problems of the pupil. These professionals must not only obtain a general understanding of learning disabilities, but also be fully informed regarding the specific perceptual pathologies which may still be influential in the learning and achievement of individual students.

In the past vocational counselors have relied heavily on standardized testing as a basis for counseling. We have stressed in this book that the usual standardized instruments for whatever purpose have very limited values with learning disabled students because of the inherent reading and written communications problems. Qualitative assessment is essential as well as on-the-job prevocational exploration discussed later in this chapter. When adequate psychological services are available in the school system, it is likely that no further "testing" will be needed if information sharing and interdisciplinary conferencing is a policy.

Traditionally high school guidance and counseling services have been focused essentially on the college-bound student. With new state education department regulations and state laws in place, personnel in these services simply must turn their attention toward the unique and interesting problems of the learning disabled student. Not only is careful prevocational counseling involved, but often continuous personal counseling is needed to assist the youth to achieve a more adequate personal adjustment in the face of the typical long history of failure.

The Career Center

Many states are encouraging the development of local or county-wide skill or career centers. These are proving to be a boon to the youth with learning disabilities. For example, the Sanilac Career Center (Michigan) serving a large rural county and its citizens offers daily instruction in the following areas:

Agriculture Power & Machinery	Food Management
Auto Mechanics	General Merchandising
Auto Body & Fender Repair	Graphic Arts
Bookkeeping & Accounting	Health Occupations
Building Trades	Machine Trades
Child Care	Ornamental Horticulture
Cosmetology	Specialized Secretarial Lab
Custodial Services	Welding & Cutting
Electronics	

This center is open to learning disabled students, and the staff of the center has attempted to become aware of the unique needs of teaching disabled pupils. A 16-year old youth, for example, has reading problems and memory and sequencing problems. After some careful assessment he was entered into the building trades program where experiences in carpentry (cutting, following instructions, nailing in patterns), brick laying (careful aligning), plumbing (eye-hand coordination), and electrical wiring all requiring a minimum of reading skills appeared to counterbalance the youth's deficiencies. What if Scott had experienced the auto mechanic's program, Andy the custodial training, Ron the bookkeeping and accounting instead of the academically oriented programs for college admissions? The career center is an excellent step between the formal school program and the work world after high school.

The career center, usually attended for five half-days a week, permits rather extensive vocational exploration and gives the youth a remarkable opportunity to determine his vocational strengths and weaknesses. The balance of the time is spent in the regular high school building in classes which we hope are geared to the needs of the learning disabled student.

Post-School Planning

The school's responsibility cannot stop with graduation or with the completion of the program of the career center. If the programs of the elementary and secondary schools for learning disabled students have been successful, if the student has been able to experience appropriate vocational counseling and prevocational exploration—very large "ifs" in today's educational and economic situation—then a next step of *liaison* is in order. There is life after high school, although rarely, other than in commencement speeches, is this fact recognized by educators. We tend to be myopic to the lifelong needs of many pupils. We sigh with relief when a student's program is in some degree a success and is brought to an end. This may appear to be a harsh statement in view of the excellent preparation, at least for college or the university, which many students received in high school. Not so for the majority of learning disabled students who have managed to survive through the high school years. The educator's responsibility to provide necessary services until the chronological age of 26 years ought to give pause to those who look forward to an early exit from the school on the part of unique groups of students. Labor unions and employers likewise resist both early school leaving and the lack of basic positive work attitudes and skills on the part of young people.

Just as prevocational training required the assistance of good vocational counseling, so the independence of the first community-based job may require similar services. Some years ago the Bureau for Children with Retarded Mental Development of the New York City Public Schools employed a number of persons well oriented to the nature and needs of the retarded youth to assist the latter in job finding, placement, and holding. Although this program did not last long due to problems inherent in the system, it was eminently successful while it was in operation. A similar type of program serving as a liaison between school and community employment and utilizing state employment service personnel, counselors of the Vocational Rehabilitation Service, or specially employed public school personnel is undoubtedly going to be required for the young man or woman with continuing learning disabilities. Job success, as Jim (Chapter 13) and Scott (Chapter 9) so clearly demonstrate, is absolutely essential for secure adult adjustment.

Scott shows what a seriously handicapped learning disabled person can accomplish in adulthood. While he has circumnavigated the pervasive issues of learning disability and has learned how to avoid others completely, he recognizes that his life could have been different under other circumstances. Nevertheless he has achieved a high degree of happiness, successful marriage, home ownership, and parenthood. This is the birthright of every learning disabled individual, and it is the pattern achieved by many in spite of inadequate school programs. What indeed could be the record if there were well-conceptualized public school programs, well-prepared teachers and administrators, and knowledgeable psychologists and counselors? Parent organizations have accomplished much with programs for learning disabled children at the elementary school level. They, along with public school educators, must turn their attention now to the secondary schools and to community agencies which will help to ensure positive social adjustment for the young adult with learning disabilities.

A KIT FOR TEACHERS OF ADOLESCENTS
WITH LEARNING DISABILITIES

Books

Bailey, E. *Academic Activities for Adolescents with Learning Disabilities.* Evergreen, Col.: Learning Pathways, 1975.

Cutler, A., and McShane, R. *The Trachtenberg Speed System of Basic Mathematics.* Garden City: Doubleday, 1960.

Fernald, G. *Remedial Techniques in Basic School Subjects.* New York: McGraw-Hill, 1943.

Johnson, D., and Myklebust, H. *Learning Disabilities: Educational Principles and Practices.* New York: Grune and Stratton, 1967.

Kirk, S.; Kliebhan, J.; and Lerner, J. *Reading for Slow and Disabled Learners.* Boston: Houghton Mifflin, rev., 1978.

Marsh, G.; Gearheart, C.; Gearheart, B. *The Learning Disabled Adolescent Program Alternatives in the Secondary School.* St. Louis: Mosby, 1978.

Myers, P., and Hammill, D. *Methods for Learning Disorders.* New York: Wiley, 1977.

Salvia, J., and Yseldyke, J. *Assessment in Special and Remedial Education.* Boston: Houghton Mifflin, 1978.

Shefter, H. *Six Minutes a Day to Perfect Spelling.* Rev. ed. New York: Pocket Books, 1976.

Weis, H., and Weis, M. *A Survival Manual, Case Studies and Suggestions for the Learning Disabled Teenager.* Great Barrington, Mass.: Treehouse Associates, 1974.

Wiig, E., and Semel, E. *Language Disabilities in Children and Adolescents.* Columbus: Merrill, 1976.

Miscellaneous

1. Typewriter(s), electric if possible
2. Touch typing book
3. Tape recorder, blank tapes, and hand calculators
4. *Talking Books* (both records and tapes) and matching books in print
5. Talking Book Machine (record players) and Talking Book Tape Recorders; forms for the *Talking Book* materials and equipment may be obtained from Library of Congress, Washington, D.C., or from local libraries or American Printing House for the Blind
6. Cassette tape recordings of frequently used classroom texts and required novels, plays, poetry, etc.
7. Several copes of: *20,000 Words* by Louis A. Leslie (New York: Gregg Division, McGraw-Hill, 7th ed., 1977).
8. Dictionaries with thumb index
9. Array of appealing literature

    comics
    newspapers
    magazines
    cookbooks
    newspapers
    high interest–low reading level paperback books
    atlas
    maps and charts
    photo-commentaries on a variety of subjects
10. Micro computer or terminal to local computer center
11. *The Tuned In, Turned On Book About Learning Problems* by Marnell Hayes. San Rafael, California; Academic Therapy Publisher (with accompanying tape)

References

Ackerman, P. T., *et al.* "Teenage Status of Hyperactive and Non-hyperactive Learning Disabled Boys." *American Journal of Psychiatry* 47 (October 1977):577–95.

Bailey, E. *Academic Activities for Adolescents with Learning Disabilities.* Evergreen, Col.: Learning Pathways, 1975.

Boder, E. "Developmental Dyslexia: Prevailing Diagnostic Concepts and a New Diagnostic Approach." In *Progress in Learning Disabilities,* edited by H. Myklebust. New York: Grune & Stratton, 1971.

Bryan, T. "Learning Disabled Children's Comprehension of Non-Verbal Communication." *Journal of Learning Disabilities* 10 (October 1977):36–41.

Cruickshank, W. M. *Learning Disabilities in Home, School and Community.* Syracuse: Syracuse University Press, 1977.

Cruickshank, W. M., ed. *The Teacher of Brain-Injured Children: A Discussion of the Bases of Competency.* Syracuse: Syracuse University Press, 1966.

Cruickshank, W. M.; Bentzen, F.; Ratzeberg, F.; and Tannhauser, M. *A Teaching Method for Brain-injured and Hyperactive Children.* Syracuse: Syracuse University Press, 1961.

Cruickshank, W. M.; Paul, J. L.; and Junkala, J. B. *Misfits in the Public Schools.* Syracuse: Syracuse University Press, 1969.

Deno, E., "Special Education as Developmental Capital." *Exceptional Children.* 37 (1970), 229–237.

Fernald, G. *Remedial Techniques in Basic School Subjects.* New York: McGraw-Hill, 1943.

Frauenheim, J. G. "A Follow-Up Study of Adult Males who were Clinically Diagnosed as Dyslexic in Childhood." Doctoral dissertation, Wayne State University, 1975.

Gillingham, A., and Stillman, B. *Remedial Training for Children with Specific Disability in Reading, Spelling, and Penmanship,* 7th ed. Cambridge: Educator's Publishing Service, 1965.

Gordon, S. "Reversing a Negative Self-Image." In *Helping the Adolescent with the Hidden Handicap,* edited by L. E. Anderson. Los Angeles: Academic Therapy, 1970.

Gordon, S., and Conant, R. *You.* New York: Quadrangle/New York Times, 1975.

Irvine, P.; Goodman, L.; and Mann. L. "Occupational Education." In *Teaching the Learning Disabled Adolescent,* edited by L. Mann, L. Goodman, and J. Wiederholt. Boston: Houghton Mifflin, 1978.

Jessor, R., and Jessor, S. *Problems, Behavior, and Psychosocial Development.* New York: Academic, 1977.

Johnson, D., and Myklebust, H. *Learning Disabilities: Educational Principles and Practices.* New York: Grune & Stratton, 1967.

Keyes, R. *Is There Life After High School?* Boston: Little, Brown, 1976.

MacMillan, D., and Cauffield, S. R. "Outer-directness as a Function of Success and Failure in Educationally Handicapped Boys." *Journal of Learning Disabilities* 10 (December 1977):48–59.

McGlannan, G. "Empathy in Learning Disabled Children." *Journal of Learning Disabilities* 10 (October 1977):42–43.

Morse, W. C., and Ravlin, M., "Psychoeducation in Schools." *Basic Handbook Child Psychiatry* (in press).

Myklebust, Helmer. *Picture Story Language Test. The Development and Disorders of Written Language,* Vol. 1. New York: Grune & Stratton, 1965.

Rosenthal, J. H. "Self-Esteem in Dyslexic Children." *Academic Therapy* 9 (1973): 27–29.

Shefter, Harry. *Six Minutes A Day to Perfect Spelling.* Rev. ed. New York: Pocket Books, 1976.

Thomas, A., and Chess, S. *Temperament and Development.* New York: Brunner/Mazel, 1977.

Weis, H., and Weis, M. *A Survival Manual, Case Studies, and Suggestions for the Learning Disabled Teenager.* Great Barrington, Mass.: Treehouse Associates, 1974.

Wilson, Y., and Mann, A. *The Haptic Perceptual-Motor Program.* Marysville, Mich.: St. Clair County Intermediate School District, *circa* 1975.

Index

LEARNING DISABILITIES
The Struggle from Adolescence toward Adulthood

was composed in 10-point Compugraphic Palatino and leaded two points,
with display type also in Palatino, by Metricomp Studios, Inc.;
printed offset on 55-pound Warren Antique Cream acid-free paper stock,
Smyth-sewn and bound over 80-point binder's boards in Columbia Bayside Linen,
by Maple-Vail Book Manufacturing Group, Inc.;
and published by

SYRACUSE UNIVERSITY PRESS
SYRACUSE, NEW YORK 13210